The Tribe of Pyn

The Tribe of Pyn

LITERARY GENERATIONS IN THE POSTMODERN PERIOD

David Cowart

University of Michigan
Ann Arbor

Published in the United States of America by the
University of Michigan Press
Printed and bound by CPI Group (UK) Ltd, Croydon, CR0 4YY

2018   2017   2016   2015   4   3   2   1

A CIP catalog record for this book is available from the British Library.

ISBN 978-0-472-07288-0 (hardcover : alk paper)
ISBN 978-0-472-05288-2 (cloth : alk. paper)
ISBN 978-0-472-12144-1 (ebook)

For my father, Eugene Guyland Cowart

Every human generation has its own illusions with regard to civilization; some believe they are taking part in its upsurge, others that they are witnesses of its extinction. In fact, it always both flames and smolders and is extinguished, according to the place and the angle of view.

—IVO ANDRIĆ, *THE BRIDGE ON THE DRINA*

Each age, it is found, must write its own books; or, rather, each generation for the next succeeding.

—RALPH WALDO EMERSON, "THE AMERICAN SCHOLAR"

Acknowledgments

"Proem: Postmodernism (Again)" and "The Jeffersonian Vision in Steve Erickson's *Arc d'X*" are excerpted from my address at the 2005 Kyoto American Studies Summer Seminar, "Heteroclite Historiography: Representations of the Past in Contemporary American Fiction," in *Proceedings of the Kyoto American Studies Seminar, August 1–August 3, 2005,* edited by Hiroshi Yoneyama (Kyoto: Center for American Studies, Ritsumeikan University, 2006), 179–99; a version of "Introduction: Literary Generations in the Postmodern Period" originally appeared as "The DeLillo Era: Literary Generations in the Postmodern Period," in *Terrorism, Media, and the Ethics of Fiction: Transatlantic Perspectives on Don DeLillo,* edited by Peter Schneck and Philipp Schweighauser (New York: Continuum, 2010), 223–42. Versions of "Fantasy and Reality in Ingalls's *Mrs. Caliban*" and "Heritage and Deracination in Walker's 'Everyday Use'" originally appeared in *Critique* 30, no. 2 (Winter 1989): 77–83, and *Studies in Short Fiction* 33, no. 2 (Spring 1996): 171–84, respectively. "Braid of Blood: Dorris's *A Yellow Raft in Blue Water*" is the revision of a revision. It appeared under that title in *Other Americans, Other Americas,* edited by Magdalena J. Zaborowska (Aarhus, Denmark: Aarhus University Press, 1998), 140–49, and, in an earlier version, as "'The Rhythm of Three Strands': Cultural Braiding in Dorris's *A Yellow Raft in Blue Water,*" in *Studies in American Indian Literatures* 8, no. 1 (Spring 1996): 1–12. "Matriarchal Mythopoesis: Naylor's *Mama Day*" appeared in *Philological Quarterly* 77, no. 4 (Fall 1998): 439–59; "Passionate Pathography: Narrative as Pharmakon in *Operation Wandering Soul*" appeared in *Intersections: Essays on Richard Powers,* edited by Stephen J. Burn and Peter Dempsey (Normal, IL: Dalkey Archive Press, 2008), 117–33; "Anger, Anguish, and Art: Palahniuk's *Choke*" appeared in *Chuck Palahniuk: Fight Club, Invisible Monsters, and Choke,* edited by Francisco Collado-Rodríguez (New York:

Bloomsbury, 2013), 157–74; "Thirteen Ways of Looking: Jennifer Egan's *A Visit from the Goon Squad*" appeared in *Critique* 56, no. 3 (2015): 241–54.

I am grateful to the University of South Carolina and its keen students for allowing this Uncle Toby to ride his contemporary fiction hobbyhorse in class after class. Together, we have launched many a flaming arrow at the circled wagons of literature. Or perhaps it was the literati who launched flaming arrows at us. Thanks, especially, to those whose dissertations have taught me so much in recent years: Theda Wrede, Natalie Leppard, Carl Jenkinson, Jeremey Cagle, Kevin Trumpeter, Michael Rizza, Craig Gibbs, and Dawson Jones (who jogged my mind at a crucial juncture).

I have often noted that American academics stand to learn a great deal from their peers abroad. For hosting me at Tsinghua University in Beijing, I thank Wang Ning and his students, especially Yao Lingling, Liu Hui, and Su Ping. I have had the good fortune to serve on some extraordinary extramural dissertation committees, including those of Rebecca Rey at the University of Western Australia, Sam Thomas and Anthony Leaker at the University of Sussex, Theo Finigan at the University of Alberta, Tiina Käkelä-Puumala at the University of Helsinki, Rod Taveira and Sam Dickson at the University of Sydney, Creon Upton at the University of Canterbury, New Zealand, Farouq Rezq Bekhit Sayyid at Al-Azhar University in Cairo, Nick Prescott at Flinders University in Adelaide, Australia, and A. Marie Josephine Aruna at Pondicherry University in Puducherry, India. Special thanks to the dissertation directors or supervisors who allowed me to share in the harvest of new knowledge: Stephen Chinna, Peter Boxall, Michael O'Driscoll, Hannu Riikonen, Melissa Hardie, John Newton and Anna Smith, Ahlam Hassan, and N. Natarajan.

Others who helped this book into print are Stephen J. Burn, University of Glasgow, who asked me to write something on Richard Powers at just the right moment; Francisco Collado-Rodríguez, University of Zaragoza, who persuaded me to overcome my disinclination to take Chuck Palahniuk seriously; and Nobuo Kamioka, Gakushuin University in Tokyo, who brought me to Steve Erickson. I thank my English Department colleagues Elise Blackwell and Susan Vanderborg for their good offices as well. Elise nudged me toward a closer look at the work of Jennifer Egan; Susan provided moral support as, *Laocoön*-like, I writhed in the great web of Mark Z. Danielewski's *House of Leaves*.

That I am able to write with joy I attribute to my splendid family; wife Pamela, son Chase, daughter Rachel, and my father, Gene Cowart, who wrote me.

Contents

Proem

Postmodernism (Again)

Announcing itself in the work of certain writers born in the 1920s (Joseph Heller, Kurt Vonnegut, Flannery O'Connor, Grace Paley, sometimes Norman Mailer), literary postmodernism seems to have come into its own in the fictions of a cohort born a decade later. The careers of Thomas Pynchon, Don DeLillo, and Cormac McCarthy—all born in the 1930s—represent the full flowering of the aesthetic variously contested, interrogated, and carried forward into the new millennium by such younger writers as Richard Powers, William Vollmann, David Foster Wallace, Maxine Hong Kingston, Carole Maso, and Steve Erickson. Postmodern fiction, in other words, already boasts its apostolic succession, its generational filiation. I propose, then, some defining of terms and a brief review of theoretical formulations of postmodernism and its antecedents. But I invite attention to what might be called theory's dirty little secret: it avoids coming to cases—and for good reason. Actual praxis has a way of giving theory the lie. So, fair warning: the theory surveyed may prove somewhat limited when specific works of the imagination come under review.

NEW, NEWER, NEWEST

Modern. Postmodern. Contemporary. As moving targets, semantic shape-shifters, these terms make lexicographers and cultural historians weep. Definitions remain at best provisional or evolutionary. "Modern," for example, can mean "everything since the Middle Ages," or "pertaining to the Enlightenment and its continuing epistemic dictates," or "characterizing the early decades of the twentieth century." Depending on one's definition of modernism, then, postmodernism represents a greater or lesser epistemic shift. As modernism's ostensible successor in the historical parade of cultural paradigms, postmodernism would seem to interrogate or overturn certain epistemological assumptions: recognition of cause and effect, respect for the empirical, belief in the ability of words to represent things. *Logos*, the principle of phallocentric reason, finds itself variously embattled. Logic, once unitary, becomes localized; new logics emerge as one passes in review ideas of language, culture, and history congenial to that protean contemporaneity we call the postmodern.

One begins, nonetheless, with a brief charting of the modernism that emerged in the earlier twentieth century. For all their iconoclasm, all their repudiation of the social and cultural and sometimes artistic corruption of the current order and the recent past, the moderns were a remarkably backward-looking lot. Formally they broke rules, they innovated. But culturally and politically they were conservative, even reactionary (at least until the Spanish Civil War concentrated a few minds). For every leftist John Dos Passos, every Ernest Hemingway who briefly entertained Marxist ideas, there were ten who like Ezra Pound and T. S. Eliot were anti-Semitic, or like William Butler Yeats drawn to Eoin O'Duffy's blue-shirted Irish fascists, or like F. Scott Fitzgerald's Nick Carraway enamored of the idea that everyone might once again stand to moral attention. Anyone who studies the great writers of this period soon discovers their nostalgia, their marked tendency to cultural retrospection. Seeking some still-valid model of civilization, for example, Yeats looks to Byzantium, Henry Adams to the High Gothic achievements seen at Mont St. Michel and Chartres, Willa Cather to an ideal of pioneer integrity, E. M. Forster to the Florentine Renaissance or to Alexandria under the Ptolemies. Pound ranges from ancient China to Rome, from Florence under the Medici to the Provençal culture that produced Arnaut Daniel. Anticipating Steve Erickson, he also scrutinizes the dynamic vision of Thomas Jefferson.

Early in the twentieth century, and especially in the years after World War I, artists held the mirror of art up to a civilization in ruins. In addition to the war's immediate and literal destruction, ancient ideas of civility and cultural authority collapsed. "Everywhere," says Yeats, "the ceremony of innocence is drowned." Modernist iterations such as Yeats's center that cannot hold or Eliot's fragments shored against ruins iterate and reiterate the idea of a civilization coming apart, going to pieces. As represented in art, however, this fragmentation invites and rewards reassembly. *The Waste Land* presents itself as a puzzle that the resourceful reader puts together as an exercise in cultural recuperation: fully to understand this great poem is to contemplate a kind of *quondam et futurus* vision of civilized order. In Eliot's later work the vision becomes explicit. Famously declaring himself "classicist in literature, royalist in politics, and anglo-catholic in religion," Eliot strove to reassert the validity of cultural ideas discredited by the Great War, as well as spiritual ideas battered by decades of doubt.[1]

But "the king's combined cavalry and foot," to borrow Richard Powers's artful rephrasing of the familiar nursery rhyme, could not put this Humpty Dumpty together again.[2] Culture had to go somewhere else—especially when the carnage broke out anew, and on an even larger scale (fifteen million died in World War I, sixty million in World War II). A postmodern Ezra Pound might say that the age demanded an image of its accelerated grimace. As Thomas Docherty has pointed out, the word "post-modern" first appeared in print, in a book by Arnold Toynbee, in 1939—an especially fateful year for Europe and the West.[3] By the time Eliot died in 1965, the new episteme had begun to manifest itself in palpable ways. Paradoxically, the modern began to seem old-fashioned.

Serviceable to new ways of thinking, perceiving, and representing, the new, postmodern aesthetic offered a different response to the twice-told collapse of Western civilization—either a vision of multiplicity (of cultures, of realities, even) assembled from the shards of the old perceptual and political hegemonies (one sees that the postmodern subsumes the postcolonial) or an artistic preoccupation with the creation of self-contained, self-referring worlds that either mock mimesis or have no mimetic function at all (according to Brian McHale, this "ontological" element lies at the heart of the postmodern aesthetic).[4] Vladimir Nabokov, in *The Real Life of Sebastian Knight* (1941), at one point depicts his title character, a novelist, "lying spread-eagled on the floor of his study." Sebastian's explanation characterizes Nabokovian art as well as his own. "I'm not dead," he says. "I have finished building a world, and this is my Sabbath rest."[5]

Another way to throw the transition into bold relief is to consider the way twentieth-century moderns and postmoderns conceptualize language. Pound, Eliot, Robert Frost, and Hemingway all inveigh against a lexicon cheapened by bad art and political dishonesty. All aspire to restore the precision of words. Hemingway dispenses with abstraction, Pound keeps his erasers in order. Though Eliot recognizes the liability of language, he believes, first and last, in the ideal he finds in Stéphane Mallarmé: *donner un sens plus pur aux mots de la tribu*. But this idea of language falters before postmodern theory and praxis, in which signification itself—the relation of words to reality—comes to be seen as fluid and unanchored. Endlessly deferred, meaning retreats down the signifying chain, nor will any degree of linguistic precision arrest signification's flux in such a way as to privilege any final referent. Not that the postmoderns become indifferent to their medium—on the contrary, these writers become almost obsessive over words. They take full advantage of the extraordinary range of English vocabulary, and well-educated native speakers encounter many an out of the way word for the first time as they read Nabokov, John Barth, Pynchon, Cormac McCarthy, and David Foster Wallace. These writers' attention to nuance, moreover, makes even Henry James look slipshod. But rather than think of words as perfectible instruments of representation, postmodern writers seek constantly to make language draw attention to itself as a performative and reflexive medium.

Too often invoked indiscriminately, "postmodern" proves a term resistant to succinct lexicography. Many have pronounced on the subject: Jean-François Lyotard, Frederic Jameson, Jean Baudrillard, Ihab Hassan, and Linda Hutcheon, in addition to Brian McHale. Not surprisingly, definitions accumulate and inculcate a first lesson: postmodernism's elements and characteristics often contradict each other. Perhaps every pronouncement about the new episteme should echo Walt Whitman's charming confession:

> Do I contradict myself?
> Very well then I contradict myself.[6]

Postmodernism resists its own totalization, just as it resists the straightforward periodization it seems, nominally, to claim (in the work of Miguel Cervantes and Laurence Sterne, for example, one encounters elements as postmodern as anything in Jorge Luis Borges or Italo Calvino). As ethos or aesthetic or episteme, postmodernism subsumes all that problematizes representation, worries the uncloseable gap between signifier and signified, disbelieves in metanarratives, denies foundations, and embraces—in language, in consciousness—an epistemology of the surface. The true postmodernist resists formulations that threaten to betray the multiple realities of individuals, societies, and, as will be seen, history. Where the modernists remain nostalgic for social, economic, aesthetic, and political hierarchy (to the point of flirting with—and in Pound's case embracing—fascism), the postmodernists recognize the essential arbitrariness or groundlessness of all such forms of authority. Among the implications: anyone writing from the margins—women, minorities, the colonized or formerly colonized—can find shelter under the postmodern umbrella. One appreciates the inclusivity, for otherwise, in its purely technical trappings, postmodernism can look suspiciously (the occasional Kathy Acker or Ishmael Reed notwithstanding) like another all-male and nearly all-white club.

But what about postmodernism and the past? Richard Powers characterizes history as an "army of occupation" that makes us "all collaborators."[7] If we parse Powers's somewhat difficult metaphor, this pronouncement suggests that our collective relation to history must perforce be shameful, in that we lack the moral backbone to join the implied resistance. But the difficulties of a moral or ethical relationship to the past pale beside the postmodern crisis of representation, which falls with particular weight on history and historiography. Fredric Jameson characterizes the postmodern as, among other things, "the aesthetic situation engendered by the disappearance of the historical referent," which "finds itself gradually bracketed, and then effaced altogether, leaving us with nothing but texts." He laments a culture-wide "waning of . . . historicity."[8]

One thinks of history as an essentially depth-oriented enterprise. The present, according to a familiar figure, has its "roots" in the past. Exploration of that past, like similar explorations of consciousness and the unconscious, was an important part of the "modern" (i.e., Enlightenment) project. But the new historiography, to paraphrase John Donne, puts all in doubt. Problematic and postmodern, the new historiography involves not so much a concatenation of facts—even "emplotted" facts—as a keen awareness of the provisionality of all representations of the past. Under the postmodern dispensation, the commonsense distinctions between history and fiction fall away. Metahistory subverts the old relationship with Clio, puts the past into postmodern play. Root gives way to rhizome.

Postmodern historiography, after all, restores recognition of what was always already the case at the etymological level: in English and many other languages, "story" and "history" are the same word.[9] Contemporary novelists who engage history in their fictions often intimate, as reverse corollary to their own enterprise, that fiction must also figure to a greater or lesser degree in the writing of history. In his 1988 novel *Libra*, for example, Don DeLillo

goes back precisely a quarter of a century to the watershed event that many
see as an annunciation of the postmodern: the assassination of President
John F. Kennedy in November 1963 (that such a shallow-draft past can be
regarded as "historical" is itself symptomatic). In this metahistorical meditation on "the seven seconds that broke the back of the American century," De-
Lillo describes an elaborate conspiracy, and he has been misread as having
joined the swelling chorus of disagreement with the Warren Commission's
"single gunman" conclusion.[10] But DeLillo is after bigger historical game: not
so much the raw event as its transformations in memory and chronicle. De-
Lillo affirms that, all documentation and research and logic notwithstanding, the events of November 1963 must remain mired in the conditions of
postmodern knowing. All versions of what happened to Kennedy seem to
have epistemological standing; like every other instance of the signified, the
definitive version absconds.

Introduction
Literary Generations in the Postmodern Period

Reflecting on the idea of literary generations in, say, the last five or six decades, one swiftly moves beyond isolated instances of the filiation that Harold Bloom sees as so problematic and vexed. One engages larger—and what may appear untimely—questions of periodization. As Brian McHale points out in a witty discussion in the *electronic book review*, postmodernism differs from its predecessors in that it was always already self-periodizing. "Periods in literary history are typically constituted retrospectively," he remarks. "Modernism," for example, "can 'appear' as a period with a canon of its own only forty years after the fact, around 1960." But "[f]rom the very outset, postmodernism was self-conscious about its identity as a period."[1] Perhaps, then, readers and critics these days must expect a certain speeding up of literary history, even as they accept the acceleration of other historical processes.

What remains unclear, however, is whether postmodernism's successor will be as "self-conscious about its identity as a period." Can the cultural historian, through thoughtful and attentive scrutiny of contemporary letters, discern the kind of shift in literary energies that normally, according to McHale, becomes plain only in retrospect? Are we, early in the twenty-first century, witnesses to the displacement of postmodernism by some kind of post-postmodernism? Conversely: Might what swims before our optics be a repudiation of all the pastiche, all the ironic self-referentiality, all the incredulity towards metanarratives, and all the hand-wringing about representation? If so, are we in for mere literary retrogression—to remodeled Modernism, perhaps, or Realism revisited? If not, what continuities will manifest themselves, what prospects for an aesthetic with "legs," as they say in the entertainment business?

These questions are not new to me. My work on Pynchon and DeLillo grounds my thinking about their literary sons, daughters, and grandchildren. By the same token, curiosity about the grammar of periodization anchors my long-standing interest in the mechanics and meanings of allusion, in history and the novel, and in what I call "symbiotic" writing—the practice of contemporary authors, from Jean Rhys and Tom Stoppard to John Gardner and Jane Smiley, who reframe (or appropriate and rework) characters, actions, and whole plots from the great bran pie of prior literature (I borrow that figure from Virginia Woolf). My work on contemporary immigrant fiction also represents engagement with questions central to the present study. Dwelling in one or more of postmodernism's parallel universes, Chang-rae Lee, Junot Díaz, Jamaica Kincaid, Wendy Law-Yone, Aleksandar Hemon, and other immigrant writers take naturally, I have found, to an aesthetic predicated on apprehensions of alterity, on the lability of self, on the constructedness of identity, and on ontological provisionality. Every immigrant knows at least two worlds, two selves, two realities. Thus I find myself in disagreement with Rachel Adams's observation that the immigrant author "reacts against the aesthetic sensibilities of high postmodernism while providing American literature with a new set of genealogical, geographic, and temporal referents."[2] I would argue, rather, that the postmodern project naturally subsumes writing from the margins, whether it come from the pens of immigrants, ethnic minorities, women, or other subalterns.

I am mindful, nonetheless, of how atomized, balkanized, and globalized contemporary writing has become. The literary historian must keep in mind that the post–1945 literary fashion was never wholly "postmodern." Modernism took its time dying (it staged something of a comeback, it seems to me, in the shock-the-middle-class aesthetic of the Beats). Meanwhile realist and naturalist fiction continued to be written, authors such as Saul Bellow, John Updike, Joyce Carol Oates, and the early Mailer vying honorably with the glamorous iconoclasts (Barth, Vonnegut, Pynchon, and company). One thinks, too, of what has been called the *New Yorker* school—J. D. Salinger, John Cheever, Updike, Ann Beattie, and the Nabokov who published fiction and memoir in that magazine. When one considers the great outpouring of fiction foregrounding the experience of women, the increasing prominence of gay and lesbian writing, and the vitality of various ethnic, immigrant, and transnational literatures, one recognizes the profound branching or eddying of whatever might once have figured as literary mainstream. This manifold division or furcation, of course, merely bears out one of postmodernism's basic premises: the multiplicity of cultures and realities and aesthetic legitimacies. But the literary scene remains a tangled bank, its denizens in busy competition for readers, sales, attention, prizes, fame, and, yes, canonical status. Generational conflict may or may not figure, but we err to think that the many voices will naturally blend together, as Thomas Pynchon once said, "like the Hallelujah Chorus done by 200 kazoo players with perfect pitch."[3]

I come to this discussion in hopes of moving beyond my special interest in certain writers who have the power, over and over, to move me with their language, their insight, their originality, and their attunement to the circumstances of life at a millennial cusp. My pantheon is personal, but its gods have spoken to one who has been reading and writing about contemporary fiction, however quixotic the enterprise, for several decades now. Among the happy few who share my passion, there is some agreement about the stature of Thomas Pynchon, Don DeLillo, Cormac McCarthy. Any given reader will have her or his own additions: Toni Morrison for many, the Canadian Margaret Atwood for me. I am, however, a member of that minority that never really took to Philip Roth. I am also among those who continue to affirm the importance of Norman Mailer. One cannot gainsay Updike's importance, even though he seems, like Joyce Carol Oates, to be overcommitted to what Andreas Huyssen characterizes as "the dogma of mimetic referentiality."[4] These names constitute a generation, beyond which lies a kind of literary terra incognita—or at least a conspicuous lack of consensus. As Andrew Hoberek has observed, "The pleasure and the danger alike of thinking about contemporary literature lie in the tenuous nature of any hypotheses we might put forward—a fact that we should keep in mind but that should not stop us from proceeding."[5] One can only keep one's ear to the ground, read the reviews, talk to others who specialize in the study of current fiction. Ultimately, one reads as widely as possible and gauges one's honest responses.

ULYSSES OR TELEMACHUS

According to a Chinese proverb, "One generation plants the trees, and another gets the shade." Unless, of course, the trees fall to axes wielded by a generation wanting its place in the sun.[6] Thus it is, sometimes, with literary generations. Younger writers, finding all pedestals on Mt. Parnassus taken, may resort to toppling certain of the more recent monuments. Such ruthlessness in making space for themselves suggests the need to amend T. S. Eliot's picture of young artists gently immersing themselves in the great river of literature. Eliot famously affirms that "tradition" accommodates "individual talent." Harold Bloom, however, asserts that the literary past produces an "anxiety of influence" in young writers. Arguing that these "ephebes" (a decidedly noninclusive term, one notes) must realize themselves by repudiating, subverting, or rewriting their predecessors, Bloom has proposed an elaborate typology of the literary displacements occasioned by filiation. Though he characterizes the relationship of ephebe to precursor as "filial," the word seems, in the Bloomian lexicon, not to imply much in the way of "dutiful," "respectful," or "loving." Bloom, after Sigmund Freud, emphasizes the combative relationship between offspring and parent. One wonders, then, whether Bloom's model takes properly into account the ways in which certain artistic generations, "filial" in a more positive sense, might be disinclined to an aesthetics of subversion and displacement. One wonders, too, whether breaking with an inherited aesthetic should be viewed as intrinsically superior, somehow, to artistic activities aimed at building on the achievements of a parental generation.

Ulysses and Telemachus, as they appear in the familiar Tennyson poem, may figure for readers the two kinds of literary sensibility under consideration here. Tennyson, one recalls, makes his Homeric figures appeal to the imagination of an age much exercised by the problems of empire. As the metaphorical distillation of a particularly Victorian contrast, father and son embody twinned ideals: the risk-taking, heroic explorer on the one hand, the responsible consolidator of civilization on the other. By the same token, the literary historian should recognize that a Telemachus of letters can do as much to advance literary art as some bold, bourgeois-shocking, manifesto-writing Odysseus. But anyone scrutinizing generational identities among writers publishing in the decades after, say, 1945 may well ask: Does postmodern literary art owe less to its Telemachuses than to its Odysseuses?

Which is to say: Must sons always slay fathers? Are literary mothers, for that matter, exempt from the Oedipal violence? In the literary culture of "democratic nations," Alexis de Tocqueville observes, "each new generation is a new people."[7] José Ortega y Gasset, however, argues against the idea "that the life of each generation consists of struggling against the previous generation, and Hélène Cixous urges ʼ ʼ to "get away from the dialectic which has it that the only good father is a dead one."[8] What, then, of the mechanics of literary filiation in our time? Do they foster anxiety or *Bildung*? For that matter, does our age foster the kind of bold pronouncements that character-ized notable literary paradigm shifts in the past—William Wordsworth's Preface to *Lyrical Ballads*, Woolf's "Modern Fiction," or the pronunciamen-tos that issued from the pen of Ezra Pound, each dedicated to butchering some sacred cow of Victorian or Edwardian literary aesthetics? Postmod-ernism, as it happens, left the polemics to the critics, who made reputations with book titles such as *What Was Literature?* and *Against Interpretation*. (In the previously noted "What Was Postmodernism?" McHale argues—mischievous title notwithstanding—against premature pronouncements about the directions taken by contemporary letters.) Setting aside *On Moral Fiction* (John Gardner's prickly plea, in 1978, for a literature of affirmation, with characters recognizable, like those in classic literature, as "models of virtue"), the closest thing to a bourgeois-shocking iconoclast among the real literati was probably John Hawkes, who in 1965 denounced "plot, character, setting, and theme" as "the true enemies of the novel."[9] John Barth's highly influential and frequently cited essays "The Literature of Exhaustion" (1968) and "The Literature of Replenishment" (1980) were by contrast not incendi-ary but rather explanatory, even apologetic.[10]

If more recent disquisitions tend, still, toward the polite and mannerly, we may deduce that the dominant aesthetic remains viable—and ready to accommodate new practitioners as yet unready to declare themselves op-pressed. But styles evolve, and the young cannot indefinitely reframe the questions of the old. I undertake, then, to consider whether that old ghost, influence, continues to haunt the inheritors of a greatness that, having an-nounced itself first in the sixties, continues to monopolize readers decades later. That greatness, by the way, complicates the task of the would-be as-sessor of the younger generation's work. As one tries to gauge the achieve-ment of a Richard Powers or a David Foster Wallace or a Gloria Naylor, out tumble fresh masterpieces from Pynchon, DeLillo, Roth, Oates, Morrison, Cormac McCarthy—masters undiminished, who give every indication that, out-Bellowing Bellow, they will continue to publish significant fiction for years to come.[11] But sooner or later these exemplars (all born in the thir-ties) will join the late Norman Mailer, Joseph Heller, Kurt Vonnegut, Grace Paley, William Styron, Ronald Sukenick, John Hawkes, William Gaddis, and Gilbert Sorrentino (all born in the twenties) in the effulgence or obscu-rity of the hereafter. It is instructive, by the way, to consider our perceptions of post–World War II writers who died betimes, for example, Flannery

O'Connor (born 1925), Donald Barthelme (born 1931), John Gardner (born 1933), Raymond Carver (born 1938), or Kathy Acker or Octavia Butler (both born in 1947). Because of their premature deaths (O'Connor died in 1964, Gardner in 1982, Barthelme in 1989, Carver in 1988, Acker in 1997, Butler in 2006), these writers can seem temporally disconnected from their surviving contemporaries, who continued—and continue—to write and publish. One comes to balk at the thought of John Gardner, say, as a member of the generation born in the thirties (admittedly, Gardner attempted to define himself against the trends of his time). Gardner's untimely death in a motorcycle accident, along with the eclipse into which he drifted, creates something of the perception one hears about from old combat veterans: their fallen comrades remain, in memory, forever youthful and red-cheeked. As Laurence Binyon wrote,

> They shall not grow old, as we that are left grow old:
> Age shall not weary them, nor the years condemn.
> At the going down of the sun and in the morning
> We will remember them. ("For the Fallen")[12]

DEFINING GENERATIONS

Artists cannot seal themselves off in some social or professional equivalent of Marcel Proust's cork-lined room. They must interact with their contemporaries and with predecessors—many of them still living. If a literary tradition or style proves robust, with more than a single season of legitimacy, one may wonder about the locus of maximum energy and purpose: in the founding generation or in its successors? One wonders, too, how to characterize or define a generation—especially a postmodern one. Although a uniform generational time span has always eluded precise quantification (twenty years? thirty?), attempts to theorize this problem have yielded some worthwhile considerations. Certainly the idea of generations has fascinated culture critics for a long time. A quick survey reveals that it exercised Charles Augustin Sainte-Beuve, Wilhelm Dilthey, François Mentré, Ortega y Gasset, Eduard Wechssler, Henri Peyre, Wilhelm Pinder, Julius Petersen, Karl Mannheim, Julián Marías, and Auguste Comte. If in recent years we seem to have abandoned attempts at definition, we may still situate ourselves to advantage if we think beyond mere sequentiality or contemporaneity with regard to established and emergent authors.[13] Most of those scrutinizing this question agree that those born or living at the same time do not necessarily constitute a generation. Early and late, analysts view the shared experience of important historical developments as crucial to a generation's ability to recognize itself and speak with something like a collective voice. The struggle to theorize generations seemed to become more urgent early in the twentieth century. In 1910, the Spanish writer who called himself Azorín coined the term "Generation of '98" to describe certain of his Spanish contemporaries early in the twentieth century.[14] Here and in subsequent essays, notably "Generaciones de Escritores" (1912) and "La Generación de 1898" (1926), he suggested that a literary generation might be recognized through the refurbishing or refashioning of styles and forms on the part of its members, through their penchant for social and political analysis and criticism, and through the group's eventual rethinking or reframing of the larger patterns of literary history. In 1923, Ortega y Gasset augmented Azorín's analysis: "The changes in vital sensibility which are decisive in history," he observes, "appear under the form of the generation. A generation is not a handful of outstanding men, not simply a mass of men; it resembles a new integration of the social body. . . . The generation is a dynamic compromise between mass and individual, and is the most important conception in history."[15] In Germany, meanwhile, sociologists Julius Petersen and Karl Mannheim engaged in their own version of this discussion. Petersen undertook to devise a kind of grammar of the cohort: he affirms with his predecessors (notably Dilthey) that those within a given generation have witnessed certain events important to their nation and the world; they are shaped by similar educational experience (*Bildungselemente*); they often share perceptions of a stiffening up (*erstarren*) of style in the preceding generation; they address themselves, as artists, to similar themes; and they speak—in both the literal and figurative sense—a common language or *Generationssprache*.[16] Mannheim, like Ortega y Gasset, argued that "[m]ere contemporaneity becomes sociologically significant only when it also involves participation in the same historical and social circumstances." Mannheim suggested, moreover, that some age groups falter in creating their own "entelechies" (a term he borrows from Wilhelm Pinder): they attach themselves to older or younger generations.

> [I]t is characteristic of cultural life that unattached elements are always attracted to perfected configurations, even when the unformed, groping impulse differs in many respects from the configuration to which it is

attracted. In this way the impulses and trends peculiar to a generation may remain concealed because of the existence of the clear-cut form of another generation to which they have become attached.[17]

Recognizing the staying power of certain cultural developments, both historic and artistic, Mannheim implies that criticism need not disparage the integrity or originality of artists who of necessity enlist under the banner of their age's dominant aesthetic.

Within any such dominant, of course, artistic growth eventually peaks, and often one sees a slide into mannerism—the easy, unfresh consolidation of a once-powerful style. The epigone displaces the genius. But this routinization is not—at least historically—the work of two or three decades. What follows a particular climacteric in the history of any art, in other words, can as easily be the fuller realization of something present only as potential in the work of the innovator's generation. One thinks of the comprehensive fulfillment of Giotto's promise in the full efflorescence of the Quattrocento in Florence, followed in its turn by the high Renaissance of the Cinquecento (nor was late fifteenth-century mannerism such a decline if it could boast a Greco, a Tintoretto, a Bronzino). If one discerns successive generations building on the work of their predecessors here, why not in contemporary literary art? In other words, what prospects for surpassing the achievements of the first-generation postmodernists, those who, in the 1960s, shaped the new literary aesthetic?

Before trying to answer that question, I must be a little more specific about that first generation. Consciously or unconsciously realizing tendencies annunciated by Gertrude Stein, Nathanael West, Samuel Beckett, and Vladimir Nabokov, these are the writers who charted a somewhat different literary course from that of their contemporaries the Beats, whose prodigal energies were so obviously self-consuming and self-exhausting. Though mindful of an element of difference in their achievement, I group writers born in the 1920s (Joseph Heller, Grace Paley, Flannery O'Connor, Paule Marshall, Kurt Vonnegut, Gilbert Sorrentino, Norman Mailer, Ursula Le-Guin, Paula Fox) with those born in the 1930s (Barth, Pynchon, DeLillo, Ishmael Reed, Toni Morrison, Robert Coover). I realize that the work of the first group may seem slightly more tentative than that of the second, in which the full paradigm shift manifests itself. I realize, too, the temptation to recuperate the early fictions of older writers (Heller, Hawkes, Gaddis), to late-phase modernism—and those of writers a decade younger

(Pynchon, DeLillo, McCarthy) to a somehow more valid or recognizable postmodernism. I am uncomfortable, however, with the notion of claiming separate generational status for these two neighboring decades—especially when both gave us writers who in the 1960s published work establishing the new, postmodern aesthetic. By the same token, setting aside the Dos Passos-influenced *Naked and the Dead* (1948) and the Joyce-influenced *Invisible Man* (1952), I sometimes think I discern more traces of residual modernism in the work of Pynchon and DeLillo than in the work of predecessors who, though a decade or so closer to the moderns, would probably not have encountered them in the course of their formal education (one recalls that anecdote about Thomas Pynchon and his friend Richard Fariña gotten up as Fitzgerald and Hemingway, respectively, for a costume party at Cornell).

Given the exuberance of the first postmoderns, it can seem that their successors—those born in the forties, fifties, sixties, and seventies—must represent a falling off. But who are they, these second- and third-generation postmodernists, and have they erected new wings to—or attempted to bulldoze—the splendid edifice erected by Heller, Paley, Pynchon, DeLillo, and company? Or have they settled into a merely custodial relation to the achievements of their predecessors? Whose is the voice of the new generation?

Early in the twenty-first century, Lev Grossman speculated in the pages of a popular news magazine about whether one could discern a single voice (or voices) amid the under-forty generation of novelists. In the past, the generational voice was always that of some white male—now Fitzgerald, now Hemingway, now Salinger, Jack Kerouac, Heller, or Vonnegut. But Grossman wryly notes the essential puerility behind any such notion. "The paradox of every Voice novel," he says, lies in its gathering "a generation of readers together around the idea that they alone are the single badass misfit truth teller in a world full of phonies." Grossman eventually decides that ours is not an age congenial to the Voice novel. But "[i]f the novelists under 40 have a shared preoccupation, it is—to put it as dryly as possible—immigration. They write about characters who cross borders."[18]

Although Grossman seems to mean borders of all kinds, he may be credited with recognizing that the storytelling of immigrants constitutes a real literary phenomenon in the United States (one observes parallel trends in England, Germany, and France). Publishers have caught on to the seemingly insatiable appetite of readers for narratives of the border-crossing experience, and fictions by new immigrant literati seem to turn up in every issue of the *New York Times Book Review*. Immigrant writers have won all of the major literary awards, including MacArthur Foundation grants (Charles Simic, Walter Abish, Aleksandar Hemon) and even the Nobel Prize (Isaac Bashevis Singer, Saul Bellow, Joseph Brodsky, Derek Walcott). Moreover, as previously noted, the postmodern seismograph spikes every bit as sharply at immigrant fictions as at those of native-born literati—who might be thought to enjoy greater ludic latitude, more license to experiment.

A "GREAT DIVIDE"

As I set to work on this project, my pulse quickened at a line in Andreas Huyssen's superb 1986 study, *After the Great Divide: Modernism, Mass Culture, Postmodernism*: "I will now suggest a historical distinction between the postmodernism of the 1960s and that of the 1970s and early 1980s." If not exactly the project I was undertaking, the proposed "historical distinction" might, I thought, yield a useful methodology or terminology. Describing, first, the vexed relationship between modernist high art and mass culture, Huyssen emphasizes the ways in which postmodernism mediates or transcends this "great divide." Initially part of an avant-garde (in the sixties, that is), postmodernism presently—in the seventies and eighties—evolved fresh forms to register "the emergence of a culture of eclecticism" that to some degree obviated "critique, transgression or negation." At the same time, along a parallel track, postmodernism continued its "resistance, critique, and negation of the status quo in non-modernist and non-avantgardist terms." I am not altogether convinced, however, that "the postmodernism of the 1960s tried to revitalize the heritage of the European avant-garde and to give it an American form along what one could call in short-hand the Duchamp-Cage-Warhol axis."[19] I resist the implicit characterization of early postmodernism as warmed-over Dadaism, which could at times make common cause with its more strategically disruptive cousin, mainstream modernism. As Huyssen himself points out, avant-gardist intersections with modernism took place largely in Europe, where the unimaginative middle classes had co-opted high art as a validator of social status. Because high art in the United States never enjoyed the status it enjoyed in Europe, he observes, American modernists remained especially passionate in their claims for art's legitimacy and importance—they took relatively little interest in the European avant-garde's attacks on the cozy relationship between art and bourgeois culture. Rather, as one sees in the musings of the dying writer in

Hemingway's "Snows of Kilimanjaro," American modernists reproach their native culture for its general philistinism. For the student of current trends in American literary art, then, the historicizing of questions about the avant-garde's role in postmodernism can seem oversubtle (except insofar as one thinks of the Beats as both avant-garde and postmodern).

But even if Huyssen offers little help with the question most under scrutiny here—what differentiates the writers who came to prominence in the 1960s from the succeeding generation or generations?—one should note some of his more cogent observations. An example: "Pop in the broadest sense was the context in which a notion of the postmodern first took shape, and from the beginning until today, the most significant trends within postmodernism have challenged modernism's relentless hostility to mass culture." In the sixties, he notes, "[t]here emerged a vigorous, though again largely uncritical attempt to validate popular culture as a challenge to the canon of high art, modernist or traditional." Thus he concludes: "the great divide that separated high modernism from mass culture and that was codified in the various classical accounts of modernism no longer seems relevant to postmodern artistic or critical sensibilities."[20] These pronouncements would seem to be borne out when a Thomas Pynchon—arguably Zeus in the postmodern Pantheon—can supply the voice in depictions of himself on *The Simpsons* or when curmudgeonly Cormac McCarthy agrees to an interview—his first in fifteen years—with Oprah Winfrey, the same daytime television personality whose embrace so troubled Jonathan Franzen (about whom more presently).

Certainly one discerns abundant cross-fertilization between the contemporary novel and popular genres. One has seen what Don DeLillo can do with the thriller (*Running Dog*); or John Gardner with the spirit of Disney (in *Grendel* or *The Sunlight Dialogues*); or Thomas Pynchon with cartoonist/animators Chuck Jones and Tex Avery (in *The Crying of Lot 49*), with film culture (*Gravity's Rainbow*), with television (*Vineland*), and with the detective novel (*Inherent Vice*); or any of a number of writers with the idea of the theme park (I think of Pynchon again—Zwölfkinder in *Gravity's Rainbow*—or George Saunders in the title story of *Pastoralia*, or Richard Powers in *Prisoner's Dilemma*, or, less seriously, Michael Crichton in *Jurassic Park*). This granted, I squirm to read novelists who reveal cultural poverty (rather than some principled postmodern egalitarianism) in their inability (not, that is, unwillingness) to include some reference to art and ideas outside the pop-cultural matrix. There is, alas, a body of work—sometimes tak-

ing itself quite seriously—that references only brand names and the productions of recent popular culture. I was struck, some years back, while enjoying
Stephen King's *The Stand*, to realize that the range of high-cultural reference
in it amounted to a single, rather predictable echo of Yeats. By the same token, the hackneyed apocalypticism of the novel's conclusion (complete with
the staging of a new Calvary) made me nostalgic for the day when biblical
allusion actually carried some conviction. O Tempora! O Milton!

Still, the much discussed 2001 case of Jonathan Franzen *contra* Oprah
may in fact be understood as a vestige of what Huyssen calls "the modernist
dogma that all mass culture is monolithic Kitsch, psychologically regressive
and mind-destroying."[21] Franzen's alarm at the prospect of mass-media commodification, along with his apparent conviction that a popular book club
posed a threat to his artistic purity and autonomy, does seem to be the reas-
sertion of an older, pre-postmodern contempt for or fear of mass culture.
"[T]he artist who's really serious about resisting a culture of inauthentic
mass-marketed image must resist becoming an image himself."[22] However
ungracious, Franzen poses an interesting problem to the literary historian.
His case prompts one to perpend the passionate attention to craft on the part
of many of our most serious contemporary writers. Can the artists themselves have become a little uncomfortable with the collapse of boundaries?
The correspondence between Franzen (born in 1959) and Don DeLillo (born
in 1936) suggests a quiet—or not so quiet—insistence on discrimination.
Authors write, DeLillo told Franzen, to deliver themselves from "mass identity."[23] Thus DeLillo speaks sympathetically, in an interview, of the "writer . . .
working against the age," the writer who "feels some satisfaction at not being
widely read," the writer "diminished," even, "by an audience."[24]

Franzen is not alone in seeking inspiration and example (if not outright
mentorship) among writers of the older generation. A central character in
Richard Powers's *The Gold Bug Variations* declares Thomas Pynchon his
"favorite living novelist," and the novelist narrator of *Galatea 2.2* (he calls
himself Richard Powers) mentions having read *Gravity's Rainbow* in high
school.[25] Among the innumerable counterparts of these fictional sons of Pyn,
one includes the real-life Powers, along with George Saunders, Rick Moody,
Jeffrey Eugenides, Lorrie Moore, Lydia Davis, Joanna Scott, Percival Ever-
ett, Kathryn Kramer, Carter Scholz, Trey Ellis, Jim Shepard, Emily Barton,
Jay Cantor, and Steve Erickson—all contributors to the 2005 special issue
of *Bookforum* devoted to Pynchon. These writers practice discipleship in
various ways. Delighting in the anatomy, the catalogue, and the endless list,

many write fictions of "encyclopedic" inclusiveness, often embedding salutes to the master in their texts. One notes, in passing, that Pynchon occasionally returns the compliment—and not just in the blurbs that his bibliographers cherish like the fewmets of some elusive literary prey. In *Against the Day*, for example, he pauses at one point over stories that disguise ancient atrocity, as if to tip his hat to the Richard Powers of *Operation Wandering Soul*. In much the same way, when a character in the Pynchon novel wakes up beside the body of his victim in a surreal Los Angeles, one recalls the similar scene in Steve Erickson's *Arc d'X*.[26] In *Bleeding Edge* (2013), with its fraud investigator protagonist, Pynchon seems to be reimagining the accountant at the center of David Foster Wallace's posthumous *The Pale King* (2011).

In a 1996 article, the critic Tom LeClair speculated on the emergence of a post-Pynchon, post-DeLillo poetics, especially visible in the work of younger writers "educated in the Age of Information." LeClair notes that "Powers, born in 1957; [William] Vollmann, born in 1959; and [David Foster] Wallace, born in 1962," all profess in various ways to admire and look up to Pynchon, twenty or so years their elder. But where polymathic Pynchon tore down the wall between science and the humanities, his successors were born, as it were, into the information culture, which they take for granted and manipulate in ways that seem impossible to authors whose demographics make them prisoners (one is tempted to say "virtual" prisoners) of an analogue sensibility.[27] Supremely comfortable with the new technology and the new science, the postmodern ephebes are the literary equivalents of kids who can program the DVD player to interface with the stereo system, the cell phone, the digital camera, the camcorder, and the MP3 device. Powers is a kind of reverse version of Ken Jennings, the *Jeopardy* champion who majored in English and became a software engineer. The author of the immensely original *Three Farmers on Their Way to a Dance* (1987), the stunning *Gold Bug Variations* (1991), and the disturbing *Operation Wandering Soul* (1993), Powers has worked as a programmer but found his real calling as one of the most accomplished novelists of his generation. His characters often share his background in or aptitude for computer (and other) technology.

But a single swallow (or even three) does not make a summer. One must remember that many important younger authors take relatively little interest in information technology. Many, in fact (Anne Tyler, Ann Beattie, Kent Haruf, Jane Smiley), flourish as writers of what might be called the postmodern novel of manners. Again, we are left with the problem of competing postmodernisms, tidal pools instead of the tide itself.

I do, however, see considerable continuity between the David Foster Wallaces, the William Vollmanns, the Mark Z. Danielewskis and such older writers as Barth, Pynchon, Gaddis, and DeLillo. In that they perfected a style that remains fresh in the hands of their successors, the first postmodernists resemble such great modernist counterparts as Joyce and Eliot (though not, perhaps, the Hemingway whose style, often characterized as influential, actually resists imitation, except to parodic ends). Thus Gaddis, Barth, Pynchon, and McCarthy may plausibly be said to inspire Richard Powers, David Foster Wallace, and, less convincingly, Chuck Palahniuk or Michael Chabon. Certainly one sees, across this spectrum, an immense and unflagging delight in the possibilities afforded by an extensive vocabulary, deployed with wit and precision. Not that clever wordsmithing always translates to great achievement. An ability to pyrotechnicalize on the page cannot obviate the need for passionate ideation and a larger artistic vision. But the best of our younger writers, as I have noted previously, strive to write fictions of encyclopedic scope, novels with "Menippean" credentials. Subject to what Janette Turner Hospital calls "the God itch," all delight as much in creating worlds as in representing them.[28] If in fact they view referentiality in language as problematic, language yet remains for them the tool to keep ever sharp. The younger postmodernists, like their older counterparts, delight in supple, ludic, performative prose.

TRACING THE MAINSTREAM

My problem here turns out to be the conflict between a perceived splintering of fictive practice and a felt need to discern some kind of larger continuity— the continuity that will presumably become plain to later observers and literary historians. After all, we seldom think of previous periods of literary history as congeries of competing aesthetic visions and goals—in retrospect, at least, the contending politics (University Wits–Upstart Crows, Catholic-Protestant, Roundhead-Cavalier, Whig-Tory) are subsumed within the larger, epistemic order. With the passing of the years, a true dominant emerges, an entity that mutates, adapts, and survives to redirect the trajectory of culture. As Mannheim would say, "entelechies" materialize and gather in the disparate strands of the cultural moment.

But how long do artistic or musical or literary styles hold their own? Do their life spans become progressively shorter as time goes on? Can one still imagine the emergence of an era that, in its music, its art, and its literature, might vie in authority and longevity with, say, the Renaissance or the Augustan Age or the Victorian period? Are new movements—black humor, surfiction, minimalism, K-Mart realism—doomed to brief transits across the cultural heaven? Does even genius get only fifteen minutes? Every literary age has its short-lived sensations, but our own can be especially quick to dismiss. How troubling to think of all the gifted, often prolific writers who have in recent years proved to be meteors, not new planets: William Goyen, John Gardner, D. M. Thomas, Charles Frazier, Kaye Gibbons, Jayne Anne Phillips, Stewart O'Nan. Along with these, one ranges the one-book wonders, living proof of Fitzgerald's dictum: "There are no second acts in American lives."[29] Ross Lockridge comes to mind, along with such admitted titans as Ralph Ellison, who achieved planetary status on the strength of a single great book, or Joseph Heller, who wrote several novels but only one great one (much the same, of course, can be said of Herman Melville).

It can be instructive to ask colleagues who study, teach, and write about contemporary fiction to name the authors whose work they feel obliged to read promptly, as soon as it appears. Which authors do they merely sample? How much of a sample do they consider adequate? Which respected authors do they gradually stop keeping up with? The other day, asked whether I had yet read the latest Paul Auster, I found myself thinking: no—I've read all the Auster I need to, especially when I consider all the as-yet-unsampled authors who await my attention. Better to read more Ben Marcus, ZZ Packer, Mark Richard, Charles D'Ambrosio. As for the authors whose books I myself always read as soon as they appear (or, by going online in search of "ARCs" or Advanced Reader's Copies, before they appear), the list bears repeating: Thomas Pynchon, Don DeLillo, Cormac McCarthy, Margaret Atwood, Richard Powers, Chang-rae Lee.

Not that reliable prognostication always figures in the likes and dislikes of specialists in contemporary fiction. Doubtless we have neglected our share of Chattertons and Melvilles, and doubtless we have embraced this or that equivalent of Colley Cibber or James Branch Cabell. Indeed, reflection on the last two, both famous literati in their day, should prompt worried questions about which of our current stars will, a hundred or two hundred years hence, elicit incredulous chuckles among those who read the classics—if such things still exist—of the late twentieth and early twenty-first centuries. The unrecognized, of course, we have always with us. One thinks of John Kennedy O'Toole as our Chatterton, that marvelous boy. What might he have accomplished had he not given up and, anticipating David Foster Wallace, violated what Hamlet calls the "canon 'gainst self-slaughter"? Others, perhaps equally gifted, survive amid exiguous applause from a tiny readership: Rachel Ingalls, perhaps, or Curtis White, or almost anyone published by the visionary folks at Dalkey Archive Press.

By way of conclusion, I should like briefly to comment on the narrowness of my focus. I realize that much artistic energy has been shunted into film, contemporary music, graphic fiction, and other genres, but my interest remains fixed on the contemporary American novel, however precarious its appeal to consumers of literary and other art. I do not, that is, repine at the thought of merely documenting the decline of a once robust form. After all, "[i]f serious reading dwindles to near nothingness," as Don DeLillo has remarked, "it will probably mean that the thing we're talking about when we use the word 'identity' has reached an end."[30] I would be more worried, of course, if the novel were not so frequently—and prematurely—pronounced dead; nor is it particularly worrisome if the fictions and authors adduced here subsist at the margins. "If I were a writer," says Owen Brademas in DeLillo's 1982 novel *The Names*, "how I would enjoy being told the novel is dead. How liberating to work in the margins, outside a central perception."[31] These sentiments seem to echo those of the author himself: Adam Begley observes that "[i]f everything in the culture argues against the novel, that's what DeLillo's going to make. If celebrity is the expected path, he'll find a detour. He chooses to set up shop on the far periphery, in the shadows—out of sight, but with a clear view of the center."[32] The margins, then, afford a good vantage from which to observe a culture, and the critic, one hopes, may profitably share that perspective with the serious novelist.

Thus one makes no claims regarding the ability of contemporary literary artists to be, as it were, "players" (the word echoes another DeLillo title). Indeed, the inability really to shape public perception—or even to aspire to do so—may constitute another of those modern-postmodern demarcations that critics from Ihab Hassan to Fredric Jameson like to enumerate. As recently as 1959, Norman Mailer could aspire to effect, single-handedly, "a revolution in the consciousness of our time," but by century's end such vaunts gave way to recognition, in some quarters, that certain tectonic shifts in the culture had sidelined its most gifted literary artists, however cogent and perceptive their thought.[33] DeLillo's Bill Gray makes the point most trenchantly: "Years ago I used to think it was possible for a novelist to alter the inner life of a culture. Now bomb-makers and gunmen have taken that territory. They make raids on human consciousness." This painful recognition recurs in his thought: "For some time now I've had the feeling that novelists and terrorists are playing a zero-sum game. . . . What terrorists gain, novelists lose. The degree to which they influence mass consciousness is the extent of our decline as shapers of sensibility and thought. The danger they represent equals our own failure to be dangerous."[34] Critics rightly decline to see Bill Gray as DeLillo's Mauberley-like self-portrait. In the end, the fictional writer in *Mao II* enacts an authorial paralysis that seems never to have troubled his creator. Bill's oft-quoted remarks, however, suggest that he has been brought low by the great paradox of modern and postmodern poetics: politicized expectation diminishes the art it affects to take seriously. Bill remembers Beckett but forgets Sir Philip Sidney, who understood that "the poet nothing affirmeth." To paraphrase that famous line from W. H. Auden, the novel makes nothing happen.

That said, one can also paraphrase William Carlos Williams: "It is difficult / to get the news from novels / yet men die miserably every day / for lack / of what is found there."[35] Great fiction, like the poetry to which Sidney and Auden and Williams actually refer, distills the experience of living and captures the human condition in all its variety. Great contemporary fiction, by the same token, orients us to the business of living with and in the sprawling, vital, endlessly vulgar culture of the American moment. In 1923 T. S. Eliot imagined that the modern novel, as newly configured by James Joyce, might give its readers a handle on "contemporary history," which the author of *The Waste Land* characterized as an "immense panorama of futility and anarchy."[36] In 1961, Philip Roth lamented that the contemporary novelist "has his hands full in trying to understand, describe, and then make credible" an "American reality" that so "stupifies," "sickens," and "infuriates" that it becomes "a kind of embarrassment to one's meager imagination."[37] Over half a century later, the "American reality" has become, if anything, even more appalling. But whatever its capacity for beggaring the imagination, it continues to register—often in unique ways—on the constantly calibrated instrument that is the contemporary American novel. Those of us who read serious fiction have at least the comfort of a heightened knowledge, however Cassandra-like and apologetic our pedagogy.

Beyond these considerations abide the questions of who or what comes next. One often hears (in Walter Jackson Bate, in John Barth, in Harold Bloom) that every succeeding literary generation has to come to terms with its sense of inadequacy before the achievements of its predecessors. Johann

Wolfgang von Goethe, one recalls, was relieved not to have been born an English writer—having to make it new after William Shakespeare would be, he felt, just too daunting. But in theorizing such anxieties (Bloom's word remains compelling), one need not capitulate to the doctrine of imaginative entropy. Literary creativity delights in fresh challenges and meets them, often as not, without throwing over its models. Which is not to say that young writers must be content with the blunted tools of secondhand language. Every new literary generation purifies the Pierian Spring in its own way.

* * * * * * *

A word, finally, about my specimen texts, ten fictions published at the end of the twentieth century and the beginning of the twenty-first. A glance at the table of contents will show that I do not see literary postmodernism as another club for white males. But I have also made a point of not rounding up quite the usual suspects. That is, disinclined to join the journalistic chorus characterizing David Foster Wallace, say, or Jonathan Franzen as their generation's most important voices, I have opted to revisit certain fine writers who strike me as unjustly neglected (Michael Dorris, Gloria Naylor) or unjustly patronized for their popularity (Chuck Palahniuk, Ann Patchett). By the same token, though mindful of current critical claims for the legitimacy and value of genre fiction, I am less interested in assessing the latest graphic novel or science-oriented fabulation or young adult vampire fantasy than in analyzing the many ways that more serious fiction incorporates elements of popular narrative. Viktor Shklovsky was right to argue that literature has always renewed itself by such "canonization of the junior branch," that is, the inclusion and making respectable in high art of features previously encountered only in genre fiction and related popular forms.[38] Whatever their pop culture accommodations (I think especially of the punk rock ethos of Jennifer Egan's A Visit from the Goon Squad), the works adduced here merit their place on the shelf reserved for serious writing. More interesting for his literary journalism, in my view, than for his fiction, Jonathan Franzen suggests that "good fiction is defined, in large part, by its refusal to offer the easy answers of ideology, the cures of a therapeutic culture, or the pleasantly resolving dreams of mass entertainment."[39] Continuing to differentiate the good from the bad, the common from the canonical, such observations reaffirm with Ralph Ellison, that "[o]ne function of serious literature is to deal with the moral core of a given society."[40] Yet despised popular entertainments often reveal themselves as trenchant critiques of that "moral core," and postmodern practitioners have done much to discredit the low-brow, high-brow dichotomy. Thus does a Joss Whedon film, a Chuck Palahniuk novel, a *Simpsons* episode edge its way into the precincts of serious art, recognizable, even, as what an aesthetic conservative might embrace.

I think of the generational question as a kind of ground bass in these chapters, above which varying themes are announced and developed: the role of irony in turn-of-the-millennium writing, the challenge to the storyteller of metahistory's ascendancy and metanarrative's decline, the role of the artist under the postmodern dispensation. Without, I hope, becoming thesis-bound or schematic, I recur periodically to the proposition that one can often think profitably about this or that foregrounded theme in terms of just how its development differs from or resembles that of similar material in the work of a first-generation postmodernist. This dynamic receives more attention as the study progresses. Thus chapters 1 and 4, devoted to fictions in which Rachel Ingalls and Gloria Naylor reframe Shakespearean archetype (the one reimagines Caliban, the other Prospero), feature only passing notice of the intertextual presence of such pioneering postmoderns as Grace Paley, Toni Morrison, Kurt Vonnegut, and John Fowles. In chapter 2, however, I suggest that negotiations with Flannery O'Connor figure importantly in Alice Walker's anguished meditations on the politics of African American identity and experience. In chapter 3, I turn to a Native American, Michael Dorris, who, like his contemporaries James Welch and Leslie Marmon Silko, must reframe the already postmodern aesthetic of their predecessor, N. Scott Momaday (all must reconcile postmodern storytelling with tradition as they treat themes of assimilation and racial difference). In chapters 5 and 6, reading works by Steve Erickson and Richard Powers, I look at the benefits—and costs—of postmodern discipleship, for both writers plainly express their admiration for Thomas Pynchon and revisit certain of his themes: the problematic coalescence of story and history, the radical question of the storyteller's legitimate or perhaps profoundly illegitimate mendacity. Where these writers worry about dishonest storytelling and tendentious historiography, others grapple, on the very eve of 9/11, with the question of irony's legitimacy as rhetorical default in the age of terrorism. In chapter 7, then, I consider the ways in which one can situate Chuck Palahniuk in the apostolic succession of postmodern ironists. In chapter 8, I reflect on Ann Patchett's post-DeLillo treatment of terrorism and art. I then proceed, in chapter 9, to differentiate competing figures of the postmodern (and post-Nabokovian) artist-protagonist in Mark Z. Danielewski's vast and ambitious *House of Leaves*. Lastly, in chapter 10, I consider how Jennifer Egan, like Patchett, embraces a postmodern aesthetic that has passed beyond the need constantly to rehearse its iconoclastic superiority to modernist antecedent. All of these writers, I suggest, work fresh veins in a postmodern mine in which the canaries are still singing.

Appendix

A Selection of Contemporary American Fiction Writers by Birth Decade

1920s William Gaddis (1922), Grace Paley (1922), Kurt Vonnegut (1922), Jack Kerouac (1922), John Williams (1922), Paula Fox (1923), Joseph Heller (1923), Norman Mailer (1923), James Baldwin (1924), William H. Gass (1924), John Hawkes (1925), Flannery O'Connor (1925), Alison Lurie (1926), Richard Yates (1926), David Markson (1927), Cynthia Ozick (1928), Kate Wilhelm (1928), Ursula LeGuin (1929), Paule Marshall (1929), Gilbert Sorrentino (1929)

1930s: John Barth (1930), Maureen Howard (1930), Paul West (1930), Walter Abish (1931), Donald Barthelme (1931), E. L. Doctorow (1931), Toni Morrison (1931), John Updike (1932), Robert Coover (1932), John Gardner (1933), Cormac McCarthy (1933), Philip Roth (1933), Joan Didion (1934), N. Scott Momaday (1934), E. Annie Proulx (1935), Don DeLillo (1936), Clarence Major (1936), Tom Robbins (1936), Thomas Pynchon (1937), Robert Stone (1937), Renata Adler (1938), Raymond Carver (1938), Ishmael Reed (1938), Lynn Sharon Schwartz (1939)

1940s: Maxine Hong Kingston (1940), Bobbie Ann Mason (1940), Rachel Ingalls (1940), James Welch (1940), Anne Tyler (1941), John Edgar Wideman (1941), Rikki Ducornet (1943), Kent Haruf (1943), Richard Ford (1944), Eric Kraft (1944), Alice Walker (1944), Robert Olen Butler (1945), Michael Dorris (1945), Jim Dodge (1945), Tobias Wolff (1945), Tim O'Brien (1946), Stephen Wright (1946), Paul Auster (1947), Kathy Acker (1947), Ann Beattie (1947), Ron Hansen (1947), Octavia Butler (1947), Lydia Davis (1947), Marilynne Robinson (1947), T. Coraghessan Boyle (1948), William Gibson

(1948), Alan Lightman (1948), Leslie Marmon Silko (1948), Dorothy Allison (1949), Richard Russo (1949), Jane Smiley (1949)

1950s: Kate Braverman (1950), Steve Erickson (1950), Charles Frazier (1950), Gloria Naylor (1950), Jean Thompson (1950), Amy Hempel (1951), Oscar Hijuelos (1951), Ted Mooney (1951), Bob Shacochis (1951), Curtis White (1951), Geoffrey Green (1952), Alice Hoffman (1952), Walter Mosley (1952), Amy Tan (1952) Sandra Cisneros (1954), Louise Erdrich (1954), Ken Kalfus (1954), Siri Hustvedt (1955), Gish Jen (1955), Barbara Kingsolver (1955), Jay McInerney (1955), Mark Richard (1955), Mark Leyner (1956), Carole Maso (1956), James McBride (1957), Lorrie Moore (1957), Richard Powers (1957), Donald Antrim (1958), Charles D'Ambrosio (1958), Ben Fountain (1958), George Saunders (1958), Jonathan Franzen (1959), William Vollmann (1959)

1960s: David Bajo (1960), Joanna Scott (1960), Marisa Silver (1960), Susan Straight (1960), A. M. Homes (1961), Rick Moody (1961), Mark Costello (1962), Jennifer Egan (1962), Julie Otsuka (1962), Chuck Palahniuk (1962), David Foster Wallace (1962), Michael Chabon (1963), Tom Franklin (1963), Shelley Jackson (1963), Randall Kenan (1963), Ann Patchett (1963), Christopher Sorrentino (1963), Donna Tartt (1963), Elise Blackwell (1964), Jonathan Lethem (1964), Bret Easton Ellis (1964), Jim Knipfel (1965), Matt Ruff (1965), Jess Walter (1965), Sherman Alexie (1966), Mark Z. Danielewski (1966), Claire Messud (1966), Allegra Goodman (1967), Adam Johnson (1967), Ben Marcus (1967), Sam Lipsyte (1968), Emily Barton (1969), Aimee Bender (1969), Amy Waldman (1969), Colson Whitehead (1969)

1970s: Dave Eggers (1970), Nathan Englander (1970), Matthew Guinn (1970), Adam Haslett (1970), Atticus Lish (1971), Benjamin Kunkel (1972), Michael James Rizza (1972), Anthony Doerr (1973), ZZ Packer (1973), Joshua Ferris (1974), Nicole Krauss (1974), Philipp Meyer (1974), Teju Cole (1975), Chad Harbach (1975), Jonathan Safran Foer (1977), Garth Risk Hallberg (1978), Ben Lerner (1979), Benjamin Percy (1979)

1980s: Nathaniel Rich (1980), Karen Russell (b. 1981), Brian Ray (1982)

The immigrants: Charles Bukowski (1920), Bharati Mukherjee (1940), Janette Turner Hospital (1942), Ursula Heyi (1946), Wendy Law-Yone (1947), Art Spiegelman (1948), Jamaica Kincaid (1949), Julia Alvarez (1950),

Abraham Verghese (1955), Ha Jin (1956), Achy Obejas (1956), Anchee Min (1957), Cristina García (1958), Lan Cao (1961), Mylène Dressler (1963), Colin Channer (1963), Aleksandar Hemon (1964), Joseph O'Neill (1964), Khaled Hosseini (1965), Chang-rae Lee (1965), Colum McCann (1965), Jhumpa Lahiri (1967), Junot Díaz (1968), Edwidge Danticat (1969), Gary Shteyngart (1972), Dinaw Mengestu (1978)

CHAPTER I

Fantasy and Reality in Rachel Ingalls's Mrs. Caliban

Misery acquaints a man with strange bedfellows.

—WILLIAM SHAKESPEARE, *THE TEMPEST*

Rachel Ingalls, an American who has long resided in England, drew little attention in this country until the British Book Marketing Council declared her 1982 novel *Mrs. Caliban* one of the twenty greatest American novels after World War II. According to Jack Beatty, the book had originally sold only 500 copies in the United States.[1] A brief though positive notice in the *New Yorker* (25 July 1983) was virtually the only review. But the British pronouncement (like the French appreciation of a nearly forgotten Faulkner in the forties) prompted belated cis-atlantic attention to a remarkable talent. Enthusiastic articles and reviews appeared in the *Atlantic* (April 1986), the *New York Times Book Review* (28 December 1986), and *USA Today* (25 April 1986). Ingalls began to be widely read in her native country; four years after its original publication, the novel became a kind of academic bestseller. While the students were reading Bret Easton Ellis's *Less Than Zero* (1985), their teachers were reading *Mrs. Caliban*.

The reader of *Mrs. Caliban* encounters considerable mythic, literary, and psychological depth. Though not overtly allusive (only the title points clearly to literary antecedents), the novel seems to invite connections with a number of related fictions that enhance and extend its meaning. It seems at times a paradigm of intertextuality—of the tendency, that is, of a text to echo and imitate and rewrite other texts. A postmodern psychological novel, *Mrs. Caliban* reveals an awareness on the part of its author that the definitive venue of intertextuality, the supreme palimpsest, is the mind. Ingalls explores the fundamental conflict between the pleasure principle and the reality principle in terms of one woman's experiences with love, sex, mother-hood, friendship, social integration, and fate.

Born in 1940, Ingalls is the oldest of the authors treated here as second-generation postmodernists. That is, I place her with figures such as Bobbie Ann Mason (also born in 1940), Alice Walker (born in 1944), Octavia Butler (born 1947), and Gloria Naylor (born 1950), rather than with such pioneers of postmodernism as Flannery O'Connor and Grace Paley (both almost twenty years older than the author of *Mrs. Caliban*).[2] I admit, however, that a case could be made for including Ingalls—only three or four years younger than Pynchon and DeLillo, after all—in the first generation, and perhaps, given the memorable amphibian she creates ("Larry the Monsterman"), it will be just as well to treat her as his literary equivalent, a bridge between first- and second-generation postmodernism. Certainly one discerns links and affinities between this writer and both her older and younger fellows. Like Gloria Naylor, she rewrites Shakespeare's *The Tempest*; like Octavia Butler, she liberates science fiction and fantasy from the genre-fiction ghetto. Yet like the older writers, O'Connor and Paley, she favors short forms (only *Binstead's Safari* is long enough to be called a novel). By the same token, Ingalls's West Coast gothic (in *Mrs. Caliban*) displays affinities with the cele-brated southern variety as it figures in O'Connor. More importantly, Ingalls's powerful representations of women's experience reframe, in some degree, those of the Grace Paley who in a 1982 interview characterized "[t]he dark lives of women" as "what made me a writer to begin with."[3]

These affinities aside, *Mrs. Caliban* subsumes or parodies several literary and cinematic genres, in both romance and realist modes. These include, besides the psychological novel, science fiction, fantasy, monster movies, and soap opera. Ingalls also invokes the spectrum from "women's fiction" to feminist literature. This generic multivalence complements more spe-cific affinities with such fictions as Fitzgerald's *The Great Gatsby*, Fowles's *The Collector*, Pynchon's *The Crying of Lot 49*, and *Beauty and the Beast* in both its traditional and cinematic versions. The *Wizard of Oz* also figures, for *Mrs. Caliban* concerns a Dorothy with a remarkably rich fantasy life. In Ingalls's version, however, the adorable terrier has long since perished, and an unreal Southern California replaces both real Kansas and fantastic Oz. Like Fowles's *The Collector*, the novel invites its reader to reflect on the contemporary significance of the Caliban myth. Fowles's Caliban, a psycho-pathic clerk, exemplifies what Hannah Arendt famously called the banality of evil; Ingalls's Caliban, on the other hand, is a largely sympathetic portrait of embattled nature itself. Ingalls glances at Pynchon's *The Crying of Lot 49* in that she depicts a psychologically marginal housewife whose bizarre experiences alienate her forever from the dreary, unimaginative lives around her in wasteland suburbia. As an erotically charged fantasy about the female encounter with the sexual other as a beast at once fearsome and splendid, *Mrs. Caliban* has a mythic side that links it to *Beauty and the Beast* and the rest of what Bruno Bettelheim calls "the animal-groom cycle of fairy tales."[4] As in *The Great Gatsby*, finally, characters' driving habits symbolically suggest their moral identities.

The references to automobiles and driving, in other words, do more than authenticate the Southern California setting. Cars traditionally suggest responsibility, a means of freedom, a potential danger to oneself and to others. Dorothy's husband, Fred, for example, drives a car described as old and frequently in need of repair. It resembles his marriage, and indeed he must rent a car or call a cab to pursue erotic opportunity. The pursuit proves costly when he and his teen-aged lover perish in a fiery car crash.

Larry, another male who makes the automobile his means of freedom, hot-wires cars and roams far and wide. Dorothy's friend Estelle enters the novel with a comic crash of surrogate cars, supermarket carriages; the narrator subsequently describes her—with transparent symbolism—as a "natural speeder."[5] As she drives, so does she roll over marriage vows and personal friendship. Ironically, at one point she complains about her daughter Sandra's having taken their car, which no doubt facilitates Sandra's own pursuit of Dorothy's husband. As for Dorothy herself, she appears as a "careful driver" (18), considerate, thoughtful of others.

Literary affinities like those noted above provide intertextual buttressing for the meaning or meanings intimated in the novel's title, which invites connections with Shakespeare's *The Tempest* and perhaps with Browning's "Caliban Upon Setebos." Ingalls suggests with her title that she will somehow androgynize the monstrous Caliban, reluctant servant of Prospero in Shakespeare's play. Since the protagonist, Dorothy, is something of a despised servant who shops, cooks, cleans, gardens, and mothers, the novel's title can be construed to announce a meditation on Caliban as woman. Yet the title can also refer to an idea of woman as spouse of Caliban. Dorothy, in fact, is Caliban's woman twice over: wife and servant to the moral monster, Fred; lover of the physical monster, Larry.

If Dorothy embodies an idea of female subalternity in her relationship with Fred, the more refined feminist polemic figures in her relationship with Larry, which also allows for a more subtle exploitation of the Shake-speare paradigm. Shakespeare's Caliban symbolically represents what one critic calls "brute-matter"—that which human ingenuity, in the form of the magician-scientist Prospero, must bend to its will to improve the quality of human life.[6] But the mastery of nature, begun so necessarily and gloriously in Shakespeare's Renaissance, has come in the twentieth century to mean the violation of nature. Science seems now to result in increasingly ambigu-ous advances, as experimentation with animals becomes indistinguishable from abuse of animals, and as new knowledge issues in weapons and pol-lution as often as in life-enhancing technology. Larry, brutally tamed at the Jefferson Institute for Oceanographic Research by Kelsoe, Wachter, and Forest, is Shakespeare's Caliban in the twentieth century, an embodiment of nature as helpless victim of modern science.

As Caliban-nature, Larry exhibits a simple affinity not with coercive, logocentric science but with woman. What is done to "Aquarius the Mon-sterman" is done by male scientists; only a woman can respond appropriately to this symbolic projection of nature itself. The nonrational, nonanalytic relationship with nature finds expression in Dorothy's instinct for garden-ing. She easily makes it a common cause with her Hispanic gardener, Mr. Mendoza, who represents an exploited minority as traditionally powerless as women. Together they make a point of gardening ecologically—without artificial fertilizers and pesticides. Dorothy even imagines on one occasion that Mr. Mendoza shares her secret about Larry.

But Ingalls looks to *The Tempest* for more than Caliban. Shakespeare's play provides an ironic counterpoint to the bleak worldview that figures in this novel. The play concerns an island realm perfectly ordered by a benign magus or artist-figure, the powerful Prospero. His power makes him almost, symbolically, God, and with it he not only subdues and chastens the bestial Caliban but also obtains justice for himself and love for his daughter and Prince Ferdinand. At the same time, he neutralizes the machinations of vil-lains like Antonio and Sebastian.

In other words, *The Tempest* is a near-utopian vision of an ordered world, a world in which virtue flourishes and evil falters because of the ac-tive involvement of a benign supernatural power. But in *Mrs. Caliban*, the reader enters a world filled with brutality and disorder both natural and so-cial: children die or mothers miscarry; people betray their spouses and their friends; Tinseltown Lotharios enjoy sixteen year olds as sexual playthings, while other children seduce their parents' lovers; street gangs wreak havoc;

pets get run over; scenes of carnage ensanguine the highways; scientists torment animals sadistically; the press battens onto every horror like a vampire; cheese and people are processed.

No Prospero, no Ariel, no God. The subject of religion comes up only to be dismissed as superstition. Dorothy "had asked herself was religion really the only thing that kept people together, wrongly believing bad things will happen after death?" (23). She has, then, nothing to fall back on as her hopes for fulfillment dwindle: fate closes off every possibility of escape from her increasingly desperate circumstances.

In this benighted world, science and the press, charged with providing some understanding of the natural and the social disorder respectively, prove corrupt; their corruption, indeed, sometimes mirrors and sometimes promotes the disorder they investigate. This perception may account for Ingalls's dark picture of scientific inquiry. Like William Kotzwinkle in *Dr. Rat* (1976), this novelist takes an unsparing view of what animals are subjected to in the laboratory. The experiments with Larry proceeded simultaneously with instruction in language and behavior, but Dorothy recognizes in his pacific demeanor only evidence of how cruelly he has been treated: "He was always scrupulously polite. Now that she knew of the brutal methods that had been used to ram home the Institute's policy on polite manners, she found these little touches of good breeding in his speech as poignant as if they had been scars on his body" (36).

When Larry turns on his tormentors, he reenacts the fury of another sympathetic monster, the literary creation of another woman who examines the problematic relationship between nature and science. Mary Shelley's nightmare creature embodies the repressed id of her protagonist, Dr. Frankenstein, but as Sandra M. Gilbert and Susan Gubar argue in *The Madwoman in the Attic*, the monster also projects the largely unconscious anxieties of the woman ultimately responsible for him.[7] By contrast with the Frankenstein monster, Larry has no psychologically symbiotic relationship with an irresponsible scientist. He reifies, rather, the unconscious of the woman who succors him.

One notes, in this regard, the parallel between Dorothy and Larry as lab specimens. Larry has been injected, tormented, toyed with, sexually abused, and made superficially polite by draconian methods of behavior modification. He is not so much a clockwork orange as "Alex," the protagonist of Anthony Burgess's famous novel, but he is clearly made him something unnatural by the scientists' methods. Dorothy, too, is an experimental subject.

Rushing to get dinner ready for her husband and a guest, she recognizes herself as performer in a maze: "it was like some sort of test or race. Perhaps, like her, laboratory rats took a pride in solving the puzzles scientists set them" (24). But Dorothy is a specimen in the laboratory of cosmic caprice, the subject of a senseless but even more sustained course of torments at the hands of existence itself. She loses two children, a dog, her husband, a lover, a friend, and perhaps her mind. The extent of her bad luck seems like something almost metaphysically malign—God as mad scientist or as the capricious deity imagined by Caliban in Browning's "Caliban Upon Setebos." Both she and Larry are subjected to the most sadistic and cruel treatment imaginable; both are, as a result of their suffering, gentle and considerate.

Larry answers Dorothy's mental, emotional, and physical desperation so specifically as to suggest an answer to every reader's first question about this book: is Larry supposed to be real? The negative answer to that question comes in a variety of forms, beginning with the radio messages ostensibly intended for Dorothy alone. One notes, too, the suggestive passage that follows her initial encounter with Larry. Driving home after a shopping expedition, she sees, "up in the sky . . . a gigantic mounded cloud, as large and elaborately molded as a baroque opera house and lit from below and at the sides by pink and creamy hues. It sailed beyond her, improbable and romantic, following in the blue sky the course she was taking down below. It seemed to her that it must be a good omen" (38). No more substantial than this lovely cloud, "improbable and romantic," Larry exists only in her fevered and desperate mind.

The novelist's undeviating commitment to Dorothy's point of view supports the argument that Larry is imaginary. One notes a similar technique in Margaret Atwood's *The Handmaid's Tale*, published a couple of years after *Mrs. Caliban*. Atwood's novel also concerns the life of a woman cut off from meaningful activity—even reading. Atwood's Offred, like Ingalls's Dorothy, plays Scrabble with a disagreeable spouse named Fred and suffers the loss of a child. The first-person narration of *The Handmaid's Tale*, like the scrupulously limited third-person narration of the Ingalls novel, contributes to a sense of claustrophobia and exitlessness.

Dorothy never shares her knowledge of Larry with any of the people around her, and the narrative technique contributes to the likelihood that Larry exists only in her desperate imagination. Although press reports seen by characters other than Dorothy would seem to confirm that something has in fact escaped from the Ocean Research Laboratory, the reader has only

Dorothy's perceptions for such corroborative testimony. Perhaps, like the neurasthenic governess in *The Turn of the Screw*, she surrenders to psychosis. From first to last, Larry remains her personal secret, never to be shared—except perhaps with a psychiatrist.[8]

But the madness of women, in the present literary and cultural environment, is hardly to be settled thus casually. Linda S. Pickle, citing Mary Carruthers, notes that "madness is one tag attached to 'women whose lives no longer serve a function for men.'"[9] One is tempted, therefore, to honor Dorothy's conjuring of Larry as an imaginative act rather than to pity her mental buckling. Sandra Gilbert and Susan Gubar have argued persuasively that creative women, producing art in isolation, have historically suffered an "alienation that felt like madness" (51). The fact that women artists in the present have more cultural support for their activity happily obviates this sense of mental estrangement, but for a woman with no consciousness of artistic possibilities—for a woman like Dorothy, that is—the act of creation that alleviates half-grasped victimization remains psychologically problematic. Unfortunately, Dorothy lacks sufficient awareness of her plight or of legitimate imaginative responses to it.

Interpreted symbolically, Larry gives expression to Dorothy's every secret fear, anger, and desire; his symbolic multivalence ultimately provides the most cogent argument for his being a fantasy and at the same time makes the novel such a tour de force. Larry's capacity for violence, for example, represents Dorothy's repressed rage at life's injustice—and at the multiple betrayals around her. Because it is repressed, such rage cannot be properly focused or openly expressed. But Larry's violence is visited on entities obliquely representative of those that oppress Dorothy: masculine authority (the abusive scientists) and the son of the perfidious Estelle (whose betrayal Dorothy must unconsciously realize).

Yet Larry is also the child Dorothy has twice lost. Just before the description of the cloud (cited above), Dorothy explicitly links her feelings about Larry to feelings experienced in pregnancy: "Her happiness returned, like a glow, as though she had swallowed something warm which was continuing to radiate waves of warmth. It was a secret thing of her very own, yet she also wanted to talk about it to someone. This was the way she had felt the last time she was pregnant" (37). When Larry tells her that "music" surrounds him when he dwells in the sea, she thinks, "Perhaps it was like a child floating in its mother's womb and hearing her voice all around him" (45).

He is, finally, the consummate sexual fantasy—though as monster and lover he remains a version of her husband. His head is suggestively described as phallic, "quite like the head of a frog, but rounder, and the mouth was smaller and more centred in the face, like a human mouth. Only the nose was very flat, almost not there, and the forehead bulged up in two creases" (26). He is Anne Sexton's "Frog Prince," about whom the poet says, "Frog is my father's genitals."[10]

As the psychological projection of a woman in extremis, then, Larry represents (1) Dorothy's sense of herself as a strange life-form, at once wonderful and loathsome, (2) her need for love and gentleness and purpose, (3) her need for freedom and a "place," (4) her rage, (5) her child, and (6) her husband as monster and lover. At the end, in the cemetery, she gives her husband's name as both "Fred" and "Larry": "His name was actually Frederick. But I called him Larry" (124).

Unlike the problematic secret world discovered by Oedipa Maas in Thomas Pynchon's *The Crying of Lot 49*, Dorothy's fantasy cannot be construed as an essentially healthy illusion in an insane and brutal world, an illusion that promotes a desirable awareness of truths ignored or missed by more psychologically integrated citizens. At the end, she is utterly bereft of both real and imaginary sources of love, comfort, and human community. Her condition is depicted as unsparingly as anything in Beckett—but without the comforting determination of Beckett's characters to go on when they think they cannot go on. Waiting at the beach for the lover who "never came" (125), Dorothy faces an entropic finality. Defeated socially, emotionally, even biologically, this is a Dorothy without Toto, without Oz, without the happy ending.

Dorothy's condition at the close hints at a grim thematic resolution. In the closing pages of this story, the reader encounters three bereaved women: Dorothy, Estelle, and the nameless woman in the cemetery. The author seems to suggest that all women come at last to a barren coast, where that great sweet mother, the sea, mocks their expectations of fulfillment and even their pretensions to fertility. Thus John Updike, in his dust-jacket endorsement, marveled at *Mrs. Caliban*'s "opening up into a deep female sadness that makes us stare."

The final coalescence of Dorothy and Estelle merely caps the relentless irony of the whole novel's structure. Rereading it, one discerns the irony of every conversation between these two characters, every mention of Sandra or of Stan and Charlie (who represent Estelle's own version of Larry, the fantasy with which she handles her inability to have Fred). Irony, of course, is the rhetorical mode appropriate to the worldview at the heart of this novel. As discursive default, such irony figures as an ideational bridge between the modern and the postmodern. It also signals a continuity, rare in contemporary letters, with ancient ideas of tragedy.

CHAPTER 2

Colonized Tongue, Colonized Pen

Heritage and Deracination in
Alice Walker's "Everyday Use"

When the ax came into the forest the trees said the handle is one of us.

—TURKISH PROVERB, EPIGRAPH TO ALICE WALKER,
POSSESSING THE SECRET OF JOY

Postmodern irony differs from that of modernism in that it becomes more and more inclusive, as if sincerity in any sphere might lay one open to error more catastrophic, even, than the Great War that gave the lie to the old abstractions: honor, glory, sacrifice, in vain. Some deplore the universalization of irony as ultimately nihilistic, but it actually promotes a desirable recognition of perspectival fallibility and an understanding of the referential complexity of language. Irony in African American discourse, as Henry Louis Gates has shown, at once functions as critique and maps literary filiation. Like *Mrs. Caliban*, Alice Walker's "Everyday Use" proves ironic in all its parts, but the tone is comedic, even though the story unfolds in the vast and troubled shadow of African American history. In this story, included in her 1973 collection *In Love and Trouble*, Walker addresses herself to the dilemma of African Americans who, in striving to escape prejudice and poverty, risk a terrible deracination, a sundering from all that has sustained and defined them. The story concerns a young woman who, in the course of a visit to the rural home she thinks she has outgrown, attempts unsuccessfully to divert some fine old quilts, earmarked for the dowry of a sister, into her own hands. This character has changed her given name, "Dee Johnson," to the superficially more impressive "Wangero Leewanika Kemanjo"—and thereby created difficulties for the narrator (her mother), who tries to accustom herself to the new appellation but cannot quite repudiate the old one.

She tries to have it both ways, referring to her daughter now by one name, now by the other, now by parenthetically hybridized combinations of both. The critic, sharing Mrs. Johnson's confusion, may learn from her example to avoid awkwardness by calling the character more or less exclusively by one name. I have opted here for "Wangero"—without, I hope, missing the real significance of the confusion. Indeed, in this confusion one begins to see how the fashionable politics espoused by the central character of Walker's story becomes the foil to an authorial vision of the African American community, past and present, and its struggle for liberation.

The problem addressed in the present study—that of continuity or discontinuity between literary generations—has its own special history in African American letters. African American writing, according to Henry Louis Gates, enjoys its own distinctive brand of intertextuality, and I should like to begin this discussion by glancing at a couple of the ways in which "Everyday Use" exemplifies the theory developed by Gates in *The Signifying Monkey*. Borrowing a term from the vernacular, Gates argues that texts by African-American writers "Signify" on prior texts: they play with their predecessors in a perpetual and parodic evolution of meanings congenial to a people whose latitude for direct expression has been historically hedged about by innumerable sanctions. Gates explains Signifyin(g) with reference to Mikhail Bakhtin's idea of a "double-voiced" discourse, in which one hears simultaneously the present text and the text being augmented or ironically revised. Not that Signifyin(g) need always be at the expense of its intertext: in one of the analytic set pieces of his book, as it happens, Gates reads Walker's *The Color Purple* as what he calls "unmotivated" (that is, nondisparaging) Signifying on texts by Rebecca Cox Jackson and Zora Neale Hurston.

In "Everyday Use" one encounters Signifyin(g) in both its street sense and its literary sense. "To rename is to revise," says Gates, "and to revise is to Signify."[1] Thus Wangero thinks she is Signifyin(g) on white culture when she revises her name, but inadvertently she plays false with her own familial culture, as her mother's remarks about the history of the name Dee allow the reader to see. Indeed, if the mother were not so thoroughly innocent, one would suspect her of Signifying on her daughter's misguided aspirations. The master manipulator of the intertexts is of course Walker herself as she Signifies on Africanist pretension, calling into question the terms with which a number of her contemporaries are repudiating the language and culture of what Wangero calls "the oppressor."

Though Gates more or less exclusively considers how African Americans

Signify on the discourse of other African Americans, his theory also lends itself to sorting out relations between the shapers of a "minor literature" and the mainstream or majority writers encountered on the road to a problematic literary autonomy. Gates himself dismisses as "reductive" the idea that the Signifying Monkey's adversarial relationship with that ubiquitous authority figure, the powerful but unsubtle Lion, can be understood as symbolically representative of power relations between black and white.[2] But I would argue that insofar as those relations are literary, they prove interesting and complex. The critic interested in them ought only to keep in mind Gates's assertion that when "black writers . . . revise texts in the Western tradition, they . . . do so 'authentically,' with a black difference, a compelling sense of difference based on the black vernacular."[3] Surely, then, one can legitimately consider the possibility that Walker plays the Signifying Monkey to a white literary Lion more or less literally in her own Georgia backyard. To come to cases: what is the relationship between Walker's story and the respected and influential body of short fiction about the rural South written by Flannery O'Connor?

Walker considers O'Connor an influence, and Margaret D. Bauer, who has remarked on some of the parallels in the work of these two artists, tends to see their relationship as healthily nonagonistic.[4] But anyone who dips into the essay on O'Connor that appears in *In Search of Our Mothers' Gardens* will be struck by the ambivalence of the younger author's feelings about the elder. "I have loved her work for many years," declares Walker, but she goes on to gauge feelings of "fury" and "bitterness" when she visits O'Connor's house outside Milledgeville, Georgia.[5] Thus one should not be surprised to discover something other than simple homage in "Everyday Use," the little comedy of superficial sophistication and rural manners in which Walker replicates and plays with the many such fictions of O'Connor.

O'Connor contrasts intellectual pretension with certain transcendent realities: Original Sin, Grace, prospects for redemption. Walker, meanwhile, assesses ideas of cultural identity within a community only a few minutes' drive from the home in which O'Connor spent her last years. O'Connor relentlessly exposes liberal pieties—notably regarding race—as humanistic idols that obscure the spiritual realities central to her vision. Writing at the height of civil rights agitation, she delights in characters like Asbury in "The Enduring Chill" or Julian in "Everything That Rises Must Converge"— characters who have embraced the new ideas about race only to be exposed for their concurrent spiritual folly. With similar daring, Walker satirizes the heady rhetoric of late sixties black consciousness, deconstructing its pieties (especially the rediscovery of Africa) and asserting neglected values. At the same time, however, she revises—Signifies on—the O'Connor diagesis, which allows so little real value to black aspiration. Thus Walker parodies the iconoclastic tricks that O'Connor deploys over and over again. As Wangero meets in Maggie the self she wants to deny, Walker Signifies on O'Connor's fondness for characters that psychologically double each other. Walker Signifies, too, on the O'Connor moment of divine insight, for Mrs. Johnson's decision to reaffirm the gift of the quilts to Maggie comes as heaven-sent enlightenment. Mrs. Johnson, however, enjoys a positive moment of revelation—unlike Mrs. May in "Greenleaf," Mrs. Turpin in "Revelation," or the Grandmother in "A Good Man Is Hard to Find." When, finally, Walker represents Wangero's intellectual posturing as shallow beside the simple integrity of her mother and sister, she plays with the standard O'Connor plot of the alienated and superficially intellectual young person (Hulga, in "Good Country People," is the definitive example) who fails conspicuously to justify the contempt in which she or he holds a crass, materialistic, and painfully unimaginative female parent. Walker tropes even the O'Connor meanness. Where O'Connor allows at best that the petty complacency and other failings of the mothers in "The Comforts of Home" and "The Enduring Chill" are venial flaws beside the arrogance, the intellectual posturing, and the spiritual blindness of their children, Walker declines to qualify her sympathy and admiration for Maggie and Mrs. Johnson.

One of the ironies here is that both Walker and O'Connor are themselves intellectuals struggling to make their way in a world of competitive ideas and talents—not to mention competing ideologies. Each critiques herself through mocking self-projection, and each stakes out an ideological position at odds with prevailing thought. O'Connor addresses herself to the spiritual folly of a godless age, Walker to a kind of social shortsightedness. The measure of Walker's success may be that one comes to care as much about the question she poses—"Who shall inherit the quilts?"—as about the nominally grander question posed by O'Connor: "Who shall inherit the Kingdom of Heaven?"

Walker contrives, withal, to make the situation of Wangero, the visitor, analogous to the cultural position of the minority writer who, disinclined to express the fate of the oppressed in the language and literary structures of the oppressor, seeks a more authentic idiom and theme. Such a writer, Walker says, must not become a literary Wangero. Only by remaining in touch with a proximate history and an immediate cultural reality can one lay a claim to the quilts—or hope to produce the authentic art they represent. Self-chastened, Walker presents her own art—the piecing of linguistic and literary intertexts—as quilt-making with words, an art as imbued with the African American past as the literal quilt-making of the grandmother for whom Wangero was originally named.

The quilts that Wangero covets link her generation to prior generations, and thus they represent the larger African American past. The quilts contain scraps of dresses worn by the grandmother and even the great-grandmother, as well as a piece of the uniform worn by the great-grandfather who served in the Union Army in the War Between the States. The visitor rightly recognizes the quilts as part of a fragile heritage, but she fails to see the extent to which she herself has traduced that heritage. Chief among the little gestures that collectively add up to a profound betrayal is the changing of her name. Mrs. Johnson thinks she could trace the name Dee in their family "back beyond the Civil War," but Wangero persists in seeing the name as little more than the galling reminder that African Americans have been denied authentic names. "I couldn't bear it any longer, being named after the people who oppress me."[6] She now styles and dresses herself according to the dictates of a faddish Africanism and thereby demonstrates a cultural Catch-22: an American who attempts to become an African succeeds only in becoming a phony. In her name, her clothes, her hair, her sunglasses, her patronizing speech, and her black Muslim companion, Wangero proclaims a deplorable degree of alienation from her rural origins and family. The story's irony is not subtle: the visitor who reproaches others for ignorance of their own heritage (a word that probably does not figure in the lexicon of either her mother or her sister) is herself almost completely disconnected from a nurturing tradition.

Wangero has realized the dream of the oppressed: she has escaped the ghetto. Why, then, is she accorded so little maternal or authorial respect? The reason lies in her progressive repudiation of the very heritage she claims to revere. I say progressive because Walker makes clear that Wangero's flirtation with Africa is only the latest in a series of attempts to achieve racial and cultural autonomy, attempts that prove misguided insofar as they promote an erosion of all that is most real—and valuable—in African American experience. Wangero's mental traveling, moreover, replicates that of an entire generation. Her choices follow the trends in African American cultural definition from the simple integrationist imperative that followed

Brown v. Board of Education (1954) to the collective outrage of the "long hot summer" of 1967 and the rise of an Islamic alternative to the Christianity that black America had hitherto embraced. Proceeding pari passu with this evolution was the rediscovery of an African past, a past more remote—and putatively more authentic—than that of the preceding two hundred years.[7] The epoch-making decade of the 1960s was punctuated by a number of sensational defections to Africa. In 1961 the ninety-three-year-old W. E. B. Du Bois, having been denied a passport and investigated by the House Un-American Activities Committee, moved to Ghana and renounced his American citizenship. In 1967, Bob Moses fled to Canada and thence to Tanzania to avoid the draft. In 1968, Eldridge Cleaver made a similar gesture when he left the United States on an odyssey that would eventually take him, too, to a new home on the African continent. Stokely Carmichael rounded out this pattern of expatriation when, in 1969, he moved to Guinea and changed his name to Kwame Touré. Midway through the decade, in 1964, Walker herself traveled to Africa, and one imagines her character Wangero among the enthusiastic readers of the enormously popular *Roots* (1976), in which Alex Haley memorably describes the researches that eventually led him to the African village from which his ancestor, Kunta Kinte, had been abducted by slavers.

In other words, the Africa-smitten Wangero one meets in the opening pages of the story is a precipitate of the cultural struggles of a generation—struggles adumbrated in the stages of this character's education. She had left home to attend school in Augusta, where apparently she immersed herself in the liberating culture she would first urge on her bewildered mother and sister, then denounce as oppressive. Now, with her black Muslim boyfriend or husband in tow (her mother hears his name as "Hakim-a-barber"), she has progressed to an idea of nationality radically at odds with all that has hitherto defined the racial identity of African Americans.

Though Walker depicts "Hakim-a-barber" as something of a fool, a person who has embraced a culture as alien as anything imposed on black people by white America, her quarrel is not with Islam, for she hints (through the perceptions of Wangero's mother) that a nearby Muslim commune is an admirable, even heroic, institution. But the neighboring Muslims have immersed themselves in agrarian practicality. They are unlikely to view relics of the rural life as collectors' items. Their sense of purpose, their identity, seems to contain no element of pose. Wangero and her companion, on the other hand, are all pose.

Wangero despises her sister, her mother, and the church that helped to educate her. Her quest is ultimately selfish, and Walker focuses the reader's growing dislike for the heroine in her indifference to Maggie, the pathetic sister she seems prepared to ignore in a kind of moral triage. Maggie represents the multitude of black women who must suffer while the occasional lucky "sister" escapes the ghetto. Scarred, graceless, "not bright" (50), and uneducated, Maggie is a living reproach to a survivor like her sister. Maggie is the aggregate underclass that has been left behind as a handful of Wangeros achieve their independence—an underclass scarred in the collective disasters Walker symbolizes neatly in the burning of the original Johnson home. Wangero had welcomed that conflagration. Her mother remembers the "look of concentration on her face as she watched the last dingy gray board of the house fall in toward the red-hot brick chimney. Why don't you do a dance around the ashes? I'd wanted to ask her. She had hated the house that much" (49–50). Wangero did not set the fire, but she delighted in its obliteration of the house that represented everything she sought to escape. When, predictably, the house reappears as before, she may have understood that fire alone cannot abolish a ghetto. This burned house, however, represents more than a failed attempt to eradicate poverty. It subsumes a whole African American history of violence, from slavery (one thinks of Maggie's scars multiplied among the escaped or emancipated slaves in Morrison's *Beloved*) through the ghetto-torching riots of 1964, 1965, 1967, and 1968 ("Burn, Baby, Burn!") to the pervasive inner-city violence of subsequent decades. The fire, that is, is the African American past, a conflagration from which assorted survivors stumble forward, covered like Maggie with scars of the body or like Wangero with scars of the soul.

Assimilation, torching the ghetto, Islam, the Africanist vision—Walker treats these alternatives with respect, even as she satirizes her character's uncritical embracing of one after another of them. The author knows that each represents an attempt to restore a sense of identity terribly impaired by the wrongs visited on black people in the New World. Wangero, however, fails properly to appreciate the black community's transformation of these wrongs into moral capital. She does not see the integrity of African American cultural institutions that evolved as the creative and powerful response to the general oppression. In simpler terms, she is ashamed of a mother and a sister who, notwithstanding their humble circumstances, exemplify character bred in adversity.

"It all comes back to houses," Walker remarks in her essay on Flannery

O'Connor.[8] Freud associates houses with women, and this story of three women is also the story of three houses, one that burned, one that shelters two of the fire's survivors, and one, never directly described, that is to be the repository of various articles of this family's past, its heritage. This last house, owned by and symbolic of Wangero, embodies also the cultural problem Walker seeks to address in her story. How, she asks, can one escape the margins without a catastrophic deracination? Is the freedom Wangero achieves somehow at odds with proper valuation of the immediate cultural matrix out of which she comes? Can she, like Charles Dickens's Pip, embrace a grand heritage only by betraying the simpler heritage necessary to emotional and psychological wholeness?

Wangero claims to value heritage, and Walker is surely sympathetic to someone who seems to recognize, however clumsily, the need to preserve the often fragile artifacts of the African American past. But Walker exposes Wangero's preservationism as hopelessly selfish and misguided. Though the author elsewhere laments the paucity of photographs in the African American historical record, she evinces little patience with Wangero's desire to photograph mother and cow in front of the house.[9] Wangero's desire is to have a record of how far she has come. No doubt she will view as "quaint" these images of a rural past. She wants the photographs—and presently the churn lid, the dasher, and the quilts—for purposes of display, reminders that she no longer has to live in such a house, care for such a cow, have daily intercourse with such a mother and sister. She "makes the mistake," says Donna Haisty Winchell, "of believing that one's heritage is something that one puts on display if and when such a display is fashionable."[10] Wangero seems to think the African American past can be rescued only by being commodified. She wants to make the lid of the butter churn into a centerpiece for her table. She wants to hang quilts on the wall. She wants, in short, to do what white people do with the cunning and quaint implements and products of the past. Wangero fails to see the mote in her own eye when she reproaches her mother and her sister for a failure to value their heritage— she, who wants only to preserve that heritage as the negative index to her own sophistication.

One wonders if Wangero's house, unlike the houses of her childhood, will have a lawn. Doubtless she has never paused to think about the humble yard of her mother's house as anything more than another shabby badge of poverty. But like the more obviously significant quilts, this yard—a description of which opens the story—is another symbol of the cultural something produced out of nothing by people lacking everything:

A yard like this is more comfortable than most people know. It is not just a yard. It is like an extended living room. When the hard clay is swept clean as a floor and the fine sand around the edges lined with tiny, irregular grooves, anyone can come and sit and look up into the elm tree and wait for the breezes that never come inside the house. (47)

A paragon of meaningful simplicity, this yard. The grooved borders even put one in mind of the artfully raked sand in a Japanese *hira-niwa* garden (indeed, the breezes sound like a plural visitation of *kamikaze*, the "divine wind"). In Japan, such a garden affords emotional balm and spiritual serenity to those who tend or contemplate it, and Walker implies similar restorative properties in the uncluttered plainness of the narrator's yard. Mrs. Johnson mentions neither grass, nor shrubs, nor (surprisingly for Walker) flowers. In its stark vacuity the yard evokes the minimalist lives of poor people; yet the author describes that emptiness in terms suggestive of spiritual wealth.[11]

If conversely Wangero is described in language evocative of spiritual poverty or confusion, the reader does not completely despise her, for even as it satirizes her pretensions, "Everyday Use" hints at an affinity between its author and its central character.[12] "Walker's *writing*," says Marianne Hirsch, "constitutes a form of distance" from the real-life mother and home on which she bases the story.[13] The story can be read, in fact, as a cautionary tale the author tells herself: a parable, so to speak, about the perils of writing one's impoverished past from the vantage of one's privileged present. The deracination of Wangero, that is, can represent the fate of anyone who, like the author, goes from sharecropper's daughter to literary sophisticate. I refer here to an autobiographical dimension that proves interestingly unstable, for Walker's self-depiction as Wangero actually displaces an intended self-depiction as Maggie. That Walker would represent herself in the backward, disfigured Maggie strains credulity only if one forgets that the author was herself a disfigured child, an eye having been shot out with a BB gun. In a 1973 interview, moreover, Walker makes clear the autobiographical genesis of a poem ("For My Sister Molly Who in the Fifties" in *Revolutionary Petunias* [1973]) in which an ignorant and unglamorous girl discovers that her "brilliant" older sister, home for a visit, is ashamed of their uncouth family.[14] "Everyday Use" is the prose version of that poem.

But how many of Walker's post–*Color Purple* readers recognize its gifted author in the Maggie of the earlier story? Indeed, as Walker's literary reputation grows, her readers may with increasing frequency identify the apparently successful and prosperous sister of "Everyday Use" as some kind of distorted reflection of the author, an exercise in autobiographical self-criticism of the type that, on a larger scale, generates a Stephen Dedalus or an Invisible Man. (Toni Morrison, I have always thought, projects a male version of herself in Milkman Dead, the *Song of Solomon* character with whom she shares a birthday—and Richard Wright, Ralph Ellison, and James Baldwin all critique themselves in their protagonists.) Projections of this type constitute the examined life of the artist, at once an exorcism of unworthy versions of the self and a rhetorically effective shielding of the vulnerable ego, whose pretensions might otherwise be dismissed by captious readers.

Walker, then, actually doubles the self-mocking portrait of the artist, projecting herself as both the benighted Maggie and the sophisticated but shallow Wangero. She does so, I think, because she recognizes and wants to respond to the distorting pressures brought to bear on African American identity and the discourse that, over time, reflects or shapes it. In a sense, Walker's life as a writer has been devoted to preserving a proximate past in the form of its language (or, as will be seen, languages). In her essay "Coming in from the Cold," she discusses her desire to preserve the language of "the old people," her forebears—even when cultural displacements cause it to ring false. Thus she points out that words like "mammy" and "pickaninny" (long since appropriated in the construction of racial stereotypes) actually figured in the speech of earlier African Americans. These words, and the language of which they are part, constitute an irreplaceable record of otherwise unchronicled lives, generations denied the "visual documentation of painting and . . . photography." By transmitting the words of the ancestors "in the context that is or was natural to them, we do not perpetuate . . . stereotypes, but, rather expose them. And, more important, we help the ancestors in ourselves and others continue to exist. If we kill off the *sound* of our ancestors, the major portion of us, all that is past, that is history, that is human being is lost, and we become historically and spiritually thin, a mere shadow of who we were, on the earth."[15]

In short, to preserve the sound, the artist must preserve the words. To preserve the words, the artist must preserve the meanings and the sense of linguistic difference. Thus the great challenge of Walker's career (met most memorably in *The Color Purple*) has been to write a language at once true to "the old people" and viable in the marketplace of mainstream American ideas. Thus, too, like the poets of every literary renascence, Walker engages in a necessary program of linguistic reclamation. Like Wordsworth, she aspires to recover "the language actually spoken by men"—and women. Like the Frost of "The Pasture," she clears the leaves of linguistic debasement and co-optation away from the Pierian source of linguistic purity and good art. Like the Jean Toomer or Zora Neale Hurston she admires, she insists on recapturing the authentic African American voice—whether in dialect, as they do, or in standard English, as in "Everyday Use" and the other stories in *In Love and Trouble*.

But things are never this simple. When Wangero greets her mother in Lugandan ("Wa-su-zo-Tean-o!" 52), she affirms her repudiation of English, the language of slavery.[16] By implication, she indicts the practice of authors—Joyce, for example, or Walker herself—who decline to abandon that language at the bidding of political visionaries. Thus Walker remains enmeshed in problems of cultural access and linguistic authenticity, for writers at the American margins have long struggled with a paradox basic to their artistic identities: their language and their craft are inextricably intertwined with the hegemonic Anglo-Saxon culture that has systematically denied them their own voice, their own autonomy, their own identity. Black writers, their very tongues colonized, find themselves torn between the language they grew up speaking and some more authentic language or cultural orientation. How, demand artists like the American James Baldwin or the Caribbean George Lamming, can they ever achieve a voice of their own, a cultural authenticity, when they remain in linguistic bondage? Such writers fashion work that exists in a precarious and almost parasitic relation to a dominant and more or less unfriendly cultural and linguistic mainstream. They create what has been called a "minor literature."

Gilles Deleuze and Félix Guattari, who refer briefly to "what blacks in America today are able to do with the English language," say that in "minor literatures . . . everything . . . is political" and that "everything takes on a collective value."[17] They argue, too, that the minor writer—notably Franz Kafka—often effects revolutionary advances in literary sensibility. But I remain doubtful that such an argument is really needed to explain the ability of marginal writers to produce substantial work across a broad spectrum. I would argue that in the hands of a sufficiently resourceful literary practitioner language can always be made to subvert hegemonic structures. Walker casts her lot with writers who remain confident of the boundlessness of literary affect achievable in English—writers like the Nobel laureates Derek Walcott and Toni Morrison, who seem effortlessly to transcend the kind of anxieties Deleuze and Guattari would wish on them. These writers believe that culture is naturally enough eclectic, and that a language as rich as English, not to mention the manifold cultures that speak or are spoken by it, provides plenty of latitude for new voices, however subversive. They seem to view the possibilities of literary art as affording sufficient latitude to circumvent linguistic colonization. They prefer to see the resources of the English language and its canonical literature, as well as the larger cultural resources of the West, as theirs for the appropriating. Thus Derek Walcott, in *Omeros*, reimagines several millennia of colonial history and culture to shape a vision that remains wholly of its Caribbean time and place. Thus in *Beloved*, as Ellen Pifer has argued, Morrison rewrites *Huckleberry Finn*.[18] Thus, too, Walker loses nothing when she opts not to write in dialect—or Lugandan.

Walker refuses, then, to write "'protest literature,'" in which "the superficial becomes . . . the deepest reality." She credits Leo Tolstoy with showing her "the importance of diving through politics and social forecasts to dig into the essential spirit of individual persons."[19] (Here she echoes Ralph Ellison, who resists "sociological" fiction, including that of Richard Wright: "I have no desire to write propaganda.")[20] In "Everyday Use" Walker explores with great subtlety the demands—often conflicting—of ideology and art. She contemplates the culturally distorting pressures brought to bear on another kind of language, another vehicle whereby African American experience is embodied and transmitted. This other language—the quilts—exhibits a special integrity resembling that of the language in which the author writes her story. As this story engages the theme of heritage, it resolves the dilemma inherent in ideologically self-conscious art (how simultaneously to be politically engaged and free of a limiting topicality) by inviting a connection between writing and quilt-making, a connection between types of textuality that prove complementary.

"In contemporary writing," Elaine Showalter observes, "the quilt stands for a vanished past experience to which we have a troubled and ambivalent cultural relationship."[21] Certainly the quilts over which Wangero and her mother quarrel represent a heritage vastly more personal and immediate than the intellectual and deracinated daughter can see; indeed, they represent a heritage she has already discarded, for she no longer shares a name with those whose lives, in scraps of cast-off clothing, the quilts transmute. Moreover, Wangero herself has not learned to quilt—the art will die if women like Maggie do not keep it up. Yet as Barbara Christian observes, a "heritage . . . must continually be renewed rather than fixed in the past."[22] Thus for Maggie and her mother the idea of heritage is perpetually subordinate to the fact of a living tradition, a tradition in which one generation remains in touch with its predecessors by means of homely skills—quilt-making and butter-churning, among others—that get passed on. The quilts remain appropriate for "everyday use" so long as the art of their manufacture remains alive. They can be quite utilitarian, and indeed, they are supposed to be a practical dowry for Maggie.

Of course the quilts, like this story, are beautiful and merit preservation. Walker seems to intimate, however, even in her own literary art, a belief in the idea of a living, intertextual tradition, a passing on of values as well as skills that ought only occasionally to issue in canonization or any of the other processes whereby something intended for "everyday use" ends up framed, on a wall, on a shelf, in a library or museum. Indeed, as Faith Pullin notes with regard to the quilts, "the mother is . . . the true African here, since the concept of art for art's sake is foreign to Africa—all objects are for use. Dee has . . . taken over a very Western attitude towards art and its material value."[23] Walker, by the same token, seems to conceive of her own art as part of a dynamic process in which utility (domestic, political) meets and bonds with an aesthetic ideal. Her story/quilt is intended as much for immediate consumption—that is, reading—by the brothers and sisters of these sisters as for sacralization on some library shelf or college syllabus.

Thus Walker, though she mocks Wangero's idea of heritage, nevertheless aspires to project herself as sensitive artist of the African American experience, and she does so by inviting recognition of a further parallel between the contested quilts and her own fictive art. Quilts are the "texts" (the word means *weave*) of American rural life. Moreover, they are palpably "intertextual," inasmuch as they contain literal scraps of past lives. Engaged in her own version of quilt-making, Walker weaves in stories like this one a simple yet richly heteroglossic text on patterns set by a literary tradition extending into communities black and white, American and international. The interested reader may detect in Walker's work the intertextual presence of a number of writers she names as influences in the 1973 interview mentioned previously: Leo Tolstoy, Ivan Turgenev, Maksim Gorky, Nikolay Gogol, Camara Laye, Gabriel García Márquez, Flannery O'Connor, Elechi Ahmadi, Bessie Head, Jean Toomer, and especially Zora Neale Hurston.[24] Like any other writer, any other wielder of language, Walker "pieces" her literary quilts out of all that she has previously read or heard. Perhaps it is with Maggie after all that the author exhibits the most comprehensive affinity.

In "Everyday Use," then, Walker addresses herself to the problems of African Americans who risk deracination in their quest for personal authenticity. At the same time she makes the drama of Wangero and Maggie emblematic of the politically charged choices available in minor/minority writing. With wit and indirection, she probes the problem of postcolonial writers who, as they struggle with a cultural imperative to repudiate the language and the institutions of the colonizer, simultaneously labor under the necessity—born in part of a desire to address an audience that includes the colonizer and his inheritors—of expressing themselves in that language and deferring to those institutions. In her problematic repudiation of oppressor culture, Wangero represents, among other things, the marginalized individual who fails to see this dilemma as false. She seems willing to lose her soul to be free of the baleful influences that she thinks have shaped it.

Walker hints that the false dilemma behind Wangero's blindness afflicts the narrowly political writer as well. The alternative to the dilemma is the same in both instances: a living tradition that preserves a true heritage even as it appropriates what it needs from the dominant culture it may be engaged in subverting. African Americans, Walker says, can take pride in the living tradition of folk art, seen here in the example of the quilts, and they can learn from a literary art like her own, a literary art committed at once to political responsibility and to the means—through simple appropriation of linguistic tools—of its own permanence.

CHAPTER 3

Braid of Blood
Michael Dorris's *A Yellow Raft in Blue Water*

What happens when you let an unsatisfactory present go on long enough? It becomes your entire history.

—LOUISE ERDRICH, *THE PLAGUE OF DOVES*

As the African American writer makes her way into the literary mainstream (or malestream) without traducing an authentic black vernacular, so must the contemporary Native American writer occupy and transform storytelling aesthetics of great antiquity and great importance to ethnic identity. Michael Dorris, like Alice Walker and Gloria Naylor, writes from the racial and cultural margin; like Rachel Ingalls, whose *Mrs. Caliban* he praised in the *New York Times Book Review*, he looks deeply into that "deep female sadness" of which Updike spoke. In terms of race or gender (or both), these writers are always already subalterns. Their status as second-generation or junior postmoderns makes them subaltern twice over.

Responding to the work of writers such as Leslie Marmon Silko, N. Scott Momaday, James Welch, and Louise Erdrich, critics generally foreground the formal, aesthetic, and thematic elements that have always figured prominently in Native American literature. Favoring nonlinear plots, these novelists adapt and transform oral storytelling traditions. They emphasize communal remedies to individual affliction. In "homing" narratives shaped according to conventions as old, perhaps, as that primal European story of *nostos*, the *Odyssey*, they recount the struggles of errant protagonists ("errant" in all senses of the word) to effect a mythic return to the community that alone offers wholeness and healing.[1] But the hermeneutics implied here risks failing to gauge the extent to which these fictions register and perhaps incorporate the competing paradigms of the dominant culture's literary production. There is, after all, a politics as well as a poetics of Native American literature. Hence Arnold Krupat, in *The Voice in the Margin*, proposes the special category of "indigenous literature": "that type of writing produced when an author of subaltern cultural identification manages successfully to merge forms internal to his cultural formation with forms external to it, but pressing upon, even seeking to delegitimate it."[2]

As an aesthetically hybrid product of mixed-blood sensibility, Michael Dorris's 1987 novel *A Yellow Raft in Blue Water* exemplifies this indigenous literature. In this chapter I argue that Dorris's novel, even with its mimesis of oral storytelling, its nonlinear movement, its homing theme, and its emphasis on the hunger for a sense of communal belonging, addresses itself to a politics of identity less "native" American than simply American. In the linked narratives of this novel one reads—hears, actually—the witness of three generations to a bond that transcends the merely familial, a bond Dorris symbolizes in a traditional emblem of Native American culture: the braid. Though he told the Chavkins that he was not aware of just how neatly he had woven the braiding motif into this fiction,[3] it figures centrally, its implications unfolding like an exotic orchid. As hair is braided, so are lives and generations. Less obvious but equally compelling is another symbolic dimension of this image, for in America more than other nations, blood, too, has been braided, mingled with blood. As a palliative to the problems of the islanded self in a time of cultural dissolution, Dorris presents a vision of the woven, cable-like integrity miraculously surviving among the members and satellites of the unnamed tribe his story concerns. But the author seeks to braid more than the experience of a single ethnic group into his novel. He intimates that life on and off the reservation must be understood as part of a larger braiding, a larger weave. In the braid, that is, readers recognize a metaphor for the multicultural weave—or braid—that is America itself.

In modern times, every Native American story is at least tangentially concerned with the threat of assimilation. The metaphor of the melting pot, so cherished by white America, suggests the collapse of differentiation. Out of the molten soup comes a strange alloy: the American. As a *native* American, Dorris implicitly rejects this figure in favor of one that, less coercive to identity, manages still to celebrate a larger, national idea of community. Dorris proposes, as displacing figure, the metaphor of braiding, for the point of a braid is the clear integrity of each of its strands. To be sure, that integrity changes as braid becomes weave, but even here the strands retain their separate character, composing—to extend the figure yet further—identifiable figures within the carpet of national identity.

An anthropologist by professional training, Dorris studied human social relations and culture as they relate to environment and differ from one racial or national group to another, especially over time. He knew how far America is from the realization of its own collective synthesis, knew how many remain marginalized by the inexorable forces of American life. In this novel, he does full justice to the unemployment, the alcoholism, the fragmented families—in short, the pervasive misery—of Native American life. Thus he complicates the symbolism of his American theme by intimating that an individual or a whole people can be woven unwillingly into a fabric she or they may find uncongenial. To make the point in slightly different terms: Dorris registers the problematic character of America's assimilation of its minorities. What is remarkable, however, is that the author can chronicle the afflictions of Native Americans—can even set the action mostly in eastern Montana—without ever identifying the tribe to which his characters belong. By the same token, he refers to the language they sometimes speak instead of English as "Indian." Dorris seems to want an element of the generic in his depiction of Native American life.

Why? Dorris remarked that specificity regarding particular tribes led to too many letters from individuals claiming to recognize their relatives.[4] But surely there is more to it than this. Readers of Eric Konigsberg's account of the personal unraveling that issued in Dorris's suicide in 1996 know that the author suffered considerable confusion on the score of his own identity. He looked too white and had recourse to tanning salons in hopes of appearing duskier of skin. His hair curled if it grew too long. Was he "really Indian" after all? "Other native American writers" raised questions about "his blood connection to the Modoc nation." Konigsberg notes, too, that "Dorris is the only prominent Indian novelist to write only about tribes other than his own ('That just isn't done among Indians,' says the Indian writer Greg Sarris)."[5] Yet in reading *Yellow Raft* one may well sense precisely the opposite: that Dorris does not want to speak for any tribe of which he is not a member. He may wish, rather, to defer to what remains of tribal integrity. Thus the reader sees in his scenes of generic reservation life the necessary diffidence of one whose own tribe, the Modoc, has been largely assimilated.

Another rationale appears in a 1979 *College English* article in which Dorris anticipates Krupat's idea of the "indigenous literature" that results from the encounter of native aesthetics with nonnative forms. Though he deplores the Eurocentric tendency to lump three hundred or so separate peoples and languages together as an absurd monolith called "Indian" culture, Dorris argues for the emergence—in Momaday, Silko, and Welch—of a new, hybrid

Native American literature, written for a readership that includes whites as well as Native Americans of all tribes. Auguring his own *Yellow Raft*, Dorris describes the characters of James Welch's 1974 novel *Winter in the Blood* as "people who happen to be Native Americans living on a reservation in Montana." The "culture" of these people "clearly has much in common with rural, white-American society," yet

> it is also distinctly Native. It is a book about poverty but also about the survival, against great odds, of tradition and of people. Together with such works as Leslie Silko's *Ceremony* (1977), it may well be among the first manifestations of a new era in Native American literary expression; at long last a pan-tribal tradition of true "Native American literature" may be happening.[6]

In *Yellow Raft*, however, the "pan-tribal" seems naturally to engage the yet larger community of America itself. Dorris seems to be meditating on the general American culture as much as on any specifically native way of life. Certainly the ills Dorris documents are not limited to any single ethnic group. He writes of people whose mental landscape consists of the same Stephen King-inspired movies and country music songs and consumerism that shape the dreams of the entire American underclass.

Yellow Raft unfolds with a distinctive rhythm as the reader moves backwards and forwards in time, encountering first the story of Rayona, then the story of her mother Christine, and finally the story of "Aunt Ida," whose real relationship to the first two becomes one of the novel's more powerful revelations. Ray narrates in the present tense, Christine and Ida in the past. All three stories begin with the narrator at fifteen years old. Ray stays fifteen, describing her experiences "between May and August 1986," as Dorris explained to an interviewer.[7] Christine and Ida move forward in time, grow older, as their stories advance on the present. Central to the authorial purpose, the narrative's wavelike rhythm of overlapping and repetition allows the reader to see generational movement and cultural continuity as well as the reconciliation of radically different personal points of view. This last, a demonstration that truth is relative and that reality changes depending on the perspective from which it is viewed, is a commonplace of postmodern storytelling technique. From the perspective of her daughter, Christine seems a conspicuous failure as a mother, but upon reading the full story of Christine and then Ida, the reader sympathizes with—indeed, forgives—

each in succession. Thus the reader shares Christine's impercipience in a seemingly meaningless scene like the one in which she and Ida visit the dying Clara before discovering—in Ida's narrative—all that lies behind this visit. Yet the three narratives, their singularity notwithstanding, prove each to be the same profoundly human story of a struggle for integrity, growth, love, and connection—connection to family, community, and nation.[8]

The novel's backwards and forwards movement functions as a kind of cultural or anthropological analogue to psychoanalysis, in which one moves into and out of a mental past to come to terms with a psychological present. Dorris, I suspect, holds no brief for the idea of a racial unconscious, but he sketches in the practical equivalent of this familiar Jungian notion in narratives that, outwardly distinct from one another, discover common mythic ground. At the same time he never loses sight of individual or personal experience. Readers come to know Ray, Christine, and Ida at the same time that they gain insight into the race and culture that, even in their disparateness, these self-chronicling characters represent. Thus Dorris documents intersections of the individual and her community, the better ultimately to engage a larger theme of American identity in an age in which familial, cultural, and national cohesion have faltered disastrously for both dominant and subaltern ethnic groups.

Anthropologists take a special interest in coming-of-age stories. They know that one of the surest routes to understanding a culture is to study the way its young people are initiated into adulthood. Though Dorris claims not to be interested in the theme,[9] all three of these narratives exemplify it. Coming of age in fiction, however, does tend to confer a spurious order on the many phases of growing up, and part of the point about contemporary life in America (as about life in "advanced" cultures generally) is the absence or impairment of recognized rituals whereby the young can make a formal transition to the privileges and responsibilities of adulthood. Thus Dorris devises strategies to engage the theme without overdoing it; and, indeed, such maturation as occurs in these stories is tentative, perhaps temporary. The raft surrounded by water that figures centrally in the novel and provides its title is at best an image of problematic coming of age—just as it is in *Huckleberry Finn*.[10] It is also, of course, an image of isolation. For Ray, who needs a family and self-respect, the raft and the set of experiences that radiate outward from it become a focus of significance. On the raft she has a sexual encounter, perhaps (the text is obscure) losing her virginity. Of equal if not greater importance, however, is the person she subsequently sees swimming from the raft: Ellen DeMarco, the youthful ideal that, even at their most multicultural, American advertising, film, and television promote. Sleek, attractive, straight-haired, confident, and blessed with a loving and supportive family, Ellen is the person Ray longs to be.

The piece of Ellen DeMarco's letter that Ray finds is an important plot detail, for it becomes a kind of personal talisman. Her pathetic cherishing of the letter reveals the magnitude of her desire for a stable family. The separate stories of Ray and her mother converge and reach their understated climax at the moment in Christine's narrative in which Ray finally discards this epistolary reminder of normative family life. When, earlier, Ellen inadvertently exposes the lie told to Evelyn and Sky, Ray retreats to the lakeside and stares at the raft as Evelyn comes up behind her in one of the novel's most touching scenes.

> I'm not that hard for Evelyn to find. I'm stopped, halfway down the trail, with my eyes fixed on the empty yellow raft floating in the blue waters of Bearpaw Lake. Somewhere in my mind I've decided that if I stare at it hard enough it will launch me out of my present troubles. If I squint a certain way, it appears to be a lighted trapdoor, flush against a black floor. With my eyes closed almost completely, it becomes a kind of bull's-eye, and I'm an arrow banging into it head-first.[11]

Much of the novel's title-symbolism comes together in the meaningfully conflicted imagery contained in words like "launch," "trapdoor," and "bull's eye." As the place where she was seduced and where she first sees Ellen, her counterself, the raft is indeed a launching pad: because of what happens on it, Ray strikes out on her own, finds herself cared for by Sky and Evelyn, shows her mettle at the rodeo, and finally settles in with Dayton and her mother. Yet the raft is simultaneously a bull's-eye—that which violently ends the flight of missiles launched by the more primitive technology of Ray's Indian ancestors (and contemporary Native Americans are in fact torn between an incult past and a space-age present). The raft is also a trapdoor, which can be a means of escape or the vehicle of sudden disappearance. It is at once trap and door, something that arrests and denies freedom as well as the opening into fresh experience. It is, in short, the end of the old Ray and the beginning of the new.

The yellow raft, then, is a hub around which, spokewise, the author arranges elements of his maturation theme. That it figures only in Ray's narrative makes for a certain asymmetry unless the reader recognizes a thematic signature that carries over to the other narratives. In other words, as an emblem of isolation and problematic coming of age, the raft governs the stories of Christine and Ida as much as it governs the story of Ray. The novel repeatedly, in each of its constituent narratives, engages the theme of growing up in a world where the old instrumentalities for personal, familial, and cultural integration are no longer operative. Christine and Ida, too, are isolates, victims of circumstances Dorris imagines, again, as personal rather than political. The raft has been elided from the picture, but each narrator, like Ray, comes to a crossroads where her future life takes shape. Ida must come to terms with the fact that her life and reputation have been sacrificed to preserve the good name of her shallow and selfish Aunt Clara. She must also come to terms with her feelings about Christine, who is not, after all, really her daughter—and about Willard Pretty Dog, who is the father of Lee and who leaves her once plastic surgery has restored his ravaged face to something like its former comeliness. Christine, on the other hand, must accept the final breakdown of her relationship with Elgin, Ray's father, as well as her own impending death. She must sort out her unresolved feelings about the half sister/half cousin she thinks is her mother ("Aunt Ida") and about the half or quarter nephew she thinks is her brother Lee. She must also face her guilt at Lee's death in a stupid war, for Lee went to Vietnam in part to flee the destructive rivalry of Christine and Dayton, his best friend. When, years later, the rivals stumble into a comfortable cohabitation, Christine finds that her troubled daughter can, with remarkable ease, be introduced into the new relationship. In Christine, Dayton, and Ray, the reader sees another human braid, a functioning family.

Dorris's images of braiding complement and metonymically reify the novel's backwards-and-forwards narrative movement. Though the author begins with Christine braiding Ray's hair in the hospital, one must wait until the last page—indeed, until the last sentence, after Ida and Father Hurlburt have crawled onto the roof in the dark—for the symbolism fully to jell:

> The cold was bearable because the air was so still. I let the blanket slip from my shoulders, lifted my arms about my head, and began.
>
> "What are you doing?" Father Hurlburt asked.
>
> As a man with cut hair, he did not identify the rhythm of three strands, the whispers of coming and going, of twisting and tying and blending, of catching and letting go, of braiding. (372)

Ida's language is suggestive: the three strands are at once hair, lives, and stories—the stories of the three women the reader comes to know in the course of the novel. The author takes as his subject, in other words, the "coming and going," the "twisting and blending," and the "catching and letting go" of human beings, of mother and daughter, of one generation and another.

The phrase "as a man with cut hair," on the other hand, reveals the curiously mixed perspective from which Ida speaks and Dorris writes. It is, of course, the mixed perspective of most Native Americans. "Cut hair," that is, is the marker of maleness only from the point of view of the larger culture within which Dorris's characters have their being. From the point of view of the subaltern culture it is the marker, rather, of whiteness; for at a number of points the author reminds his reader that Native American men have not, traditionally, worn their hair short.[12]

One may wonder at the absence of male voices, especially when women's experience does not prove to be the whole story. After all, the reader also hears a good deal about Lecon, father to both Ida and Christine, and about Lee and Dayton and Foxy Kennedy. Perhaps Dorris means to remind his readers of the familiar sociological point about the pervasive dereliction and absenteeism of fathers in American ghettos. Perhaps, too, he wants a particular type of marriage between form and content—between the theme of braiding and the narrators who embody that theme. The author, that is, seems aware of the ancient tradition of women's being at once weavers and woven in the human community.

Dorris's real sympathy, however, remains with the vision of a national (as opposed to a tribal) braided wholeness. Moreover, one credits this novelist with resourceful exploitation of weaving's gendered imaginary—for he knows that women in literature perennially engage in catching and letting go, in twisting and blending. Shuttle or needle in hand, they occupy themselves with weaving, embroidering, and quilt-making. One thinks of Eve spinning ("When Adam delved and Eve span"), of Arachne's contest with Athena, of Philomela making of her loom a prosthetic tongue, of Penelope weaving and unweaving, of Queen Matilda and the Bayeux Tapestry, of the Wife of Bath and her cloth-making, of the weaving of Tennyson's Lady of Shalott, and of the quilt-making tradition in Gloria Naylor's *Mama Day*, in Margaret Atwood's *Alias Grace*, and in such stories as Alice Walker's "Everyday Use" or Bobbie Ann Mason's "Love Life." This, archetypally, is what women do: they weave, they quilt, they work cloth, they embroider. In doing so they compose for themselves a myth of womanist purpose, a myth of what women always represent in human society. Women are weavers of their culture and of their world.

In opting exclusively for female narrators, Dorris endorses the ancient view of women as what the Anglo-Saxon poets call "weavers of peace." But he himself, along with Melville's mat-weaving Ishmael, embodies the possibility that men, too, can promote relationship, connectedness, community, family, and all the other cultural desiderata contained in the imagery of braiding and weaving. Though wholly the activity of women and the metaphor for their writing of themselves, the narrative braiding here nevertheless figures in a work signed by a male author, who thereby resists female hegemony in the realm of the weave, the realm of relation, the realm of human connectedness.

Feminism has contributed the phrase "the personal is political" to the lexicon of ideological analysis. But Dorris resists this formulation, too. Binding himself to the unsophisticated perspectives of his narrators, he emphasizes the personal in opposition to the political and thus declines to produce what one might expect from an author so acutely conscious of the plight of Native Americans in our time. Even in his references to Vietnam (potentially a matter of great passion) he avoids the easy scoring of points: he has no desire, for example, to underscore the irony when Lee, last scion of a warrior race, allows the hegemonic Anglo-Saxons to dispose of his energies and his life (not to mention those of so many black and Hispanic Americans) to subjugate, on the other side of the world, yet another pigmented population. The author carefully underplays the larger political dimensions of his story, as if to resist Fredric Jameson's reductive formulation for "third-world" literature, in which *"the story of the private individual destiny is always an allegory of the embattled situation of the public third world culture and society."*[13] Dorris lays greater emphasis on the intimate, familial tragedy of Christine's thoughtless shaming of Lee into participation in a fight that was never his own.

Similarly, Dorris is uninterested in an easy demolition of the spiritual chauvinism of Christian missionaries. Although the decent, humane, and part Senecan Father Hurlburt (322), a good shepherd to Ida, gives way presently to the loathsome Father Novak (a priest guilty, in John Milton's memorable image, of climbing into the sheepfold),[14] Dorris emphasizes not the fact of Christian hypocrisy but rather the universal attenuation of a spiritual life of great importance, historically, to Native Americans. What is central to the lives of Ida and the young Christine (Father Hurlburt on the one hand, the nuns and the promised end of the world on the other)[15] proves, by the time Ray is coming of age, to be almost lifeless. For Ray, a rich and distinctive spiritual heritage exists only vestigially, in the half-remembered dream of a bear (totemic emblem of power among northwestern tribes) and in her negative initiation in the middle of Bearpaw Lake. Latitude for a spiritual life, in other words, dwindles from generation to generation.[16]

This is not a condition experienced exclusively by Native Americans—it is part of the American heritage in modern times. Such considerations, it seems to me, lie behind the author's making Ray a half-breed. The racial makeup of this first narrator (unlike that of the similarly burdened Tayo in Silko's *Ceremony*)[17] is part of Dorris's statement about the legitimate submersion of tribal or racial identity in the larger identity of Americanness. That the social, economic, and cultural plight of Native Americans is indistinguishable from the more widely recognized situation of African Americans is, then, only one of the messages contained in Ray's half-black, half-Indian racial makeup. Another, more pointed message concerns an idea of racial synthesis. The point behind Ray's name, which derives from the tag in her mother's gown, "rayon," is not that she is artificial. It is rather that she is, like rayon, "synthetic": she is a synthesis, after all, a braiding together, of two races. Dayton, the man who takes in first her mother and then her, is also a mixed blood.

The strange blood relationships in this novel contribute to its symbolism. Few characters enjoy uncomplicated familial relationships. The point is not "inbreeding"—there is none—but rather a meaningful disorientation of the familiar patterns of kinship (a subject, Krupat remarks in *Ethnocriticism*, with which "most Native narratives deal substantially").[18] Though the reader hears nothing about intertribal marriage, the curious relationships—where one's brother proves to be the son of the half-sister one had thought was one's mother—may reflect the distant and tangled consanguinity of all Native Americans. Yet these relationships must also reflect the shared heritage and frequently mixed bloodlines of all the immigrants to America—the black and white as well as those who migrated across the land bridge from Asia.

Dorris, then, does not seem interested in underscoring the ethnic otherness of his characters so much as their common humanity. Even though they live out their lives at the cultural margin, they are presented simply as people, Americans. It is not by accident that Ray's friends carry her back to the reservation for the second time on the 4th of July. But *Yellow Raft* is hardly a political tract. It is rather a traditional plea for recognition of the common problems that all Americans share as they negotiate their personal autonomy amid the coercive pressures of life in the twentieth century. The reader finishes this book impressed less with the disorder of these lives than with a sense of how infinitely adaptable is the human instinct for familial and societal cohesion. These stories are filled with misery, but the individuals peopling them exhibit an extraordinary resilience, a remarkably inextinguishable thirst for connection, for human braiding. This braiding of lives into something ordered, unified, and strong is the very definition of culture. Dorris views Native American culture as embattled, but he simultaneously affirms the indestructibility of the cultural braid, whether tribal, pantribal, or more broadly American.

CHAPTER 4

Matriarchal Mythopoesis

Gloria Naylor's *Mama Day*

J'entends donc par 'femme' ce qui ne se représente pas, ce qui ne se dit pas, ce qui reste en dehors des nominations et des idéologies.

—JULIA KRISTEVA, "LA FEMME, CE N'EST JAMAIS CA," *TEL QUEL*

Gloria Naylor, like Alice Walker, resists the notion that mainstream literature must be repudiated in the name of postcolonial autonomy. Indeed, like Rachel Ingalls (or Jane Smiley), Naylor appropriates and rewrites Shakespeare but with, as Henry Louis Gates says, "a black difference." As Michael Dorris, braiding the tribal and the pancultural, hybridizes a native American aesthetic, Naylor weaves African American myth into a reconfigured *Tempest*. Naylor's fictions, like Vonnegut's *Cat's Cradle* (1963), Mailer's *An American Dream* (1965), Pynchon's *Gravity's Rainbow* (1973), Umberto Eco's *The Name of the Rose* (1980), *Denis Johnson's Fiskadoro* (1985), and Pynchon's *Vineland* (1990), fall into a category of writing that naturally burgeoned as the year 2000 approached. One of the things that gave birth to postmodernism—or at least strengthened its hold on the aesthetic imagination—was the sense that history itself might be coming to a close. Naylor's linked novels, a kind of millennial roman fleuve, discover a startlingly original vision of the last days. One traces in *The Women of Brewster Place* (1983) and *Bailey's Cafe* (1992) the mythic chronicle of travail and purgatorial suffering. In the all-black real estate development that gives *Linden Hills* (1985) its title one sees a parody of white materialism conflated with the false vision of a New Black Jerusalem whose high priest, Luther Nedeed, perishes in apocalyptic flames. Only in *Mama Day*, however, with the year 1999 as its temporal frame, does the larger eschatological drama come fully into focus.

This novel's fin-de-millénium setting invites readers to reflect on the end of the drama that begins in Eden with the Fall and Original Sin, continues through the Incarnation and the fated sacrifice, and concludes with the Apocalypse and the Second Coming. But neither the virgin birth of *Bailey's Cafe*, nor the pit that yawns for Luther Nedeed in *Linden Hills*, nor the millennial promise of *Mama Day* represents an exercise in Christian piety.[1] Rather, Naylor proposes a radically feminist revision of traditional patriarchal narrative. In *Mama Day* she implies that humanity will achieve its redemption only by restoring the proper mythic/religious relations between the sexes. The larger vision here involves recognizing and re-embracing a mother-deity displaced, in remote antiquity, by a host of unhealthy patriarchal alternatives. As corollary to this restoration, she implies, the usurping son or consort of the goddess (the mythographers'"solar hero") must accept the immolation of his rationality and return to his divinely subordinate role. Ultimately Naylor subverts the linear premises of Christian eschatology. In our end, she suggests, is our beginning.

Naylor became known when *The Women of Brewster Place* won the National Book Award. As her subsequent work has appeared, readers have seen the unfolding of an experimental project of no small magnitude—realization of the author's dream of "a quartet of interconnected novels."[2] Though not so elaborately linked as, say, the fictions of William Faulkner, Naylor's novels feature abundant cross-references and a modest version of what Balzac scholars call *"retour de personnages."* Thus *Brewster Place* includes among its major characters Kiswana Browne[3] and the lesbian couple Theresa and Lorraine—all refugees from Linden Hills. In the later novel named for that upscale development, a character briefly mentions Kiswana Browne as having gone off"to live in the slums of Brewster Place."[4] In *Linden Hills*, too, a desperate Willa Prescott Nedeed recalls "being so ashamed of her great-aunt, Miranda Day, when she pulled up in that cab each summer, calling from the curb at the top of her voice, 'Y'all better be home. Mama Day done come to visit a spell with her Northern folks'" (147).

This character comes into her own in Naylor's 1988 novel, *Mama Day*, which the author seems to have conceived as the nexus or center of her larger project. Cocoa, one of the major characters of this novel, is first cousin to the Willa of *Linden Hills*, and passing reference is twice made to the fire in which she dies. In addition to a redoubtable great-aunt, Cocoa and Willa share a grandmother, Abigail, and both claim descent from the legendary Sapphira Wade. In *Mama Day*, too, Cocoa and the man she will marry, George Andrews, go through an important reconciliation scene outside of

Bailey's Cafe, which gives its name to another Naylor novel, published later but set further back in time (indeed, *Bailey's Cafe* concludes with George's birth). The understated connections reveal that all of these characters exist in the same fictive world, the same historical space. They prompt the reader's attention to some larger unfolding drama—not a *comédie humaine* but rather *the* comedy of millennial fulfillment.

In *Mama Day* Naylor reconfigures at least three Shakespearean models. *King Lear* and *Hamlet*, in particular, yield archetypes of character and situation for Naylor's postmodern palimpsest. Cocoa's real name, after all, is Ophelia, and if something is rotten in the state of Denmark, something is amiss in Willow Springs too. That something, moreover, stems from a usurpation that makes the time out of joint. In Shakespeare, the love of Hamlet and Ophelia dies aborning, as he must be about his father's business, and some such patriarchal imperative seems also to disturb the marriage of George and Cocoa. But most of the explicit allusions direct the reader to *King Lear*, and a number of situations and actions parallel similar elements in that bleak text. One notes, for example, the drama of profound suffering and final reconciliation, and one notes the centrality of a terrible storm, in which human frailty is starkly reliefed (as Faulkner would say) against the violence of nature when untrammeled by humanity's civilizing institutions. In introducing a bastard son into her narrative, and in examining the fate of three daughters in two different generations, Naylor invites further notice of a relationship between her story and *King Lear*. One notes in passing that Naylor's rewriting of Shakespeare seems to involve little of the anger encountered in, say, Jane Smiley's 1991 novel *A Thousand Acres*, in which the *King Lear* story, set now on an Iowa farm in the late 1970s, is told entirely from the point of view of the old patriarch's oppressed daughters, two of whom he has sexually abused. Naylor, too, may deploy deconstructive strategies (for certainly she resists the Shakespearean patriarchalism), but like Alice Walker or Bharati Mukherjee she disdains the role of cultural victim, preferring to challenge the literary past less in the name of a political grievance than in the name of that older, more essential (if less fashionable) ideal: artistic autonomy.

Though *Hamlet* and *Lear* figure prominently, critics rightly emphasize Naylor's engagement with *The Tempest*. As a romance, this play includes a number of fantastic elements and departs from a realistic portrayal of scene and character and action. At the same time, through the alchemy of art, it explores human and cultural reality on a vast scale, for at its heart lies a pow-

erful vision of nature made serviceable to the Renaissance intellect and com-
formable to the Renaissance will. One of the play's less grandiose features,
on the other hand, is the amorous relationship between Prospero's daughter
Miranda and Prince Ferdinand. Their eventual marriage is the seal to Prospero's righting of ancient wrongs: the usurpation of his dukedom and his
banishment to the island. In the end, having played his maieutic role in the
union of Ferdinand and Miranda and having restored familial and political
harmony, Prospero reconciles with his brother and returns to his dukedom.

Naylor appropriates some of these elements and transmogrifies others.
In her novel, also a romance, Prospero becomes Mama Day, Sycorax the
vicious Ruby. Naylor reimagines Shakespeare's magical setting as Willow
Springs, an island with a past that represents a strange eddy in the larger
stream of African American history. When Mama Day wreaks her vengeance on Ruby by conjuring a lightning storm, one recognizes the borrowing and transformation of the tempest summoned by Prospero (it is the
second, unconjured storm that comes from *Lear*—though of course Hurston's *Their Eyes Were Watching God* also features a hurricane as the oblique
agent of a sympathetic husband's demise).[5] Naylor's plot, like Shakespeare's,
concerns a troubled family, with a history of ancient suffering that a benign
sorcerer, fostering love in the younger generation, strives to reverse. In Naylor as in Shakespeare the magician demands the labor, a kind of courtly service, of the heroine's suitor. Ferdinand is presently released from servitude;
George labors and dies. Thus the author of *Mama Day*, even more than
Shakespeare, insists on a recognition of the role played by Eros—the relationships between men and women—in the larger drama of political and
cultural travail. She insists, too, on a role for Thanatos.

Though her transformation of *The Tempest* has been well canvased,[6] no
prior discussion has explored this crux. Shakespeare is incidental to a set of
ideas that swiftly move beyond the quarrel with Prospero's colonialism—
his displacement, that is, of Sycorax and Caliban as rightful owners of the
island. Rather, Naylor seeks to subvert a much older and more absolute patriarchalism, for Prospero represents a symbolic version of the male deity
who usurps the ancient place of the goddess, here tendentiously disparaged
as mere witch. The author therefore proposes a major reinterpretation of
African American history and Judeo-Christian myth.

Naylor sets *Mama Day* largely on an island off the coast of the American
southeast—an island to which neither Georgia nor South Carolina can lay
claim. Offering a somewhat romanticized version of the topography, land-

scape, and culture of the barrier islands, she asks the reader to imagine a place exempt from certain of the concrete dimensions of actual history, a place in which some kind of separate African American identity might flourish. Though Willow Springs has hardly been exempt from poverty, it has led an existence largely untrammeled by the two centuries or so of oppression experienced by other African Americans. Not that Naylor goes so far as to imagine African Americans without the heritage of slavery—the exemption is from the more debilitating elements of postemancipation misery. For in Willow Springs emancipation came (in "18 and 23") two generations earlier than it did for the rest of the country's slaves. It came, moreover, with a myth of the slaves' appropriation of themselves and their erstwhile master's other property—the land itself. In addition to this substantial patrimony, their community was exempt from the hegemony of the nearby Southern states because its first owner, Bascombe Wade, was "Norway-born or something, and the land had been sitting in his family over there in Europe since it got explored and claimed by the Vikings."[7] The Vikings, one recalls, arrived on American shores at the end of the previous millennium—a thousand years, more or less, before present time in *Mama Day*.

The internal dating here is meticulous, and even remote or casual dates point the reader toward epiphanies. Most of the story is told in flashbacks narrated by Cocoa and George, with sections told by an anonymous narrator, perhaps the same collective, communal voice heard in the prologue. The book covers the courtship of Cocoa and George in 1980, their marriage in 1981, and the disastrous events of 1985, when they finally visit Willow Springs. The hurricane, the poisoning of Cocoa by Ruby, Mama Day's vengeance, and George's sacrificial death (which saves Cocoa) all transpire in this past before Naylor, skipping forward in time again, concludes with a description of Candle Walk 1998 and, on the eve of Mama Day's death at the age of 104, an August 1999 valedictory.

Though far more attractive than Linden Hills, Willow Springs remains, as an island, a not wholly positive conceit. One recognizes in *isola*, Latin for island, the root of the word "isolation." Islands stand for separateness that is not always enabling, and from one point of view the inhabitants of Naylor's imaginary community dwell in a condition of internal exile, cut off from their brothers and sisters on the mainland. More importantly, an island can symbolize the isolation that is the fate of every human being—a universal separateness that individuals seek to circumvent by such familiar blendings of self and other as friendship, sex, love, and marriage. In this recognition

one begins to descry the true matter of Naylor's novel. *Mama Day* concerns
what seems the difficulty—heightened in the course of modern times—that
men and women face in attempting to come together. Setting her tale largely
on an island, Naylor takes up, as theme, a kind of root estrangement between male and female.

The book addresses an issue more subtle, then, than the lack of suitable
black husbands that exercises news-magazine sociologists. More a condition
of Western life than a racial matter, the difficulties of Cocoa and George lie
close to the heart of things. D. H. Lawrence, one recalls, often takes up what
he perceived as a fundamental breakdown in relations between the sexes in
the twentieth century. Indeed, from *Sons and Lovers* to *St. Mawr* and *The
Man Who Died*, this collapse of marriage was his gauge of all that had gone
wrong in modern civilization. Naylor seems to address this same dysfunc-
tion, but from a feminist perspective. The single great source of disharmony,
she intimates, lies in an overturning, centuries ago, of matriarchal authority
and its divine counterpart. The world still reels from this displacement of
the Goddess, the Great Mother.

The special distinction of Willow Springs is that a matriarchal order
has re-emerged after the long patriarchal interregnum represented by two
generations of seven sons each (Naylor glances at Du Bois, who in *The Souls
of Black Folk* calls "the Negro . . . a sort of seventh son" among the world's
civilizations).[8] The chief evidence for a matriarchal survival is in the character of Mama Day, the conjure woman who gives her name to the story,
but one recognizes it also in the way that time is conceptualized on her island, notably at the cemetery. Here, in a number of scenes, the island's living inhabitants sustain relationships with their ancestors—indeed, *worship*
them—in moments of tribal communion very much like those still common
among the Dogon, the Yoruba, the Fon, and other peoples of West Africa.[9]
But George, the outsider, can only try to put the pieces into some kind of
logocentric order:

> The tombstones—some granite, some limestone—were of varying
> heights with no dates and only one name. You explained that they were
> all Days so there was no need for a surname. But what, as in your case, if
> a woman married? You live a Day and you die a Day. Early women's lib,
> I said with a smile. A bit more than that, you answered. You showed me
> how they were grouped by generations: the seven brothers and then the
> seven before them. The sizes of the headstones represented the missing

dates—but only in relationship to each other. There was a Peace who died younger than another Peace and so her stone was smaller. There was your mother's stone—Grace—and she had obviously died younger than her sister Hope. Mama Day, you said, would have the tallest stone. She'd already lived longer than any Day before her. The closeness of all this awed me—people who could be this self-contained. Who had redefined time. No, totally disregarded it. (218)

Time in this graveyard is the cyclical and rhythmic "women's time" that Julia Kristeva describes in one of her best-known essays. One notes, indeed, that insofar as the individual components of Naylor's roman fleuve appear out of temporal order, she herself subverts—or at least puts into play—the linear model of Fall/Incarnation/Sacrifice/Apocalypse/Millennium that she inherits from patriarchal Christianity.

Naylor nevertheless realizes her parable about an island of matriarchy in the great sea of Western patriarchalism in terms that, ultimately focused on female temporality, remain accessible to those prepared to grasp only the temporal models of the dominant episteme. Thus she translates, as it were, certain important elements in her story, allowing them their traditional expression, however phallocentric. For example, the scrupulous dating within the novel—especially the general orientation to 1999—makes an obvious obeisance to the familiar linear thinking of Christian eschatology. By the same token, she allows the reader knowledge of certain facts denied to the characters who live in the novel's late twentieth-century present—facts regarding Sapphira's name and original status as slave (the name is known properly only to the ancestors, the dead, whose collective, chorus-like voice the reader hears in the prologue and here and there elsewhere in the text).

One can advance further into the meaning of Willow Springs and its history by considering for a moment its countertype, Linden Hills, that monument to African American materialism. "The original 1820 surveys" (1) of Linden Hills, which have passed to every successive descendant in the Nedeed line, reveal a temporal origin virtually identical to that of Willow Springs, which acquired its unique identity in 1819, when Bascombe Wade purchased the slave Sapphira, and 1823, when he emancipated the slaves and gave them the island. The mythic founder of Linden Hills had bought the land and sat looking at it for "exactly seven days" (2) before setting his plan in motion. The same echo of Genesis figures in Mama Day when John-Paul, speaking from the grave, characterizes the godlike activity of the mythic Sapphira and explains the origin of the family surname: "God rested on the seventh day . . . and she would too" (151). In Linden Hills, the Nedeeds explicitly court millennial expectation by offering their clients a standard "thousand-year-and-a-day lease—provided only that they passed their property on to their children" (7). In unpretentious Willow Springs, on the other hand, land is "always owned two generations down" (219) to preserve the integrity of a birthright that passed, at the moment of its realization, to the generation of 1863: emancipation by prolepsis.

Parallel at a number of points, Linden Hills and Willow Springs diverge in their destiny and moral symbolism, and in each the Judeo-Christian model undergoes meaningful alterations. What emerges in Linden Hills is an infernal rival of peaceful Willow Springs, for the Nedeeds are diabolical monsters of patriarchal ruthlessness. The fire that consumes Luther Nedeed and his wife is palpably apocalyptic, but this annihilation of a false messiah (indeed, the black Antichrist) represents only the penultimate phase of the promised end. The more spiritual community, Willow Springs, survives to await postapocalyptic revelation. Whether the thousand years of peace will emerge in Willow Springs, however, depends on an altogether different messiah and the problematic resurgence of an altogether different deity.

The subversion of familiar Christian elements in *Linden Hills* and *Mama Day* extends to parallel observances of the winter solstice. On December 22nd of every year the people of Willow Springs celebrate Candle Walk, which originated as a remembrance of the moral conscience of Bascombe Wade. In Linden Hills every Nedeed inheritor is born at the Winter Solstice because every Nedeed progenitor copulates according to ancient precept: "There must be five days of penetration at the appearance of Aries, and the son is born when the sun has died." Luther Nedeed follows this rule to the letter: "his seed was only released at the vernal equinox so the child would come during the Sign of the Goat when the winter's light was the weakest" (19). Luther's light-skinned wife, however, gives birth to what seems "a white son" (18), a parody Jesus whom Luther takes for a bastard. "The child went unnamed and avoided by his father for the first five years of his life" (18). Nedeed's hatred of his supposedly unfaithful wife grows, not least because the apparent discontinuity in the succession of coal-black Nedeeds threatens his empire: "His fathers slaved to build Linden Hills. . . . and it would be a cold day in hell before he saw some woman tear it down" (20). At last he imprisons his wife and their son in the basement, where the child soon dies and where, in the six days preceding Christmas, 1979, she lives with the corpse and plots revenge.

A more authentic Jesus perishes in Willow Springs. As the *pharmakos* or sacrificial victim of *Mama Day*, George Andrews fulfills the destiny implicit in the miraculous circumstances of his birth, recounted in *Bailey's Cafe*. There the reader learns that his fifteen-year-old mother, Mariam, was a Falasha or Ethiopian Jew. She was also a virgin. Because time and space are highly fluid in *Bailey's Cafe*, the birth is somewhat difficult to date. Expected at one point "by next summer," it seems actually to take place immediately after the New Year—perhaps on 7 January, when the Coptic Church celebrates the Nativity. Before the birth, a character says, "maybe it's meant for this baby to bring in a whole new era."[10]

In revisiting and reshaping Judeo-Christian material, Naylor also explores and deconstructs the myth of primal transgression. Where Milton briefly compares Eve, stalked by Satan, to Persephone at a similar moment of innocence, Naylor gives the pre-Christian analogue more play, allowing the classical myth to resonate in both past and present. Like Willa Prescott Nedeed, who suffers a literal below-ground imprisonment, Sapphira is a black Kore or Persephone, striving to escape the arms Plutonic. The grief of Bascombe Wade is archetypal, too—it figures the frustration of the chthonian deity, obliged to yield up his stolen bride. By the same token, one recognizes echoes of the Eleusinian mysteries (celebrated in September or October, these commemorate the passion of Persephone and Demeter) in the present-day action of *Mama Day*. In its climax, which takes place in late summer or early autumn, the title character becomes a grieving Demeter, Cocoa the resurrected Persephone, and George the divine Triptolemus.

But Naylor's overt allusions are to that plinth of patriarchal Christianity, the Eden myth. Even to a rationalist like George, Willow Springs breathes an "atmosphere" straight out of Genesis: "This place was . . . like a wild garden" (217), he says. "More than pure, it was primal" (185). At one point he imagines permanently living on the island with Cocoa and is moved to say, "Let's play Adam and Eve" (222). But in Willow Springs one recognizes a different Eden, with a different pair of "grand parents," a different Original Sin, and latter days that are differently flawed. Indeed, the book's great conundrum is its conceptualization of a sin so primal as to infect every succeeding generation—and with apparently incremental malignancy. Thus the reader learns of the accidental drowning, in childhood, of Peace, sister of Abigail and Miranda, and the subsequent suicide drowning of their mother (the first Ophelia) in the sound. All three of Abigail's daughters are dead, including Cocoa's mother Grace and the second Peace. Further back, one discovers the mysterious destiny of Bascombe Wade, who died pining for the extraordinary woman who seems to have transformed bondage into the erotic enslavement of her erstwhile master. Some of those in Willow Springs say this woman, with the Catheresque name of Sapphira, murdered Bascombe Wade after making him deed the island to his slaves; others aver that, in despair at the loss of love, he committed suicide.[11] Contemplating the "other place," the house that Wade built for himself and Sapphira, George wonders, "What caused those two people to tear each other apart in this old house with a big garden?" (225). Unwittingly he anticipates his wife's similar question, after his death, about their own unsmooth relationship: "what really happened to us, George?" (311). These twinned questions mask another: why cannot men and women overcome their differences and achieve love and peace?

The answer is that some primal transgression has poisoned the well of Hymen, leaving marriage itself perennially impaired. That primal transgression is not slavery, nor does Naylor invite the reader to see in Cocoa's mixed blood a curse that precludes her final fulfillment in this life—a curse that also hangs over the other inhabitants of the island. To be sure, Cocoa, as a schoolgirl, had nearly cut her finger off, "fearing she really had the white blood she was teased about at school" (47). But thematically this is a red herring. "No, there was something more, and something deeper than the old historical line about slave women and their white masters" (225). Though unsparing in her intimations that slavery leaves scars in generation after generation, Naylor repeatedly hints at something more insidious as the source of this community's woes.

Naylor's real energies here seem focused on an issue that transcends race—a simple question about the complexity and difficulty of love. Thus the author finds her subject and theme in the difficulties that men and women struggle with in attempting to achieve true marriage. One sees this emphasis from the level of isolated detail to fully elaborated subplot. Cocoa's embittered mother, Grace, for example, was abandoned by her husband when she was eight months pregnant. Similarly, Mama Day broods about unchosen spinsterhood in her own and subsequent generations: healthy, mutualistic love relationships were not to be had "in her time," she reflects, "and from what these young women tell her, it's rare to find it now. So a lot of 'em is waking up like me, except they're waking up young and alone" (203). On a larger scale, the one stable marriage in the story, that of Ambush and Bernice, is dogged by the infertility that they circumvent only to lose Little Caesar. One sees love at its least coherent, finally, in the sordid drama of jealousy and fecklessness that Frances, Ruby, and Junior Lee play out. These relationships provide a meaningful background to the marriage of Cocoa and George, itself threatened, like the union of Bascombe Wade and his quondam slave Sapphira, by something malevolent in the very air.

Before Carl Gustav Jung and Erich Neumann recognized the Great Mother as a psychoanalytic archetype (to the occasional distress of feminists who see an historical reality denied or finessed), she was the subject, at least in part, of the pioneering work *Myth, Religion & Mother Right* (1861) by Johann Jakob Bachofen, whose birthday— 22 December 1815—reveals another child of the winter solstice. Other studies include Sir James George Frazer's *The Golden Bough* (1890–1915) and two books by Jane Harrison: *Prolegomena to the Study of Greek Religion* (1908) and *Themis* (1912). More recently, studies of the Great Mother have included *The Cult of the Mother Goddess* (1959), by E. O. James, and *The Great Cosmic Mother* (1987), by Monica Sjöö and Barbara Mor. Still to be done is some definitive study of the Goddess in Africa, amid cultures perhaps irreparably altered by colonialism and modern political history. Thus any attempt to discuss Naylor's Black Goddess may seem to lean excessively on Eurocentric mythologies. In adducing certain white or male mythographers here (notably Robert Graves), I plead guilty to possible distortion. But at the same time I would suggest that Naylor's vision, however clearly rooted in African American experience, values, and history, engages the entire cultural spectrum, and I find that the wider the range of anthropologists, mythographers, and classical scholars brought to bear on her texts, the more they seem to foliate and expand.

Certainly the male scholars do not lack for enthusiasm and sympathy for the Goddess. Both Robert Graves and the more disinterested E. O. James explore pre-Olympian goddess worship, emphasizing the primacy of a cosmic female principle. James notes that "the Mother-goddess was assigned a male partner, either in the capacity of her son and lover, or of brother and husband." This consort "occupied a subordinate position to her" and was "a secondary figure in the cultus." James thinks "a primeval system of matriarchal social organization . . . by no means improbable" and emphasizes "that the Goddess at first had precedence over the Young God with whom she was associated."[12] Graves, famous for the iconoclastic theory of Western cultural origins that he developed in his 1948 book *The White Goddess*, argues that the familiar deities of classical mythology, led by Zeus, Poseidon, Pluto, and the lesser gods of sky, sea, and underworld, were in ancient times usurpers of this much older divine figure. Basically the earth mother, the White

Goddess is a triple deity who also reigns, in various incarnations, over birth, death, and the mysterious springs of fecundity.

The goddess chooses a consort, often a mortal, who enjoys her favor for a certain period (usually a year) before yielding himself up for sacrifice. This is the solar hero or solar king, a mythic figure born at the winter solstice. His avatars include Apollo, Dionysus, Zeus, Hermes, Hercules, Osiris, Horus, Ra, and of course the Christian savior, Jesus Christ. These avatars, in the reinscription of religious meanings carried out by the ancient displacers of the Mother, have come, in the body of patriarchal myth that dominates in the West, to outrank and displace her.[13] "Our modern patriarchal society," observes Jane Harrison, "focusses its religious anthropomorphism on the relationship of the father and the son; the Roman Church with her wider humanity includes indeed the figure of the Mother who is both Mother and Maid, but she is still . . . subordinate to the Father and the Son."[14] In other words, Christians worship Jesus—the Virgin they merely honor.

But in the old dispensation, the solar hero's sacrificial death was ordained as a means to the goddess's great ends. This is the burden of Graves's cryptic 1945 poem "To Juan at the Winter Solstice." As poet and votary of the Goddess, Graves counsels Juan, his newborn son who may also become a poet, with regard to the true bardic subject matter. Juan, as a child of the winter solstice himself, must be especially mindful that "There is one story and one story only"—that of the Goddess and her marriage to the solar hero always born when the sun is at its weakest, a marriage of sun and earth, male and female, that fructifies the universe. The fate of the solar hero is at once noble and terrible, for he will witness and fulfill the power of the goddess, the power sketched in Graves's portentous maxim: "Nothing promised that is not performed."

Graves, who spent much of his life under the influence of the Sapphira-like Laura Riding, attributed the ills of modern civilization to its repudiation of the Goddess. Enlisting under her banner himself, he argued that the West could save itself only through a return to its ancient fealty. Unlike Bascombe Wade, then, Graves gets credit for recognizing and deferring to the goddess. But perhaps he errs in calling her the "white" goddess. After all, Hecate, one of her avatars, is in fact black—and if, as some have argued, the mythologies of the West had a sub-Mediterranean genesis, Graves's deity must originally have been what Sjöö and Mor call "the Black Goddess, the Great Mother of Africa."[15]

Mama Day refers to Cocoa's ancestor as "The great, grand Mother," the "ancient mother of pure black" (48), and her words suggest at once Sapphira Wade and something older, more powerful, and truly divine. Cocoa herself passes this vision on to her baffled husband. "You told me," he muses, "that woman had been your grandmother's great-grandmother. But it was odd . . . the way you said it—she was the great, great, grand, Mother—as if you were listing the attributes of a goddess" (218).

In the absence of more information about the tribal origins of Sapphira Wade, one cannot particularize the goddess with whom she is associated,[16] but many in West Africa (notably the Fon) recognize in Nana Buruku (or Buluku) a deity so ancient as to frustrate mythography. She is, observes Pierre Verger, "an archaic deity older than all others known among the Yoruba, and very little is known about her."[17] In Sapphira Naylor imagines a priestess or indeed an incarnation of Nana Buruku—or another of her many avatars. She imagines her as nothing less than absolutely black: "the black that can soak up all the light in the universe, can even swallow the sun" (48). This engulfed or swallowed light, one realizes, is the emblem at once of classical order (Zeus and Apollo, displacers of the mother goddess, are always resplendently clothed in light) and of Enlightenment logocentrism ("More light!," breathes the dying Goethe). The sun to be swallowed is also the hero who must serve, mate with, and be slain by or for the goddess. Naylor's story comes more sharply into focus.

The reader attuned to these elements draws nearer to understanding the primal trespass and solving the enigma of Willow Springs: Bascombe Wade never surrendered to the goddess in Sapphira, and thus his gestures of emancipation could never be more than half measures, tragically guaranteed to fall short. The primal sin on this little coastal island, as elsewhere in the Western world, is displacement of the Great Mother by logocentrism—the casting out of Sycorax by Prospero. The male children of Sapphira Wade take the surname Day as if in homage to the new cosmic principle whereby the fecund darkness must give way to the light of masculine reason. Nevertheless, it was the goddess in Sapphira that created Willow Springs, and the reader sees her powerful survival in the conjure woman, Mama Day. The story allows hope for an eventual, millennial triumph of the Black Goddess.

On Willow Springs, then, one recognizes the symbolic stage on which certain great passages in the history of Western civilization are enacted and reenacted. Here one sees again the betrayal of the Goddess and her struggle with the white, rationalistic, Eurocentric order that Bascombe Wade represents. From the primal, unholy union of master and sometime slave descend fourteen sons in two generations, their very names evocative of Judeo-Christian patriarchy. In the first generation, the sons bear names from the Old Testament; in the second, names from the New Testament. The last of these is the father of Miranda and Abigail, and his name, John-Paul, reflects a significant shift from the apostolic to the patristic. But at this point the female principle reasserts itself in two generations of women, with names that, when not taken from Shakespearean romance and tragedy, hint at subtle modifications of Christianity's virtues and desiderata. Not Faith, Hope, and Charity, but Grace, Hope, and Peace. In the distaff line, only Cocoa's grandmother, Abigail, has a biblical name. It means "source of joy," for she is the passer-on of Sapphira's blood.

One hundred and sixty or so years after Bascombe and Sapphira founded their troubled line, George Andrews strives blindly to connect with a woman who is the heir-designate of all the mysteries represented by this island of matriarchal power. This woman, Cocoa, is herself tragically blind to the precise dynamic that comes between herself and her husband, who, as engineer and Republican, is a man wholly committed to the Logos, impervious to the matrifocal wisdom of the island and its current matriarch. "What do you do when someone starts telling you something that you just cannot believe?" (286), wonders George when confronted with what he attempts to dismiss as "mumbo-jumbo" (295). Mama Day offers him candor on a similar occasion: "You have a choice. . . . I can tell you the truth, which you won't believe, or I can invent a lie, which you would" (266).

Mama Day does not despise George. Rather, she recognizes his strength and seeks to convert it to her ends. That is, she asks him, in the name of his love for Cocoa, to suspend his skepticism and serve her. She knows that "he believes in himself," and she wants his belief and his "will." In short, she wants his hands, willingly given. With "his hand in hers" (285), she will prevail against the dark forces marshalled by the horrific Ruby. Thus the ancient conjure woman sends George on a strange mission to find and bring to her whatever might lie behind a certain baleful denizen of her henhouse. She knows that he will find there only his own hands, and she hopes he will return and put them at her disposal. When George does not return, she thinks that she has failed to persuade him, that "he went and did it his way" (302). But in fact George has perished in the attempt to carry out his instructions, and Naylor seems to imply that his sacrifice is instrumental in Cocoa's recovery, that his act of faith is enough to tip the balance. He has become the half-conscious instrument of Mama Day's healing. She has managed to defeat the malevolence brought to bear on Cocoa, not to mention briefly to circumvent a rationalistic hegemony some thousands of years old. She becomes the conduit whereby some power of maternal, cosmic healing comes into play.

The darker side of this rescue, not desired or understood by Mama Day, is George's present death, which is nothing less than sacrificial. Human and hence fallible, Mama Day surely errs to think this death avoidable.[18] The strain of the day and the violence of the brood hen prove too much for a heart weak from childhood (the weakness of that heart, like the strength of his intellect and will, is obviously symbolic). Like Bascombe Wade before him, George is a classic solar hero. All those stories of the hero loved by the goddess yet doomed—Endymion, Attis, Adonis—are stories, more or less disguised by androcentric revisionism, of the ancient, matriarchal order and its ritual slaughter of the young and privileged king, consort to the goddess for one splendid year before his fated end. The boar that slays Adonis becomes the old and vicious red hen with which George does battle, only to stumble away with a complete set of stigmata: the ankle, the hands, the "stitch in my side" (301). George fulfills the destiny hinted at in his dream of walking on water (183–84). He becomes the local savior, undergoes the redemptive sacrifice.

In his two desperate trips on the path between the other place and the trailer, George brings on the bursting of his heart and reenacts the passion of the island's first sacrifice, Bascombe Wade: "Up and down this path, somehow, a man dies from a broken heart" (118). The inhabitants of Willow Springs commemorate the island's emancipator in the annual ritual of Candle Walk, which the people understand differently at different moments in their history—but which always takes place on December 22, the winter solstice. This is the point in the annual round at which the tide turns in the struggle between light and dark. The winter solstice marks the birth of the solar deity, for the sun waxes from this point in the year to furnish creation with more light and heat. But when summer ends—hurricane season in the American Southeast—the solar hero must undergo his inevitable sacrifice.

Candle Walk, like any other folk tradition, evolves and changes; yet all its versions are equally valid. In Miranda's youth it seems linked to a matriarchal commemoration of Sapphira Wade's departure in—or as—a mythic ball of fire. But Mama Day remembers accounts of other meanings from the days of her father, John-Paul, and grandfather, Jonah—meanings centered in the male ancestor. Twice in the story Miranda pauses in wonder at the realization that "the light wasn't for her—it was for him" (118). George, she says,

> done opened that memory for us. My daddy said that his daddy said when he was young, Candle Walk was different still. It weren't about no candles, was about a light that burned in a man's heart. And folks would go out and look up at the stars—they figured his spirit had to be there, it was the highest place they knew. And what took him that high was his belief in right, while what buried him in the ground was the lingering taste of ginger from the lips of a woman. (308)

One errs, however, to construe the meaning in terms of an either/or. Erich Neumann observes that "the winter solstice, when the Great Mother gives birth to the sun, stands at the center of the matriarchal mysteries."[19] All meanings of Candle Walk cohere in the matriarchal vision.

"Lead on with light." The saying, like the candles, glances simultaneously at the flickering existence of the infant solar light on December 22—and at the principle of light that can come to dominate a logocentric episteme rather than casting, as it ought, glory on the Goddess. Mama Day experiences this light as the climax to the mental struggle that follows her recovery of the ledger with the "slip of paper" (279) recording the sale of Sapphira to Bascombe Wade. The ink on this document has long since run, and the name of her great-grandmother remains illegible. She can make out only a series of suggestive words: "Law. Knowledge. Witness. Inflicted. Nurse. Conditions. Tender. Kind" (280). These words contain, however, a complete gendering of psychology—from Lacan's Symbolic Order ("Law," "Knowledge") to Kristeva's chora ("Nurse," "Tender," "Kind"). The progression is at once backward and forward in time: from the law and knowledge implied in the Name of the Father backward to the tender condition of nursling, sheltered and nurtured by the body of the mother—and from the patriarchal hegemony of slavery forward to the progressive recovery, on Willow Springs, of an alternative, female order.

Why is the name, known in the prologue yet unknown to Miranda, unspoken? Evidently Naylor wants to express something of the pathos of a community denied the name of its tutelary spirit. At the same time, Naylor knows that naming, as Adamic prerogative, is intensely logocentric. This particular name, she suggests, welters in the limbo of all that fails to register on the instruments of patriarchy. "Woman," says Kristeva, is precisely "that which cannot be represented, that which is not spoken, that which remains outside naming and ideologies."[20] On the night Mama Day discovers the bill of sale, she puzzles over the obliterated name until she falls asleep, but though "in her dreams she finally meets Sapphira" (280), she still does not learn her name. Instead, "in a vast space of glowing light," she experiences an oneiric return to the prelinguistic chora and the mother's body:

> Daughter. The word comes to cradle what has gone past weariness. She can't really hear it 'cause she's got no ears, or call out 'cause she's got no mouth. There's only the sense of being. Daughter. Flooding through like fine streams of hot, liquid sugar to fill the spaces where there was never no arms to hold her up, no shoulders for her to lay her head down and cry on, no body to ever turn to for answers. Miranda. Sister. Little Mama. Mama Day. Melting, melting away under the sweet flood waters pouring down to lay bare a place she ain't known existed: Daughter. And she opens the mouth that ain't there to suckle at the full breasts, deep greedy swallows of a thickness like cream, seeping from the corners of her lips, spilling onto her chin. Full. Full and warm to rest between the mounds of softness, to feel the beating of a calm and steady heart. She sleeps within her sleep. (283)

At the end, Mama Day still has not recovered the lost name. In a reverie at the graveyard, she remarks to the dead George, "I can't tell you her name, 'cause it was never opened to me. That's a door for the child of Grace to walk through." Cocoa's mother was named Grace, but the epithet also affirms Cocoa's growing spiritual distinction—indeed, the inheritance of Mama Day's own spiritual gifts. Cocoa will one day know even as she is known. It will perhaps be a day when naming and time and light will no longer be emblems of patriarchal, logocentric division—a proximate day, perhaps, when the gender of Cocoa's children (two boys) will pose no threat to the spiritual condition of Willow Springs. When Mama Day adds that "there'll be another time—that I won't be here for—when she'll learn about the beginning of the Days," one recognizes, I think, the intimation of another, culminating stroke on Naylor's great canvas. But like Cocoa, the reader must "go away to come back to that kind of knowledge" (308).

CHAPTER 5

The Jeffersonian Vision in Steve Erickson's Arc d'X

> There is no political power without control of the archive, if not of memory.
> Effective democratization can always be measured by this essential criterion: the
> participation in the access to the archive, its constitution, and its interpretation.
> —JACQUES DERRIDA, *ARCHIVE FEVER*

The troubled relationship of Bascombe Wade and his quondam bondswoman Sapphira gives way, in the imagination of Steve Erickson, to the
historically real connection between Thomas Jefferson and his slave Sally
Hemings. But Erickson's treatment of miscegenation goes far beyond that
of Naylor. It may in fact go too far, and in the present chapter I will register some reservations regarding this author's 1993 novel *Arc d'X*. As one
who does not care for negative criticism, I tend simply to steer away from
books that strike me as clumsy or unachieved, but occasionally, asked for
an essay or a talk, I discover unnoticed virtues in fictions that had left me
unenthusiastic at a first reading. With *Arc d'X*, I have not become a believer
(much as I respect the opinions of such Erickson apologists as Larry Mc-
Caffery and Nobuo Kamioka), but I have come to see the error in thinking the novel completely without merit. One respects Erickson's epistemic
discernment and its realization, however flawed, in an ambitious narrative. I
include a brief discussion of that narrative here because it represents at once
the continuing viability and the dangers to second-comer postmoderns of
an aesthetic ripe for passage into mannerism. The author professes himself
an admirer of postmodernism's celebrated pioneer, Thomas Pynchon; on
balance, unfortunately, Erickson comes off more as epigone than as junior
partner to his great predecessor.

The plot of *Arc d'X* strikes me as too extravagant, too incoherent, too
bent on violent overthrow of received history. Erickson's primal American

pair slips the bonds of realistic storytelling in an ultimately heavy-handed exercise in historical revisionism. Invited to think less of an American icon, Thomas Jefferson, readers may find themselves merely deploring the rhetorical overkill of a writer who may have learned the wrong lessons from the writers he has named, in interviews, as influences, including (along with Pynchon) Stendhal, Faulkner, and García Márquez.[1] Like these writers, he aspires to present the great sweep of history, but the attempt at making America a continent-sized Macondo miscarries—as does the exposure of Thomas Jefferson as real-life Carothers McCaslin (the half-mythic patriarch who presides over Faulkner's Go Down, Moses). Erickson's history is too fluid, too unanchored. Like Pynchon, he aspires to powerful language and subversive historiography, but pretentiousness outpaces perspicacity—at least in Arc d'X. The transitions from an actual eighteenth century to a fanciful future in this novel may well strike the reader as short on historiographical heft. This in contrast to Pynchon, a master of ellipsis in its various forms who nonetheless weaves historical tapestries as replete with detail as those of Stendhal (one thinks of the tour de force account of Waterloo in The Charterhouse of Parma). In V., for example, Pynchon recapitulates the course of the twentieth century in a handful of powerfully realized tableaux; in Gravity's Rainbow, he treats the final phase of the European campaign in World War II (and its aftermath) with extraordinary conviction; in Mason & Dixon, he re-creates the British and American eighteenth century; and in Against the Day he patiently documents the historical and political matrix in which a worldwide century of carnage had its beginnings. Pynchon never fails to make a convincing world; Erickson sums up, describes, sketches more history than he can accommodate diegetically.

*****

Even under a postmodern dispensation routinized to the point of invisibility, most human beings continue to function according to an Enlightenment epistemology and ontology. That is, most people think that what is is, and they view as uncomplicated the difference between reality and its representation. Their physics, for that matter, remains largely Newtonian. This natural conservatism makes easy the work of those "ideological state apparatuses" that, according to Louis Althusser, foster and sustain the citizen's position as subject.[2] Ideology aside, however, governmental and religious institutions defend versions of reality (including supernatural reality) that remain mired in outmoded orthodoxies.

When we theorize postmodernism and the breadth of its cultural expression, we sometimes forget the extent to which institutions—especially government—remain unconcerned with the paradigm shifts that trouble both social and physical science. This institutional resistance to postmodern conceptualization of the real, this failure of imagination and intellect, has its instantiation in one of the central conceits of *Arc d'X*, the novel in which, Steve Erickson feels, his early work in fiction "culminated."[3] Here the reader follows Thomas Jefferson and his slave-concubine Sally Hemings from versions of revolutionary America (and France) to a strange life and death—or lives and deaths—in a varied, fluidly imagined present and near future. As an historical fiction, *Arc d'X* strikes the reader as another iconoclastic hybrid, related on the one hand to such historically predicated representations of the future as Russell Hoban's *Riddley Walker* (1980) or Margaret Atwood's *The Handmaid's Tale* (1986) and, on the other, to such alternate history (or "allohistorical") fictions as Ward Moore's *Bring the Jubilee* (1953), Philip K. Dick's *The Man in the High Castle* (1962), Keith Roberts's *Pavane* (1968), and Robert Sobel's *For Want of a Nail: If Burgoyne Had Won at Saratoga* (1973).[4] On the third hand (these fractionations, as Nabokov observes, sprout additional forelimbs all the time), one discerns elements of the chronicle fiction that traces a single family or community down through time (sometimes, as with James Michener, readers start all the way back at the geological beginning). Erickson elides the generationalism, however; like characters in some magical-realist fantasy, his freely imagined Thomas Jefferson and Sally Hemings live from colonial times into a reimagined present, the one steadily fading as a personality, the other becoming something like a pebble in the shoe of American history. The historical revisionism is as radical, in its own way, as the change in gender that Woolf's Orlando undergoes in the course of a life that extends from the sixteenth century into the twentieth. Nevertheless, one faults Erickson for his undisciplined prose, his unanchored figures, and his treatment of history as fantasia.

Liberated from time, space, and the mortal span of years, Sally Hemings figures in *Arc d'X* as an important viewpoint character. History is inscribed, as it were, on her body. As part of Jefferson's entourage, she witnesses the French Revolution, after which, according to one strand of the story, she remains in France until her death in 1835 in the room where she tacks up a tarot card that will be found a century and a half later by the French scholar Seuroq. According to another strand, Sally returns with Jefferson to the United States, where she lives on into modern times, history's plaything and ageless embodiment of that part of the American soul that is forever African or partly African.

Other characters, somewhat more anchored in time, include Etcher, the file clerk who retrieves Sally's story from historical oblivion, and Seuroq, who at the end of the twentieth century discovers a temporal anomaly, a kind of historical black hole designated "*JOUR D'X*."[5] Bearing some resemblance to the temporal lacuna that figures in *Mason & Dixon* (where calendar reform causes eleven days to disappear), not to mention the conceit that dictates the title of *Leap Year* (the 1989 book in which the real Erickson introduces Sally Hemings), DAY X concentrates and contains "all the moments over the millennium that grief and passion had consumed from memory and then dribbled back into the X of the arcs of history and the heart" (210). An international sensation, Seuroq's discovery compels a failed American novelist named Erickson—one discerns the Paul Auster touch here—to head for mythic Berlin on the eve of the millennium. Here a skinhead named Georgie Valis, another talented Mr. Ripley, murders him, assumes his identity, and travels to America to assassinate Thomas Jefferson—still alive in the year 1999—in the very room where Sally Hemings lies asleep. Before dying, Jefferson tells his assailant: "I made a country once. It was the country of redemption, somewhere this side of God's" (261).

The sprawl of the narrative strikes the reader as either a major part of its historiographic message or the latest illustration of the fallacy of imitative form. The resistance of *Arc d'X* to one's desire to summarize it, in any event, becomes a kind of postmodern credential in and of itself. Lee Spinks argues that Erickson's "writing seeks to give both structure and thematic expression to the complex relationship between temporality, history, and narrative. The involuted timescales and intricate plotlines of his novels consistently imbricate ends with beginnings and inscribe an eschatological trajectory within the discourse of American history."[6] Thus the various plots, characters, and settings of *Arc d'X* eventually prove interwoven in a "structure" that, according to Jim Murphy, "evokes the visual illusions of the interlocking corridors in an M. C. Escher print."[7] But the operative word here is *illusion*, for under scrutiny the elaborate edifice turns out to be constituted of mismatched parts, discontinuities. In Erickson as in Escher, the seemingly perfect schematicism proves instructively chimerical, a study in the postmodern distrust of totalized forms.

Reasoning, evidently, that any liaison between a white man and his bondswoman must have involved coercion (for assent cannot be freely given by a slave), Erickson depicts Jefferson as rapist, albeit on French soil, where the victim is at least technically not chattel. But this violation fosters a strange, quasi-masochistic dependency, a relationship that initially proceeds pari passu with the French Revolution—also compromised by a violent beginning and led by, among others, the Georges Danton that Erickson imagines as wondering: "My God . . . does all of history think with its dick?" (284). Where the revolutionaries view Jefferson as shining example and culture hero, however, a later age, learning of his seigneurial exploitation of Sally Hemings, will find his stature diminished, his august reputation besmirched. Erickson, to his credit, undertakes something more than simple vilification of the man who drafted the Declaration of Independence. Though he invites consideration of whether a founding father's priapism might somehow have contaminated the institutions that supposedly sustain American self-regard, the author invests more of his intellectual energy in interrogating and dismantling the Jeffersonian myth. In that he does not simply identify a hierarchy and invert it, moreover, Erickson undertakes deconstruction in its most rigorous sense: his novel makes of Jefferson a signifier in freeplay, more and more resistant to the desire of reader or historian to arrest him in some definitive posture of signification.

Arc d'X may, however, strike the reader as rather inelegant revisionism, an unsuccessful attempt to reconceptualize the invention of America ("of the American Dream," says the jacket copy) and the pursuit of happiness. At its best, the book shows that owning slaves—and violating them sexually—creates an ineradicable bond, a permanent condition of iniquity rather like Original Sin. But too often this message welters in a sea of bad prose and labored symbolism—thrown into relief if one juxtaposes a shifting but perspicuous metaphorical passage from Pynchon with an Ericksonian passage that gets out of control. Here, then, are Pynchon describing a derelict suffering from delirium tremens, and Erickson describing Jeffersonian introspection:

Cammed each night out of that safe furrow the bulk of this city's waking each sunrise again set virtuously to plowing, what rich soils had he turned, what concentric planets uncovered? What voices overheard, flinders of luminescent gods glimpsed among the wallpaper's stained foliage, candlestubs lit to rotate in the air over him, prefiguring the cigarette he or a friend must fall asleep someday smoking, thus to end among the flaming, secret salts held all those years by the insatiable stuffing of a mattress that could keep vestiges of every nightmare sweat, helpless overflowing bladder, viciously, tearfully consummated wet dream, like the memory bank to a computer of the lost?[8]

Expanding on this description, Pynchon will presently call DTs "the trembling unfurrowing of the mind's plowshare" (the figure derives its justness from *delirium's* etymon: *lira*, Latin for "furrow"). He shares with Shakespeare the ability to shift his metaphorical ground without risk of incoherence or absurdity (the kind of *sottise* the *New Yorker* has for years featured as "Block that metaphor!"). Erickson, attempting prose as performative, goes astray. "I've invented something," says the Jefferson of *Arc d'X*:

> As the germ of conception in my head it was the best and wildest and most elusive of my inventions. It's a contraption halfcrazed by a love of justice, a machine oiled by fierce hostility to those who would ride the human race as though it were a dumb beast. I've set it loose gyrating across the world. It spins through villages, hamlets, towns, grand cities. It's a thing to be confronted every moment of every day by everyone who hears even its rumor: it will test most those who presume too glibly to believe in it. But I know it's a flawed thing, and I know the flaw is of me. Just as the white ink of my loins has fired the inspiration that made it, so the same ink is scrawled across the order of its extinction. The signature is my own. I've written its name. I've called it America. (46)

The passage begins inelegantly and descends into muddle. This reader, at least, summons to his side the Polonius who firmly objects to "an ill phrase, a vile phrase" in the amorous discourse of Prince Hamlet. One winces especially at "the white ink of my loins" that "fired inspiration." Such sense as Jefferson makes here seems less than cogent: some bad angel fired some good angel out? a buildup of semen led to the creation of America? (The idea is not without its modicum of Freudian insight, but Freud was more persuasive, more rhetorically deft, in arguing a libidinal plinth to civilization-building). Verbally maladroit ("[h]e only wished she were so black that his ejaculation might be the only white squiggle across the void of his heart" [24]), Erickson makes Jefferson guilty of an uncharacteristic conceptual fuzziness. With the possible exception of the scene in which, in France, the fictional character addresses an adoring crowd (35–36), the language of the novel sorts ill with documentary evidence of the real Jefferson's eloquence. The "flawed thing" here is neither America nor its founding *philosophe* but the author who, trip-

ping over his own prose, tries unsuccessfully to say that seminal "ink" somehow impregnates history itself, that it writes America even as it signs its
death warrant. Only at the end of the passage does plausibility return, as Jefferson and his "invention" coalesce. As his "signature" and "its name" coincide,
he declares: I am America, America is I. *This* one can understand, work with,
connect with other representations of America's dual character, the strange
mix of idealism and ruthless appetite.

The novel goes further astray, however, in Erickson's attempt to develop
a complex, historicized idea of the relationship between freedom and love—
of what happens "when the thing that emerged from the collision of sex and
freedom, called love, collided with the thing that emerged from the collision
of time and memory, called history" (155). One faults the author for clumsy
prose and for the more than dubious notion that a rapist and his victim
might presently become devoted to each other. The author obscurely characterizes "the heart and memory" as "the only two things that can puncture the
flow of time through which hisses the history of the future" (195). Imagining
"a place where the static of love meeting freedom was not to be confused
with history" (199), Erickson introduces only confusion into his otherwise
compelling meditation on a past willfully forgotten or suppressed. Suggesting that what is done to the violated creates a need for or dependency on the
father/master/rapist (52) may be one kind of commentary on the claim for
American innocence, but Erickson lurches from gross sensationalism (blood
spurts across the room from the fourteen-year-old Sally's ruptured hymen)
to a highly tendentious romantic fantasy. As in the silliest of bodice rippers,
sexual violence proves somehow self-legitimating, as Sally comes to capitulate emotionally to the union with Jefferson, compelling him to a commitment to the household they share (first in Paris, later in Virginia and parts
west). In short, the depiction of Thomas Jefferson as rapist does not square
with Erickson's subsequent attempts to tell a love story predicated on what
the dust jacket copy calls "the tension between history's denial of the dictates
of the human heart and our secret pursuit of the heart's expression." Is this
really—still quoting from the dust jacket—"the emblematic dilemma that
has forged our nation's destiny?" I think not: all the reflections on giving up
freedom for love notwithstanding, the thematic idea of fulfillment on the racial boundary—fulfillment, indeed, rising above the circumstances of Sally's
defloration—remains obscure.

Back in America (according to one path of Erickson's story), Jefferson
becomes president, and Sally, seemingly abandoned, sets out on a strange,

surreal voyage. Stranger still, Jefferson follows through space and time—to the west and to "a city that lay outside of history," a city governed by "a church that presumed itself unthreatened by the collision of time and memory that named its own truth." The language here—"it was the joke of their arrogance that they presumed history might be locked away in a room without a single guard" (150)—resembles that of the 1995 essay "American Weimar," in which Erickson characterizes as "grand arrogance" the conviction that America might always "dictate its own terms to history rather than the other way around."[9] By implication, then, the setting in Erickson's novel is less dystopian future than metaphoric distortion of today's America, with its ascendant pietism, its willful forgetting of certain hideous realities of the past. This past survives, in Erickson's allegory, in an Orwellian archive housing the Unexpurgated Volumes of Unconscious History, the record of all that the culture wants kept out of sight: the slavery, genocide, rape, and miscegenation so seldom given their true weight in the scales of American historiography.

Erickson's great theme—in *Arc d'X*, in the journalism that complements it—is the problem of American innocence. In the iconoclasm with which he attacks the myth behind one founding father, Erickson seeks to contribute to some radical reconsideration of American identity. Essentially an historical project, this rebooting of the national character transforms history into a collective version of the "examined life" that Plato urged on the individual. Thus Erickson reframes the myth of the American Adam, a myth central to our national sense of identity and projected repeatedly in our literature. R. W. B. Lewis, in his much-admired 1955 study, characterizes the American Adam as an "individual emancipated from history, happily bereft of ancestry, untouched and undefiled by the usual inheritances of family and race; an individual standing alone, self-reliant and self-propelling."[10] Erickson disputes this conceit, seeks to devise a countermyth grounded in counterhistory. In the essay "American Weimar," the author speaks of "the delusion of American innocence," refusing "to call innocent a country where the original residents were systematically wiped out and the new tenants built a society in large part on the labor of people who were shipped over in chains from another continent in the hulls of boats."[11] Repeating these sentiments in the interview with Larry McCaffery and Takayuki Tatsumi, Erickson adds: "The great paradox of America has been the conflict between its true idealism and its false innocence, and this pathological contradiction is at the root of the country's current cynicism and spiritual bankruptcy."[12]

For this reader, Erickson creates his most compelling character in the myopic Etcher, who ekes out an existence as "history's file clerk" (153) and falls in love with the still-living, still beautiful Sally Hemings, chief suspect in the murder of her bedmate (not identified as the ghostly, attenuated Thomas Jefferson until late in the story). The author's real surrogate here (and the most interesting figure in this carpet), Etcher steals and rewrites the Unexpurgated Volumes. Too insignificant to "guard" the archive where he works, Etcher represents the artist in an age not of chaos (as in Erickson's *The Sea Came in at Midnight*) but of official reality, a reality presided over by puritanical authorities and answering, almost point for point, the bitter augury in Pynchon's *Vineland*: "a timeless, defectively imagined future of zero-tolerance drug-free Americans all pulling their weight and all locked in to the official economy, inoffensive music, endless family specials on the Tube, church all week long, and, on special days, for extra-good behavior, maybe a cookie."[13] More broadly, Etcher represents the artist/historian/intellectual marginalized in an apotheosis of the bureaucratic (indeed, theocratic) state that has engineered, in those Unexpurgated Volumes, a monumental suppression of the past. This encyclopedia contains "[t]he history of our secrets" (130), and it includes an entry on Sally Hemings, "the slave and mistress of the leader of a country Etcher had never heard of" (120). When Etcher purloins the forbidden texts from a locked room in his workplace, he symbolically enacts the arduous and long-resisted recovery, in the world outside the novel, of the staggering fact that Jefferson, founding father and shining beacon of freedom, actually had a sexual relationship with and fathered one or more children by a woman he owned, Sally Hemings.

Founding father, then, of a nation of bastards (in both the denotative and colloquial sense) unable ever to shake off the primal transgression.

At the end of the book, long after Sally's death, the reader sees Etcher restoring the purloined volumes, page by transcribed page. Ostensibly he does so at the sufferance or behest of the authorities, but Erickson intimates that the artist-historian—that solitary drudge—treats his material subversively. Like DeLillo rewriting the Warren Commission report (or, for that matter, Erickson himself), Etcher resists and repudiates single-perspective, monologic versions of the historical record. He reinscribes history, and this activity may help readers understand his charactonymic name. More than a pun on "Escher" (the Dutch draftsman best known for elevating optical illusion to the level of art), the name seems to invite reflection on the craft of etching as synecdoche, under the postmodern dispensation, for the whole artistic enterprise. And just here one discerns an interesting qualification of the poststructuralist idea of the work of art as always already some kind of simulacrum. According to Derrida, "engraving, which copies model art, is nonetheless the model for art."[14] Countering this deconstructive precept, Erickson invites attention to engraving's more respectable predecessor, the art of etching. An etcher scores a surface, first with the burin, then with acid. Inking the plate thus incised, the artist prints images in a process—*pace* Walter Benjamin—not quite mechanical.[15] Indeed, the pulling of prints one by one distinguishes this *techne* from the true mechanical reproduction of engraving. Yet Etcher (the character) remains very much a *postmodern* artist, "an author who imitates the role of Author," as John Barth would say, or another Pierre Menard, the Borges character who undertakes to rewrite *Don Quixote* and in the process manages to produce passages "almost infinitely richer" than the identical passages in Cervantes.[16] Etcher's page-by-page transcriptions, however, offer abundant latitude for subversion of the material copied. Therein lies the artist's power to resist the sanitized, engraved, cookie-cutter history most congenial to the state's ideological apparatuses.

Though one registers the weaknesses of the Erickson text, one also learns from it something of history's lability and susceptibility to ideological manipulation. The lesson is nothing if not postmodern, but in the execution it seems blurred—as if the mythic past, so hard to dislodge from the popular imagination, required only a different set of generalizations to be more answerable to conscience. What *Arc d'X* lacks is the rich particularity of the past, as seen in set piece after set piece in the novels of Pynchon or, as will be seen, in those of Pynchon's more accomplished disciple, Richard Powers.

CHAPTER 6

Passionate Pathography

Narrative as Pharmakon in Richard Powers's *Operation Wandering Soul*

All sorrows can be borne if you put them in a story or tell a story about them.
—ISAK DINESEN

Where Erickson projects an Orwellian distortion or suppression of history so extreme that all memory of the nation Thomas Jefferson helped to found may survive only in a secret archive, Richard Powers wonders about a more insidious forgetting, cloaked in the innocent narratives that parents pass on to their children. As Pynchon weaves the real darkness of "Hänsel and Gretel" into *Gravity's Rainbow*, so does Powers incorporate certain tendentious fairy tales into *Operation Wandering Soul*, which appeared, like *Arc d'X*, in 1993. Powers looks, in these tales, for the germ of actual events. With great originality, he unearths (or at least speculates about) the often terrible events that history has consigned to story—labeled, that is, as make-believe. This practice, which generates grave questions about both historiography and storytelling, is a brilliant extension of premises often traceable to Pynchon, but Powers makes the conceit entirely his own. No epigone, he.

Powers has, however, like Erickson, repeatedly expressed his admiration for Pynchon. He rereads *Gravity's Rainbow* every five years or so, and annually revisits one particularly moving passage as his own private Yuletide observance:

> For thirty years, early each winter, as the newspapers roll out their end-of-year obituaries and take to listing the year's proudest, most achieved disasters, I've read out loud, to myself or to anyone who will listen, a passage from that book that ruined me for science and made me think

of writing as a life. Nine pages: that battery-ringed evensong service, set somewhere in Kent—the closest thing I have to a private religious ritual. I do it to remind myself of the size of the made world, of what story might still be when it remembers itself, of the look of *our maximum reach outward*, of the devastating charge of words. I do it to remind myself of our only real medium of exchange.[1]

In the passage described here, Pynchon captures with great delicacy the feelings and perceptions of soldiers briefly remembering a powerful story of redemptive innocence. The author does not endorse the Christian message—only the ritualized expression of an immense desire for the peace promised in the Nativity narrative. Powers, like Pynchon, understands the poignant provisionality of any such story, any such myth, any such fairy tale.

Powers's *Operation Wandering Soul* presents readers with a problem: itself a work of fiction, it hints at some profound betrayal, in storytelling, of the often painful experience that fiction incorporates and transmutes. Emphasizing the horrific events that often underlie both historical and fictional narrative, the author invites readers to consider whether familiar stories for and about children—*Peter Pan*, *The Pied Piper*, and their many congeners—misrepresent and thereby perpetuate ugly realities. Thus the evacuation of children from major English cities at the beginning of World War II, normally a chronicle of the celebrated national pluck, becomes in the iconoclastic retelling a catastrophe of abuse. The displaced become "cheap labor, replacements for dead offspring, a government subsidy. The Shirley Temple look-alikes went first, to the local child molesters. . . . These children would never be found again."[2] Similarly, the Children's Crusade of the early thirteenth century eventuates in a glutting of the brothels and slave quarters of the Mediterranean littoral: "An estimated hundred thousand innocents are lost, sold, killed, betrayed, evacuated from this world by faith" (187). The Pied Piper story may enshrine or distort the memory of that "continental passage of guiltless children in pursuit of the millennium" (185), or it may disguise another event so terrible as to bring into play, in the collective unconscious we call history, mechanisms of repression. The *Märchen* "version of events—piper, rats—is all the smudged variorum left, a bastard compromise script lying somewhere between what really happened and what can bear admission" (233) Adducing a whole range of such stories, Powers interrogates each for possible contributions, however unwitting, to enormity. The author asks the same question in a variety of ways: does fiction reassure fearful children and comfort their elders, or does it merely connive at the unspeakable? Must stories predicated on actual events always represent them falsely? What justifies the essential mendacity of narrative?

The narrator of *Galatea 2.2* (1995), a novelist named Richard Powers, takes pride in that mendacity: "lying constructively was my job description, after all."[3] The adverb, of course, signals an important qualification. According to the traditional view, the validity of fiction lies in truth that is general, not mired in the circumstantial real. Indeed, Aristotle's distinction between poetry and history applies: "Poetry . . . is a more philosophical and a higher thing than history: for poetry tends to express the universal, history the particular."[4] But under the postmodern dispensation Aristotle's universal and particular have like other binaries developed an unstable relationship, and storytelling and historiography prove difficult to differentiate. Objectivity about the past proves chimerical, for "[h]istory," as Powers remarks in *Three Farmers on Their Way to a Dance* (1985), "is the army of occupation, and we are all collaborators." Even the insight of imaginative literature must, in the nature of things, be tendentious, slanted, self-deceiving. Distortions slip in, distortions dictated by an agenda of which the storyteller may scarcely be conscious, for "[a]ll observations"—again we are in *Three Farmers*—"are a product of their own times. Even this one."[5]

The central character of *Operation Wandering Soul*, pediatric surgeon Richard Kraft, has little or no respect for fiction. The author may seem to endorse this *askesis* and thereby to indict his very medium, but the troubled protagonist of this novel must not be mistaken for its comprehensive standard of insight and informed action. As "floater" resident, hovering at burnout, Kraft is the story's first wandering soul, a physician who cannot heal himself. However attractive his sensitivity, readers must see that, unbuffered, it proves debilitating and even pathological. "Part of the tension generated by the book," observes reviewer Cleo McNelly Kearns, "is our recognition that Kraft, whom we like very much, cannot possibly go on like this without turning into either a sociopath or a nullity."[6] Kraft's anguished contemplation of the suffering visited on children through the folly and stupidity of their elders leads to a breakdown that may preclude his continuing to function as an effective medical practitioner. The collateral damage extends to his relationship with the humane and heroic Linda Espera—a relationship as doomed, perhaps, as that of Stuart Ressler and Jeanette Koss in Powers's *The Gold Bug Variations* (1991). Koss, one recalls, dispatches Ressler to the library to encounter, in a famous work of the imagination (Poe's "Gold Bug"), an important clue to his life's work. Like Richard Kraft, Ressler has come to neglect such monuments of unaging intellect: "It's been years since he's read any fiction except the Oppenheimer charges."[7]

The distrust of or indifference to fiction on the part of Richard Kraft finds an ironic mirror in Joy Stepaneevong, his almost stereotypically studious Asian patient. An arch-rationalist even at the age of twelve, Joy has no time for storybooks, and even in hospital she applies herself passionately to her studies. Ironically it is the surgeon who introduces her to stories: he gives her a selection of his own childhood favorites. Their life encounters with fiction thus prove chiasmic: where one discovers the delights of fiction as a twelve year old, the other repudiates those pleasures at almost exactly the same age (Kraft is evidently thirteen when he first arrives in Thailand, having "outgrown fiction" [117] en route, halfway across the Pacific). Twenty years later this indifference to fiction remains unexamined, even when challenged by a senior colleague, "Chief of Surgery Burgess," who presses on him "convoluted, epistemological novels by Kraft's obscure, young contemporaries" (15). The younger surgeon has neither the time nor the inclination to read them and has even given up music, though he cannot bring himself to discard the French horn he was once passionate about playing. Whelmed by a world of suffering, Kraft has stripped himself of precisely those resources—literature, music, the arts—that afford comfort when the anguish of mortality proves obdurate against every advance of science, technology, and medicine.

Bitterly labeling their work "Kiddie Karpentry" (22) and characterizing themselves as "God's on-site warranty service" (23), Kraft and his hard-bitten colleagues perform daily operations on an endless stream of desperately sick or badly injured children at a Los Angeles charity hospital. According to the headnote to Kevin Berger's *Paris Review* interview with the author, Powers based elements of *Operation Wandering Soul* on the experiences of "his older brother, who was a surgeon at Martin Luther King Hospital in Watts in the eighties."[8] This confirms that it is the author, in propria persona, who in the last chapter of the novel characterizes its story as "one my older brother the surgeon gave me, his little brother the storyteller" (350). One appreciates the clarification because, as will be seen, this author delights in a variety of teasing, near-autobiographical masks. In Powers's tale Martin Luther King Hospital becomes Carver General—less to be gruesomely suggestive, as one or two critics have suggested, than to invoke the spirit of Walt Whitman, who visited wounded and dying soldiers (often little more than children themselves) at the Washington, DC, institution of that name during the Civil War. Set in a preapocalyptic 1990 (with flashbacks to Kraft's experiences growing up as the child of a CIA operative stationed in various parts of the world), *Operation Wandering Soul* looks back to the Watts riots of 1965 and anticipates the rioting of 1992 (events that figure more directly in Powers's 2003 novel *The Time of Our Singing*). The novelist narrator of *Galatea* 2.2 recalls how it was "on the day Los Angeles set itself on fire" after the Rodney King acquittal that he sent in final revisions on what he calls his "ornate, suffocating allegory about dying pedes at the end of history."[9]

Readers familiar with Powers know that, like Paul Auster, he often plays with the masks he dons as storyteller. The "Richard Powers" of *Galatea* 2.2 is only the most obvious of these personae, which include the narrator of *Three Farmers on Their Way to a Dance* (he refers to himself by the initial P) and the main character in *Operation Wandering Soul* (whose surname, Kraft, is German for "power"). The narrator of *Galatea* 2.2 has much to say about the novels he has written, which, though never referred to by title, are those of the real Richard Powers. He mentions in passing a crucial feature of his "millennial bedtime story": its "double-voiced" narration in a "style that perched on the brink of nervous disintegration."[10] In an interview, Powers (the real one) echoes this remark as he explains that the style of *Operation Wandering Soul* is determined by the narration's proximity to Kraft's tormented consciousness. Because Powers has "tried to approach each book as an experiment in finding the style that best supports and exemplifies that particular story's themes," the reader of this one constantly hears, in a kind of free indirect discourse, the tonalities if not the actual voice of the central character, "a medical resident who is falling apart, undergoing a kind of breakdown. So the style is often completely over the top, a verbal mania that is supposed to reflect Richard Kraft's increasingly apocalyptic read on inner-city Los Angeles in late-capitalist America."[11]

The style of *Operation Wandering Soul*, then, precludes casual reading. At once manic and muscular, passionate and performative, it frustrates as much as it pleases, and Powers notes ruefully that some readers resist the verbal extravagance. Cerebral and sensuous, Kraft's perfervid musings at times refuse to order themselves and communicate. But Powers depicts and realizes a mind in extremis as brilliantly as Malcolm Lowry does in *Under the Volcano*, and many readers (this one among them) find this novel's baroque style a strangely comforting reminder of language's ability to contain and neutralize horror, no matter the scale. By the same token, the "verbal mania" often issues in figures of great beauty and ingenuity, especially when the accents of the troubled but brilliant Richard Kraft frame perceptions anchored in a more stable consciousness, notably that of Linda Espera. Such figures redeem cliché (the wandering soul of meaning, as it were) and make new even the most banal of nursery truisms. Thus the calamity of Humpty Dumpty, for example, becomes an appropriately child-vectored image for the collective medical horrors canvassed in this novel. "How best"—the thought is Espera's, the rhetoric Kraft-flavored—"to reassemble what the king's combined cavalry and foot labored over impotently, powerless to transact?" (73).

The narrating voice does more, then, than simply transpose the fulminations of Richard Kraft into the third person. It accommodates the author's penchant for telling allusion, reference to the literary *disjecta membra* of a civilization at the point of collapse. When the narrator characterizes "the operating theater" as "as central a station as any in which to wait for that obscure appointment laid out for him" (19), we understand that his mental traveling will eventually carry Kraft to an inner station, a heart of darkness that will find its mirror in his own troubled psyche. Elsewhere Powers recalls Hardy's terrible child suicide ("Done because we are too menny") or echoes the famous lines from 1 Corinthians 13 ("And now abideth faith, hope, charity, these three; but the greatest of these is charity"): "The only limits hemming the surgeon in are that abiding trio: shock, self-infection, pain. And of these three, the greatest is pain" (24). Fortune's postoperative privates, meanwhile, undergo physical therapy "with whatever parts fortune has left you" (73).

But the hospital's inadequate budget and the children's condition admit little in the way of physical therapy. Thematically, in fact, Powers's novel unfolds as a pathographic meditation on the "ways of children going wrong." A single day's rounds include "the Rib Metastasis, the Crushed Kidney, the Mitral Valve, the Saturday Night Special" (53), and periodically the author pauses to resume this appalling catalogue:

> respiratory infection . . . cystic fibrosis, miliary TB. Endo, myo, pericarditis. All known blood disorders, book length in themselves. Lymphoblastic leukemia, that spring lodger come to spread its putrefying possessions into each limb of the playhouse tree. GI failures, renal annihilation, precocious or arrested endocrine systems, convulsive disorders. Palsy and a legion of other lesions and tumors, meningitis, diabetics, . . . [m]alnutrition, psychodisorientation, pellagras, anemias, dementias . . .

abuse. . . . ingestions of household poisons, the handgun mistakes, the training wheels spinning their mangled aluminum sidewalls in the air after a hit-and-run. (71–72)

Not for this author—or his characters—the treatable afflictions. With South-Central Los Angeles as his Egdon Heath, Powers obliges his reader to contemplate certain inexorabilities, somewhat in the manner of Thomas Hardy, whom he cites as "first" among his "great fictional influences."[12] At times, engaged in what one critic calls a "saturation-bombing of our neutered sensibilities,"[13] the author of *Operation Wandering Soul* (not to mention the harrowing account, in the 1998 novel *Gain*, of death by ovarian cancer) seems to suffer from a variant of the malady that, in a famous critical diagnosis, troubled Nathanael West. "West's Disease," according to W. H. Auden, dictated a constant emphasis on the bleakest features of existence.[14] As it happens, in the opening sentences of his sixteenth chapter Powers seems to evoke West's *Day of the Locust* Hollywood: "those studio lots, the instant vistas of belief shot on dislocation," those "film set cafeterias where centurions lunch with storm troopers, senators with psychopaths, fake doctors with would-be children" (236). More importantly, Powers creates in Richard Kraft another Miss Lonelyhearts, another sensitive soul overcome by the world's irremediable suffering. Powers also asks a question that Nathanael West might have posed if his genius had taken a pediatric turn: what medical or societal hope for children whose wounds and diseases and abuse defy treatment? But the author of *Miss Lonelyhearts*, though himself a storyteller, would have laughed scornfully at the answer proposed by a character in *Operation Wandering Soul. Stories?* Though no one would call her a Pollyanna (she knows actual, unrelieved suffering too intimately), Linda Espera manages nonetheless to demonstrate in "the promise of fiction" (79) one way to help sick, abused, and often doomed children: "Reading aloud helps as much as anything" (76). In a series of cryptic references the author characterizes this unorthodox therapy as the "leaping cure" (70, 71, 75), a treatment predicated, evidently, on a leap of faith in fiction itself. Telling stories, reading aloud, Espera "has something to leave in the dark reaches" of her young patients' psyches. She intuits "the space in each one where the earliest, inviolable fable of self still stands intact, ready to respond to a little food, workout, heat, and play. She can plant a start in that place waiting to be proven wrong, a plot that will still heal at the first touch of fresh, outrageously naive narrative" (72).

What plot will she plant? A child's garden of stories: "plots" children can grow into as they undertake to narrate themselves. From her seeding, in fact, springs the project that miraculously energizes her little charges: the hospital dramatization of *The Pied Piper*. The children's passionate involvement with this fiction allows them briefly to defy or escape their fate, to do in some measure what the royal horse and foot cannot. "For a day longer, they are certain of forever" (348).

Espera, however, represents only a part of the book's message about storytelling, a message complicated by certain disturbing undercurrents in the very fictions most frequently foisted on the bed-bound young. Who, Powers asks, are these Lost Boys, these kiddie crusaders, these children who follow the Pied Piper? How is it that every child in Hamelin "takes to the melody like a new soul to the amniotic bath" (227)? Children seek, in the late Middle Ages, escape from the life they lead, escape

> to a place where they will not be tied down or caged, sent off to strangers, hung up in trees or exposed on the roadside to die, whipped naked in cellars for their parents' sins, shown corpses and executions as moral instruction, locked in closets for having nightmares, seared on their softest parts, groped out in sport, strangled for saying yes, put up as collateral for debt, traded, sold at seven, sentenced to life apprenticeship. The tune piping in the distance is deliverance from evil, the end of that torture, childhood. (230)

Grounded in societal dereliction, these ills merely compound the already horrific catalogue of physical disease. Nor have disease and abuse abated in modern times: Joy Stepaneevong dies of cancer; her symbolic sister, with whom young Ricky Kraft briefly consorts during Operation Santa Claus, steps on a land mine. Both are subsumed in the unforgettable photograph of the Vietnamese girl burned by napalm, "running down the road to the nearest help, the nearest adult, who is busy photographing this kiddie nude" (276). The appalling circle keeps widening: the "recent epidemic of vanishing little ones—two million annually, a full two thirds of these abductions masterminded by estranged parents" (165)—finds its obscene mirror in "the dozen million disinherited minors on the street in the lush subtropics, down where 'disappear' has long gone transitive" (286).

What if such horrors are not merely tampered in the telling, but radically falsified and misrepresented? Too often, Kraft laments, storytelling seems only to transform the most egregious abuse and neglect of children into narrative pabulum for other children. Yet one doubts that Powers (or even Kraft) would really advocate, in the name of some rigorous avoidance of illusion, confronting children with every historical horror, every terrible truth. In story as in catechism such content would constitute yet another instance of the kind of abuse railed against, and it bears noting that all of the children's stories retold here have, within Powers's narrative, their own "double-voiced" existence: one version for actual children (without harm to themselves, Nico and Joy can identify with figures in the Pied Piper story), another for the adult reader, who encounters mythic Hamelin moralized as a place rather like America today with its public indebtedness, deteriorating infrastructure, and gutless political leaders who "mortgage the future to pay for an unsustainable, Pollyanna present" (215–16). These details oblige us to see ourselves implicated in the fate of children we might prefer to think safely quarantined in a thirteenth-century fiction. But no: we are *now* sacrificing our children's future.[15]

Powers, then, emphasizes the equivocal character of storytelling. At once pure mendacity and momentary deliverance from the darkness of our human fate, fiction resembles Shakespeare's figure of "adversity, / Which, like the toad, ugly and venomous, / Wears yet a precious jewel in his head." It also resembles mutation as Jan O'Deigh comes to understand it in *The Gold Bug Variations*: responsible for "cancer, stillbirth, blindness, deafness, heart disease, mongolism," it nonetheless facilitates that great biological boon, evolution.[16] In *Operation Wandering Soul* the narrator calls one famous story "medicinal compensation for an ill, confined child, to ease the time remaining to him" (234). The phrase brims with dark nuance: one senses that the illness is mortal, the remaining time brief. Perhaps, as will be seen, the child is metaphorically humanity, the time remaining to him now, in 1990, mere prelude to apocalypse: "only ten shopping years left until the Blowout Clearance" (53). In the choice of the term *medicinal*, of course, Powers invites recognition of a pharmacological conundrum at least as old as Plato: what cures can also kill. Medicine as strong as storytelling can be misused, harmful. Indeed, as Derrida has pointed out, the Greek word for medicine, *pharmakon*, can also mean poison.[17] In other words, it is a contronym, one of those Janus-faced "antithetical words" (e.g., *altus, aufheben,* cleave) that so fascinated Freud. Just as Derrida seizes upon this aporia in Plato's argument (in the *Phaedrus*) for the priority of speech over writing, Powers similarly performs a kind of benign deconstruction—exploratory surgery, as it were—on the equivocal character of fiction. His novel, with its bleak, unsparing conclusion, offers itself as *pharmakon* in its own right: bracing, even "medicinal," yet poisonous to Panglossian optimism. Like A. E. Housman (a motivic presence in *Galatea 2.2*), Powers insists on depicting certain harsh realities in his art. Readers thus toughened stand a better chance of emulating Mithridates, who famously inoculated himself with daily doses of poison and so "died old." Some such "homeopathy" figures here as well: in *Galatea 2.2* Powers defends the idea, in his "bleak, baroque fairy tale about wandering and disappearing children," of "narrating the worst so the worst did not happen."[18]

Not that the immunizing effect depends exclusively on introducing discrete quanta of "the worst" into the psychic bloodstream. The author of *Operation Wandering Soul* ultimately believes that all fiction—all *good* fiction—serves this end. Thus Linda Espera, reflecting on what might physic her young patients, sees in "[t]ales . . . the only available inoculations against the life they keep vomiting up for want of antigens" (76). In an interview with Sven Birkerts, Powers makes the point more broadly: "My apology for fiction has always taken the form of saying: When we live in real time, under the onslaught of the challenges of unmediated existence, we cannot solve all the problems that are thrown at us, the problems of the physical challenge of the world, the nature and needs of others, our own internal aggressions and animosities and ambivalences. Therefore, we remove ourselves into the space of symbolic transaction. And we do that with an eye toward solving in abstract those crises, getting a handle on them in the domain where time has been suspended. And then we reenter, more fully equipped, the world of reality."[19]

At the very end of the novel under scrutiny here, Powers reaffirms, beyond every Kraftian cavil, the immense, humane appeal of fiction. In a touching vignette, narrated in an italicized second person, he imagines "your" child at the top of the staircase, up beyond her bedtime, "*her eyes burning, wet, incredulous, on fire. . . . 'I finished it. That book you gave me? Your old favorite? I just finished it'*" (352). In the end, as Joseph Dewey remarks, "the power of narrative revives and resuscitates."[20] It also transports. Powers affirms the moral value of stories for the simple reason that, their occasional complicity in pathologies of denial notwithstanding, they allow us to go on. Thus Linda Espera reflects that "to *pretend*, to live as if life might yet lead all the way to unexpected deliverance, is the best way to keep from dying in midfable" (79). The italicized word represents an important element in the reception of stories, and even small and desperate children seem capable of acute distinctions between actuality and its fanciful transformations. Even the most disadvantaged "know . . . the transparency of the fables handed them" (286). By the same token, the phrase "dying in midfable" hints at something repeatedly intimated: that life itself is a narrative, a "fable" fraught with pain and beauty. Once thought to be divinely authored, the life-story has in common with folk tales and fairy stories the ability to proliferate in protean retellings, none definitive. But unlike fictions that end with a moral, life eventuates in nothing more than bodily decay and collapsing sphincters. At the risk of sounding like Wilde's Miss Prism, one can say that some chapters of the life-story may end happily, but the book as a whole must end unhappily. That is what the life narrative "means." In a last visit with the dying Joy, Kraft cannot tell her "how to do this"—how, that is, to make it through her final hours. The narrator, however, hints again that a life such as hers is itself a story; thus the unhappy physician "goes on to give her, in as many words as the telling takes, the point of starting out on any once upon a time. The surgeon's sense of an ending" (329). The narrator implies that a life, like a story, begins with "once upon a time," and the point of either, presumably, is to arrive at the end.

The surgeon's own story ends with a moment of metafictional reflexivity. Half blind with fatigue and emotional burnout, Kraft must presently operate on numerous children brought in from the latest of those ghastly scenes of gratuitous urban bloodletting that give the lie to America's notions of being an advanced civilization. Somewhere in the benighted city, in some "terminally ill . . . neighborhood" (344), someone has, as it were, "gone postal" in an elementary school, and once again, ready or not, Richard Kraft must "go surgical" (277). On this occasion, by way of valedictory, Kraft obscurely resolves to tell an eyewitness story that will not betray fact, will not misrepresent "[h]ow we murdered our children," will not be just another "[c]orrupt survival fable, deranged beyond recall. Based, as always, on actual event, but garbled in desperate retelling" (343). Perhaps Kraft's proposed narrative will concern not only those dying now on his operating table but a representative selection of their sisters and brothers victimized down through history. Perhaps, in other words, it will evolve into *Operation Wandering Soul*, as Stephen Dedalus's story emerges from the journal introduced in the closing pages of *A Portrait of the Artist As a Young Man* (Powers actually invokes the Joycean paradigm at the similarly recursive conclusion of *The Gold Bug Variations*: the "baby" Jan and Franklin will make is the story one has just read). Whatever the range of Kraft's imagined narrative, it will affirm the adult dereliction and malice complicit in the suffering of children—and it will take as premise the stark, irredeemable emptiness that undermines every religious fantasy concerning where life comes from and where it goes. "I saw them. I know where they are off to. I know where they *came* from. They have left us behind, with nothing but this thin plot to live on. To keep alive another sentence longer" (343). The "thin plot" is the ground beneath us, the earth itself, but it is also, as Kraft fails tragically to understand, any story that sustains life. "Even this one. *This one*" (348).

In one of our last glimpses of the surgeon, however, he seems to have accepted his role in the pediatric production of *The Pied Piper*, a fiction that fools none of the children yet seems at least to ease their going. Rehearsing, "no one knows opening night's hour" (244)—the phrase grimly parodies a famous biblical pronouncement regarding the promised end: "But of that day and hour knoweth no man, no, not the angels of heaven" (Matt. 24:36). In fact, progeric Nico, the little impresario, understands that when the company tours local venues with the play, they merely prepare "for the longer outing rapidly coming up" (312). The children have chosen this story to enact because they have "a latent messianic" as "ready-made piper" (237). The painful logic of their casting has to do with the conceit that this piper—a physician, after all—will lead them back through the mountain or membrane, back to home, Hamelin, and wholeness. Joy will be the one left behind when the magic mountain closes (and indeed, of the children on the ward, she is the only one whose death is not postponed at story's end). Recognizing in her role some obscure but powerful call to "sacrifice" (241), she becomes this novel's archetypal suffering innocent, not the Christ child but a child Christ, secular equivalent of the divine pharmakos. Because he carries this "girl dying on the edge of puberty" in the powerful, elegiac fantasy of departure with which his story ends, Kraft is characterized as "the giant Christopher" (344), that is, patron saint of wayfarers such as those setting out just here. According to legend, St. Christopher was in fact a giant who devoted himself to carrying travelers across a river on his shoulders. He acquired his name, which means "Christ bearer," on the day that he carries into the water a child who grows heavier and heavier as they proceed. "Had I borne the whole world on my back," the giant observes, "it could not have weighed heavier than thou then." To which the child replies, revealing his divine identity: "Marvel not, for thou hast borne upon thy back the world and Him who created it."[21] Kraft, then, despite his having reached, at thirty-three (79), what Joseph

Dewey elegantly characterizes as "the critical threshold age within Christian mythos,"²² is not the one who bears the burden of the world's suffering but the one who bears that bearer.

In the end, however unlikely the deliverance of a magic mountain, the children do better to meet their destiny, however bleak, exercising their imaginations. And so it is for all of us who sooner or later must take that road, follow that piper. For Powers intimates that his suffering children can be taken as synecdoche for the human race, especially insofar as its development remains hopelessly arrested. Thus he quotes, at one point, the verses that Lewis Carroll appended to *Through the Looking Glass*:

> We are but older children, dear,
>> Who fret to find our bedtime near. (252)

Reflecting on a dark operating room anecdote about the benighted judge who found a small child guilty of inciting her own sexual abuse, Powers characterizes all humanity as sick children who "[g]ot what we asked for. Solicited our own bloody wholesale rape like the cheap little tush-swinging toddlers we are." Nor do we ever graduate from this moral infancy. At the end of his narrative, Powers recurs to this conceit in references to the space probe *Voyager*, launched in 1977, the year of Joy's birth. A terrible irony attends the message endlessly broadcast as it travels through interstellar space: "*Greetings from the Children of Planet Earth*" (349, 352).

A kind of robotic wandering soul, this satellite. As such, it serves as a late reminder to consider this novel's title and its constantly evolving meanings. As acronym—OWS—it suggests howls of pain, especially those caused by the "real, flesh and blood owies" (59) of children. The title seems also to invoke a traditional view of mortality: the soul "wanders" from the body at death. But in the belief system of at least one culture the soul can absent itself under less extreme circumstances. The Hmong of northern Laos and Thailand (Joy's people) attribute illness to a straying of the spirit, which a shaman-physician must, to effect a cure, lure back to the body. As Kraft observes, the father of his pediatric cancer patient is precisely such a practitioner, a *Mawkhan* "[c]ertified in cures involving the recall of a person's errant soul" (94). In his native Laos, ironically, Wisat Stepaneevong performed rituals to heal the sick: wandering soul operations.

More commonly, the word "operation" denotes a medical procedure (such as Kraft devotes himself to performing) or a military or paramilitary campaign such as the project with which Kraft's father, as CIA operative, terrorized Vietnamese (and possibly Laotian) villagers. Nor has Powers imagined this psyops exercise: the American military and the CIA really did engage in an Operation Wandering Soul in the late 1960s and early 1970s. A "surreal little fairy plan" (270) that became real, it consisted of broadcasting moans and screeches to feign the night-borne lamentations of sons fallen on distant battlefields or ancestors unhappy at a village's sending its youth away to perish on alien soil, often to go unburied.[23] Happening to catch part of a televised documentary on what in *Three Farmers* Powers calls "that un- mitigated act of violence called the twentieth century,"[24] Richard Kraft hears the "omniscient narrator turning the whole crazed event"—the paramilitary operation in Southeast Asia—"back into fable" (271).

Powers, meanwhile, turns it into another kind of fable: one of many in this constantly self-referential exercise in narrative embedding. In his redac- tion, war's curious footnote becomes moralized, notably when the reader learns that one of those in the helicopters, Ricky Kraft's father, accidentally drops into nocturnal Laos a "silver bauble" (272), the little angel he has worn around his neck since his days as a choirboy. The loss of this "charm" (253), properly the hopeful sign of a soul in harmony with its corporeal, appetitive host, is transparently symbolic: a tarnished emblem of innocence, the talis- man reifies a spiritual existence cheapened by the whole sorry chronicle of Cold War intelligence operations (not least the psyops tricks designed to subvert a people's whole belief system). How ironic, then, that in the midst of Operation Wandering Soul this entity should part company with its body to do some wandering of its own. In time it comes into the possession of the Laotian girl, Joy, for whom it represents (at least from the reader's perspec- tive) something like the wholeness of her prediasporic childhood. Later, in the terrible sickness that she must comprehend as an irremediable wander- ing of her soul, she surrenders the talisman to the son of its original owner (253). Immersed in a despair that is itself a kind of Western soul-wandering, Richard Kraft retains it only briefly. His draping it "around the slender and severed neck" (340) of yet another dying child betokens not only his present professional impotence and lack of faith but also the feebleness of the whole spiritual idea here on the eve of the millennium. The little angel, after all, is made of tin.

Given Powers's awareness of Walter Benjamin (an important presence in *Three Farmers*), one may also view this trinket as shabby stand-in for the Angel of History. Benjamin, one recalls, represented history as what accumulates at the feet of an angel facing backward in time and propelled by the violence of world events toward a future he cannot see, his back being turned to it.[25] That future, obviously, is not expected to become any less violent. But Powers hints that what really accumulates at the angel's feet are stories, which are history by another, more honest name (for "history" and "story," as I have noted previously, are etymologically indistinguishable, the semantic distinction between them misleading).

Through its stories humanity strives to come to terms with the past and its carnage. As remedy for the incurable suffering depicted in *Operation Wandering Soul*, however, stories may seem as ineffectual as the "there, there" with which, in Heller's *Catch-22*, Yossarian comforts the eviscerated Snowden. Moreover, they can at times serve dishonest ends, as when society, unable to face certain enormities committed in the past, embraces repressive mechanisms that transform the unspeakable into less frightful symbolic analogue. But this process is not moral cowardice. Freud often noted the social and historical dimensions of individual mental pathology, and perhaps one can recognize in stories such as *The Pied Piper* not refusal or obfuscation but the end result of a successful "working through" of mass trauma. "The impulse to work over in the mind some overpowering experience so as to make oneself master of it," Freud observes in *Beyond the Pleasure Principle*, begins in childhood (the famous "*fort/da*" illustration) and becomes the "compulsion to repeat" with which adults undertake to process calamity.[26] Before *The Pied Piper* took its present form, in other words, there must have been a long period during which witnesses and survivors of the original experience could engage what had happened only in stunned retelling, only in the painful, *fort/da* iteration by which wounded, traumatized consciousness always seeks to master its distress. Not by accident—to put this into modern perspective—does Powers repeatedly link the fate of his hapless children to that of Jews in the Holocaust. When the author characterizes the suffering of children with reference to catastrophic Crystal Nights (11, 168), tattooed arms, and voices from ovens (263); when he ends his stunning account of the Children's Crusade with a version of the traditional Seder wish ("Next Year in Angel City" [188]); when a *Pied Piper* variant has the children emigrating to Transylvania, "crossing that little letter-juggle from *Liebestraum* to *Lebensraum*" (233)—the reader discerns traces of the repetition-compulsion whereby a whole culture seeks to work through the twentieth century's most unbearable reality. We think of Holocaust *denial* as monstrous irresponsibility. But who is to say that even this supremely terrible event will not, eight hundred years hence, be submerged in some less painful "fable" that represents not denial but reconciliation? In *Operation Wandering Soul* we see trauma's relentless logic enacted at two levels: at one, Richard Kraft's insistence on clear recognitions represents the universal first phase of dealing with loss; at the second, metafictional level, we see in narrative transformations a working through of all that so troubles the young surgeon. No "corrupt survival fable," Richard Powers's story at once tells the truth about Captain Hook's perennially realized "holocaust of children" (122) and, as an act of imagination, transcends that horror.

CHAPTER 7

Anger, Anguish, and Art
Chuck Palahniuk's *Choke*

> Butades, a potter of Sicyon, was the first who invented, at Corinth, the art of
> modelling portraits in the earth which he used in his trade. It was through his
> daughter that he made the discovery; who, being deeply in love with a young
> man about to depart on a long journey, traced the profile of his face, as thrown
> upon the wall by the light of the lamp. Upon seeing this, her father filled in the
> outline, by compressing clay upon the surface, and so made a face in relief, which
> he then hardened by fire along with other articles of pottery.
>
> —PLINY THE ELDER, *THE NATURAL HISTORY*, BOOK 35, CHAPTER 43[1]

Certain of his enthusiastic readers see the work of Chuck Palahniuk as sui
generis, but the more discriminating eye discerns affinities in every postmodern quarter. His novels offer abundant evidence of an energetic and irreverent writer's having absorbed lessons in outrage—or outrageousness—
from various points on the contemporary literary compass. Indeed, to trace
Palahniuk's literary pedigree back only half a century is to observe relationships with, if not apostolic succession from, such looming contemporaries
as J. D. Salinger, Joseph Heller, Flannery O'Connor, and fellow Oregonian
Ken Kesey. The last of these prompts notice of a temporal intersection or
two. Kesey's most famous work, *One Flew Over the Cuckoo's Nest*, came
out in 1962, the year of Palahniuk's birth. Kesey died in 2001, the year that
saw publication of Palahniuk's *Choke*, which features a medical practitioner as cracked as those she pretends to treat (not that Dr. Paige Marshall
is the pure monster seen in the loathsome Nurse Ratched). Similarly, the
nutty and at times criminal actions of Ida Mancini (who abducts a child
in Waterloo, Iowa, and tries to make him an accomplice in various hijack-
ings, pranks, and disruptive adventures) make her another Randall Patrick
McMurphy. Both will die while institutionalized. In Palahniuk's grotesque,

Jesus-obsessed humor, one encounters traces, too, of Flannery O'Connor, though without the orthodoxy. One imagines that the author of *Fight Club* and *Invisible Monsters* might well concur with O'Connor's defense of comic violence as a strategy to pierce the complacency of an audience bred to spiritual indifference: "to the hard of hearing you shout," she once explained. "And for the almost-blind you draw large and startling figures."[2] Elsewhere on the intertextual spectrum, one senses the presence of O'Connor's great contemporary, Joseph Heller. Palahniuk's penchant for medical gore may owe something to the graphic horror—Snowden's evisceration, the slicing in two of Kid Sampson by an airplane propeller, a defenestrated rape victim, bloody teeth in the street—that gradually squeezes off the laughter in *Catch-22*. The most pronounced of these affinities (one does not call them influences) might be with J. D. Salinger. When Ida Mancini deplores "education" as "[o]ur bite of the apple" and invokes a "cure for knowledge" and all the "living in our heads," she seems to be channeling the boy genius in Salinger's "Teddy."[3] More obviously, the author of *Choke* shares with Salinger a first-person narrator who, given to profane anger at a world of phonies, dreams of being a savior, a catcher in the rye.

One need not agree with the harsh assessment of Laura Miller, for whom Palahniuk's books "traffic in the half-baked nihilism of a stoned high school student who has just discovered Nietzsche and Nine-Inch Nails," to see that this author is dangerously beholden to a particular demographic.[4] Miller seconds the Janet Maslin who sees in *Choke* little more than "a working definition of the adolescent male state of mind."[5] Although Palahniuk's work discovers a postmodernism still green in the branches, I suspect that many readers expect from him something more, perhaps a truly "post" postmodernism. Born a generation after Barth, Paley, Roth, Pynchon, Morrison, DeLillo, and company (not to mention the writers already adduced), Palahniuk inherits a fully developed aesthetic that he shapes to ends that his main audience—Gen-Xers and Millennials—may mistake for the next new thing. These young readers—their keenness a wave that has borne Palahniuk to the top of the charts—find in his pages an irreverence and cynicism and anger that strike them as authentic, not already compromised by accommodation with the smug complacency of the employed and well-adjusted. Certain lines in *Fight Club* strike the generational chord:

> We don't have a great war in our generation, or a great depression, but we do, we have a great war of the spirit. We have a great revolution

against the culture. The great depression is our lives. We have a spiritual depression. . . .

"We are the middle children of history, raised by television to believe that someday we'll be millionaires and movie stars and rock stars, but we won't. And we're just learning this fact," Tyler said. "So don't fuck with us."[6]

Here and elsewhere Palahniuk knows he is recycling the F. Scott Fitzgerald who in *This Side of Paradise* famously declaimed: "Here was a new generation . . . dedicated more than the last to the fear of poverty and the worship of success; grown up to find all gods dead, all wars fought, all faiths in man shaken."[7] But the later generation, restive under a perceived "spiritual depression," enjoys a sometimes disquieting latitude for the expression of its anarchic and, yes, nihilistic humor—as if the "black humorists" of the sixties had spawned unruly grandchildren who delight in every form of advanced adolescent gross-out. Filmmakers and performers such as the Farrelly Brothers, Judd Apatow, Seth Rogen, and Zach Galifianakis have embraced a remarkably coarse comedic standard to enormous success. Called by his publisher "[ou]r funniest nihilist," Palahniuk purveys a comedy, like theirs, so raw as often to throttle the laughter it provokes. Yet here, too, one discerns the outline of an older truculence, for Updike's Rabbit Angstrom announces himself the prophet of such puerility: "If you're telling me I'm not mature, that's one thing I don't cry over since as far as I can make out it's the same thing as being dead."[8]

The sensitive, reasonably erudite reader who seeks the point of any parable may find that of a fiction such as *Choke* elusive, resistant to critical parsing. Because the narration is entirely in the first person, one cannot easily test the picture "Victor Mancini" gives of himself, his foster mothers, his work, his world. Is he really an addict? A sex addict? Has an especially bizarre Christ complex really been foisted on him—or has he embraced it willingly? Did Ida Mancini really kidnap him from a stroller in Waterloo, Iowa? One may, in fact, err to see in Palahniuk's unhappy narrator a study in genuine disaffection and alienation—as opposed to a "bogus little Benedict Arnold" (3), an elaborate fraud who does to the reader what he does to his fellow diners in the restaurants where he stages bouts of choking that become, along with his job at the appalling Colonial Dunsboro, the means whereby he supports himself and, at St. Anthony's, the demented woman who has for so many years represented herself as his mother. The anger and anguish, in other words, may seem factitious, two-dimensional, "bogus," and some readers resist taking the spiritual torpor, the sacrilege, and the unvectored anomie at face value. At a certain point, a Palahniuk novel comes to seem like a running parody of such topoi—and for that very reason a peculiarly bleak variation on the unhappiness so often reflected in twentieth- and twenty-first-century literature.

THE TRIUMPH OF PHILOMELA

If not a simple con, Victor Mancini's narrative purports to be the latest bulletin from the frontiers of human misery—a classic study in the alienation that has dogged the human spirit for decades now. As a theme, however, alienation has undergone some interesting transmogrifications since its heyday in the middle of the last century. In his 1956 essay "The Man on the Train," Walker Percy declares that, "strictly speaking . . . a literature of alienation" does not exist: "the only literature of alienation is an alienated literature, that is, a bad art, which is no art at all. An Erle Stanley Gardner novel is a true exercise in alienation. A man who finishes his twentieth Perry Mason is that much nearer total despair than when he started." Looking at more serious claimants to the cachet of alienation, Percy notes that reader and author and character, however individually alienated, escape their condition through a mutual recognition that cancels out the otherness and isolation that true alienation requires: "Neither Kafka nor his reader is alienated in the movement of art, for each achieves a reversal through its re-presenting."[9] If we update his example by substituting Salinger or Palahniuk for Kafka, we discover what may figure in every iconoclast's appeal: an audience that feels itself at odds with the straight, respectable, "phony" world—whether that of Habsburg Prague, the Eisenhower fifties, or the endless eight years of the George W. Bush presidency.

If the "literature of alienation" survived Walker Percy's calling attention to its self-contradictory premises, it stood no chance against post-Freudian psychology, which has complicated the ancient ideal of *gnothi seauton*, know thyself. There is, after all, no single self to know—and the world from which one might be estranged has long since lost its ontological uniqueness. We are all alienated all the time now, and we recognize our truest being amid the proliferating imagoes of a strange, universal psychopathology. Similarly, the

ideal of collective self-knowledge that we call history has run onto the rocks
of metahistory, where the past splinters to become many pasts, all somehow
valid, however mutually contradictory. Univocal history, we have come to
see, always falsifies. As Paige Marshall remarks, "[t]hose who remember the
past tend to get the story really screwed up" (208).

   Choke's narrator and central character, Victor Mancini, works at Colonial
Dunsboro, historical reenactment village and "site" of further literary and
cultural intersections. Like George Saunders in the title story of *Pastoralia*
(published in the same year as *Choke*), Palahniuk seems to be remembering Zwölfkinder, the strange German theme park in *Gravity's Rainbow*, not
to mention similar places in the movies of recent decades, notably *Future-
world, Jurassic Park, Adventureland.* (A similar conceit figures in films—*Fast
Times at Ridgemont High*, for example—in which a teen-aged character's
job requires that she or he dress up in compliance with some restaurant
theme.) Each of these places represents a more or less dubious or debased
congener of the Disneyland in which Baudrillard's precession of simulacra
so perfectly instantiates itself (the simulacra, at first a substitute for the real,
presently replace it altogether). Baudrillard famously suggests that Disneyland provides an "'ideological' blanket" that "serves to cover over a *third-order
simulation*: the theme park "is the 'real' country," the "'real' America." What
the French theorist says of Disneyland—"presented . . . to make us believe"
in an America that is in fact "no longer real, but of the order of the hyperreal
and of simulation"—applies as well to Colonial Dunsboro.[10] Such a theme
park is what Louis Marin, anticipating Baudrillard, calls "a utopic space"
that is always already in the process of becoming its own travesty. Here "the
utopic structure and utopic functions degenerate," revealing "how the utopic
representation can be entirely caught in a dominant system of ideas and
values and, thus, be changed into a myth or collective fantasy." Marin identifies Disneyland's axis, Main Street USA, as "an attempt to reconcile or to
exchange . . . the past and the present—that is, an ideal past and a real present." The village green of Palahniuk's Dunsboro features the same tendentious historicity. "The ultimate meaning of the center," observes Marin, "is
the conversion of history into ideology."[11]

   Locked forever in the year 1734, Dunsboro more simply represents history's calcification, the betrayal of any idea that by remembering the past
we can avoid repeating it. Indeed, Palahniuk introduces George Santayana's
famous observation only to suggest, in iteration, that knowledge of history offers few assurances about the future. In its superficiality and general

cheesiness, Dunsboro gives its visitors little more than history under the postmodern dispensation as sketched by Fredric Jameson—a place without temporal depth or nuance, a simulacrum, the "copy of a copy of a copy" invoked in *Fight Club* (21, 97). According to Victor, such places "always leave the best parts out. Like typhus. And opium. And scarlet letters. Shunning. Witch-burning" (29). He troubles himself to confirm the absence, too, of "a town whore," a "village idiot," a "[p]ickpocket," and a "[h]angman" (29). What Dunsboro replicates accurately, one realizes, is the climate of the Great Awakening (at its height in 1734), in all its puritanical rectitude ("what draws the crowds" to Disneyland, Baudrillard asseverates, "is undoubtedly much more the social microcosm, the miniaturized and *religious* reveling in real America")[12] "His Lord High Charlie the Colonial Governor" (26, 275) presides over petty officialdom in the form of a "town council" consisting of "six old guys who wear those fake colonial wigs" (29). One smiles at the redundancy of *fake* wigs—the phrase situates authenticity at a double remove. Overrun by teratomorphic poultry (about which more presently), Dunsboro is rife with sex and drugs: perennially giving hand jobs or passing on herpes (28), the staff stay blitzed on glue, weed, ecstasy, acid, hashish, crystal meth, heroin, Vicodin, and "Special K" (Ketamine hydrochloride). Victor himself suffers, he claims, from sex addiction—but better addiction in any form, he asseverates, than "sadness, anger, fear, worry, despair, and depression" (211). He recognizes what Thomas Pynchon calls the "nearly complete parallelism between *analgesia* and *addiction*. The more pain it takes away, the more we desire it."[13]

The psychological doubling so cleverly developed in *Fight Club* ("There isn't a me and a you, anymore" [164], declares one self to the other) metastasizes in this later novel. In *Choke*, the narration varies between past (in third person) and present (in first person). The narrator is at pains, moreover, to make of his childhood self and his ostensible mother figures of conspicuous alterity. Narrating the present, he favors "mom" or, occasionally, "mother"; in flashbacks to the past, he refers nearly always to "the Mommy," a person who veers between arrant lunacy and dubious theoretical patter about Michel Foucault (200) or "people's little identity paradigms" (66). He reviles his own juvenile alter ego as "the little stooge" (159), "this dumb-fuck little boy" (161), "the stupid little shit-heel kid" (196), and twenty or so other such epithets. Why such strenuous and overdetermined contempt? The definite article mocks itself: *the* mother is *any* mother, and *this* mother is eventually revealed as a simulacrum—a foster parent—herself. The "stupid kid" was, similarly, a collective of blind, uninformed, victimized selves. Thus when Victor says, "I don't even pretend to know myself very well" (21) or "it feels like I'm doing a really bad impersonation of myself" (69), the reader must not fall for the invitation to go looking for some authentic, bedrock identity, the key to poor Victor's recovering his psychological and emotional health. Ida begs the psychological question when she muses: "I wonder if Victor has a right to know who he really is" (70). Under the postmodern dispensation, no one has any such right—though everyone, tragically, has the need.

Absent knowledge of self and world, one must improvise, tell a story about oneself, become an artist, revert to creative child in a sandbox of words: "the only frontier left is the world of intangibles, ideas, stories, music, art" (285). But what is Victor's—or Palahniuk's—understanding of or goal for his own creation? Does the author, in particular, operate according to conscious artistic principle? Does a coherent aesthetic undergird the dark phantasmagoria of his "transgressive" fictions? Rather than issue a manifesto, Palahniuk presents, in *Choke*, a modest parable or two. The author's *ars poetica* appears in disguise—in "outline," as it were—in the story of a primal, sciagraphic depiction of the human form on a wall. One thinks, here, of the brilliant young artist Victor Wind in Nabokov's *Pnin*: at the age of three, invited to draw a picture of his mother (herself as dubious a figure as Ida Mancini), he executes "a lovely undulation, which he said was her shadow on the new refrigerator."[14]

Art began with some such minimalist gesture. "Before the Greeks, nobody had any art" (5), Ida explains. Her fable of "a beautiful girl in ancient Greece, the daughter of a potter" (3), introduces what will become one of the book's important self-referential motifs (277, 289, 292). "[T]he girl traced the outline of her lover's shadow so she would always have a record of how he looked" (4), and "[t]his was how painting was invented." Presently "the girl's father used the outline on the wall to model a clay version of the young man, and that's the way sculpture was invented" (5; cf. 277). Like the myth of Philomela, Ida's story—that of the potter Butades and his daughter Dibutade, as told by first-century scholar Pliny the Elder—credits a woman with the creative gesture in which art has its genesis. But whence the *potter's* art? The answer always leads to the geminate conceits of god as artist and artist as god.

Older than Butades is Keramos, mortal son of Dionysus and Ariadne and patron, in ancient Greece, of those whose work defined a complete artistic spectrum, from humble clay vessels to the most splendid kraters (according to Pausanias, their district of ancient Athens, Kerameikos, derived its name from this mythic craftsman).[15] In the mythopoesis of later ages, notably in the poetry of two exact contemporaries, Henry Wadsworth Longfellow and Edward FitzGerald, the primal potter would modulate from craftsman to demiurge to deity. The American versifier, in his long poem "Kéramos," surveys the great artistic variety of pottery and ceramics but cannot bring himself to suggest that the potter's mistakes might mirror those of the deity:

> Turn, turn, my wheel! This earthen jar
> A touch can make, a touch can mar;
> And shall it to the Potter say,
> *What makest thou? Thou hast no hand?*
> *As men who think to understand*
> *A world by their Creator planned,*
> *Who wiser is than they.*[16]

In the bitter questions that figure in the Kuza Nama sequence in *The Rubái-yát of Omar Khayyám*, FitzGerald dispenses with such pious circumspection. The question posed by a deformed pot—"What! did the hand, then, of the Potter shake"?—occurs to every generation that has come to doubt the putative perfection of God's handiwork. Sooner or later, suffering humanity wonders: "Who is the Potter, pray, and who the Pot?"[17] Is God, in other words, thrown on the potter's wheel of the human imagination? Where FitzGerald and his Persian predecessor imagine talking pots, Palahniuk briefly notes Colonial Dunsboro's "potter on methadone" (31) and invites readers to associate the damaged chickens of that benighted institution with the damaged human beings in and outside of St. Anthony's. Too many come imperfect from the palsied hand of the divine Potter, a deity as irresponsible, perhaps, as the children who delight in shaking the eggs from which the deformed chickens hatch.

In Pliny's parable, a daughter and a father create painting and sculpture; in Victor Mancini's story of a son and a mother, a third art emerges: storytelling. Though Ida introduces the myth of art's origin in the primal outlining, she swiftly moves beyond ideas of naïve representationalism to become the voice of theory-driven thinking about art and the reality (especially the social reality) it supposedly mirrors. Thus, at any rate, one understands her inchoate teachings about symbols, sign systems, and codes. She characterizes language, by the same token, as "just our way to explain away the wonder and the glory of the world. To deconstruct. To dismiss." She asserts, moreover, that "[w]e don't live in the real world anymore. . . . We live in a world of symbols'" (151). Alex Blazer, analyzing the relationship between this novel and Salinger's *Catcher in the Rye*, emphasizes the tension between phoniness and authenticity in terms derived from Guy Debord and Jean Baudrillard: "Both spectacle and simulation scar the postmodern psyche, leaving the subject feeling inauthentic, fake, phony"[18] (148). Thus it is that Ida argues against passive acceptance of the cultural moment and its simulacra. "I don't want you to just accept the world as it's given," she tells the boy who thinks himself her son. "I want you to invent it" (284). The boy must rediscover, years later, how "[t]o create his own symbols" (285).

But Ida's views are problematic in the end. The reader who considers the ambivalence with which Victor regards his mother and her lessons may come to see in her certain attitudes toward language and symbols that pose a challenge to the literary artist who has imagined both of these characters. With her graduate degree in English (133), Ida becomes at times the nonce representative, in her remarks about the lability of signs, symbols, and language, of the critic or theorist who subjects literary representation and its very medium to "deconstructive" operations. Her offspring, storyteller to a mad civilization, must in some way reinvent that medium and perhaps reality as well. Consanguineous or not (one may doubt the late assertion that she kidnapped Victor), their relationship takes on "symbolic" meaning: an example of what rhetoricians call hysteron proteron (reversal of natural order), they are critic and artist in retrograde filiation (an inversion congenial to the postmodern aesthetic). Borges says that "every writer *creates* his own precursors," and here, with something like the uncanniness that Borges saw in Kafka, the critic (Ida) precedes the artist (Victor).[19] Indeed, insofar as his performative choking precludes full ingestion, Victor invites recognition as another "hunger artist."

"Art," declares Ida, "never comes from happiness" (5). Behind this insight lies another myth, a dark parable that distills the paradoxical relationship between suffering and art. Ida's observation has its origin in the story of Philomela, the beautiful Athenian princess raped by her brother in law, King Tereus of Thrace, who cuts out her tongue to assure that the crime will go unreported. But Philomela weaves a tapestry to do the office of her severed tongue and so invents art—or at least defines its paradigmatic relation to anguish. From Thomas Kyd's Hieronymo to J. M. Coetzee's Friday (in *Foe*), the lopped tongue recurs as the wound that, by its nature, precludes direct witness. "Half of my tongue drops to the floor and gets kicked away" (201) observes the nameless narrator of *Fight Club*. Spared this particular violation, Victor Mancini will nonetheless tell a story predicated, like Philomela's, on personal pain.

To what end, however, does Palahniuk equate suffering and art, especially if the suffering is a bit cartoonish? (Who, after all, feels the pain of Wile E. Coyote?) More to the point: does the reader see Palahniuk's tapestry, like Philomela's, as beautiful? One assumes, after all, that what Philomela weaves, like any number of great works about horrific suffering, transcends its subject matter, turns it into the "thing of beauty" (16) that Victor remembers from Keats (who in "Ode to a Nightingale" discovers in supernal birdsong—that of the metamorphosed Philomela—the aesthetic principle that the more terrible the suffering, the more beautiful its artistic transformation can be). Eliot, too, invokes Philomela ("by the barbarous king / So rudely forced") in a work famous at once for showing the twentieth century its true subject—the universal spiritual aridity of the modern wasteland—and pushing the boundaries of the beautiful. The point of the original story, as Eliot understood, lies not in the horror of what happened to Philomela but in the transmutation of her anguish into something rich and strange, whether tapestry or birdsong. The suffering of certain sensitive individuals finds expression as art, in which variously painful events are ordered, universalized, given shape and meaning. However terrible the raw experience—one need only consider the actual subject matter of any Greek tragedy—the artistic representation becomes that rarity, something that legitimately exalts the human spirit, something as tragically beautiful or suggestive as the song of the nightingale. But it may be that art in our time, as a DeLillo character says, has edged up to and away from making "the horror, reality, misery, ruined bodies, bloody faces . . . so fucking pretty."[20] Richard Powers similarly wonders (in *Operation Wandering Soul*) about the frequency with which fairy tale and fable merely aestheticize ancient enormity.

Tracking the creative impulse to its anguished genesis, the Philomela myth invites even theological amplification. Her terrible victimization notwithstanding, Philomela can be, no less than the potter at his wheel, a figure of the supreme creator. God, too, suffers and, suffering, creates. Turning Milton inside out, one recognizes the Creation as Jehovah's tapestry, woven to articulate and transmute a vast, cosmic violation. In book VII of *Paradise Lost*, that is, the deity creates humanity and the world to sublimate the anguish, the trauma, of the betrayal narrated in book VI: rebellion by a third of the angels, collective Tereus to godhead itself.

WHAT WOULD JESUS WRITE?

In the narration of Victor Mancini, who comes to think himself the reincarnate Christ, Palahniuk imagines God the Son as another sufferer who must weave his own tapestry of symbolic witness. Here Palahniuk burlesques the spiritual autobiography, the genre created by St. Augustine and refined over the centuries by John Bunyan, Jonathan Edwards, Benjamin Franklin, John Henry Cardinal Newman, Henry Adams, and James Joyce. Thus one discerns in Victor Mancini's narrative a journal of the kind that anchors participants in the twelve-step program of Alcoholics Anonymous and similar programs. Like every addict, Victor wrestles with his fourth step, the writing of a "fearless and complete moral inventory" (215) of his addiction and everything that contributes to it (lengthy and complex, this document involves responses to as many as three hundred questions). Recurring frequently to this fourth step, he executes it as the novel we read: a serious, crude, nonclinical, self-reproachful, and psychologically revealing document, a postmodern Portrait of the Artist as a Young Addict (Joyce, too, one recalls, moves his narrative toward the journal entries that are at once conclusion and recursive genesis). As narrative, however, the post-Joycean text resists the reader's desire for orientation—not to mention determinacy (whether epistemological, psychological, social, or literary). As document, by the same token, it may be authentic, or it may be little more than a send-up—a case-history pastiche, like something concocted by Humbert Humbert (another "sex fiend"), who so loved to toy with the credulity of psychiatrists.

Much energy goes into making the story resemble such a case history, complete with primal scene that the protagonist, arrested, relives over and over again—whether as the crippling neurosis in which the early trauma encysts itself or as the repetition compulsion by which the death instinct gains psychic ground. "Around here," remarks Victor, "everybody's arrested" (275). Thus Victor jokes bitterly about the Oedipus complex from which he himself suffers: "every son raised by a single mom is pretty much born married" (15). When the receptionist at St. Anthony's calls Ida "Mrs. Mancini," Victor corrects her: "It's Miss Mancini. . . . My mom's not married, unless you count me in that creepy Oedipal way" (225). Previously, he has noted a significant anomaly in the relationship with Ida: "In the modern Oedipal story, it's the mother who kills the father and takes the son" (16). In the spirit of this modern—or postmodern—Oedipal story, he will reverse the archetype again (not to mention the prescribed sequence of events) when he kills not the father but the mother—as thoughtlessly and as circumstantially as Oedipus slew Laius. Gone, however, is all tragic elevation, for Victor effects the death of the Oedipal parent by spooning chocolate pudding into her mouth. Her death is the ironic consummation of the choking charade by which, on some 300 occasions, Victor has augmented his income. "'Widower' isn't the right word, but it's the first word that comes to mind" (270).

Freud saw in the tragedy of Oedipus a "family romance," the story of a child who, raised in literal or figurative fosterage, discovers the exalted identity of its frequently royal or divine real parents. Moses and Jesus also exemplify the pattern; indeed, the recurrence of this fantasy in myth and literature—its examples include Stephen Dedalus, Jay Gatsby, and more than one hero in Richard Wagner's operas—suggests its cultural and psychological validity. Stories of fabulous parentage feed or mirror a fantasy congenial to childish imagination. Evidently interested in psychoanalysis, Palahniuk seems drawn to Freudian euhemerization of religious archetype. Repeatedly in *Fight Club*, for example, one reads that "your father was your model for God" (140, 141, 186). In *Choke*, the narrator compounds mythic identity: he becomes not only Oedipus but Jesus, central figure in the supreme family romance.

Among its other features, this novel published in 2001 is a comedy of millennial expectations that have come and gone with no sign of the apocalypse, the promised end. Hence the elaborate joke on Victor's paternity, the outrageous idea of his being the son of the son of god, through the agency of DNA allegedly preserved in the "authenticated foreskin" (229, 267) of Jesus. Initially, Victor resists apotheosis. Though he claims "I'm not a monster" (62), he rejects, with increasing desperation, what he takes to be the mounting evidence of his divine identity. Christian youth affect little wristbands with the enigmatic letters WWJD, meaning What Would Jesus Do, and in time the sentiment, which might be traced back to the early fifteenth century in Thomas à Kempis's *De Imitatione Christi*, made its way into other social spheres, including the bumper stickers of green Christians (or simply environmentalists baiting those with the annoying fish symbol adorning their SUVs), which asked rhetorically: What Would Jesus Drive? In defiance of such pietism, Victor tries to live by the principle he repeats like a mantra:

"What would Jesus NOT do?" (169, 182, 186, 194, 208, 211, 216, 227). Ostensibly
a routine piece of flippancy in the vein of *Fight Club*'s "[b]elieve in me and
you shall die, forever" (145), this little epithet does something more than
declare a disinclination to imitate Christ: it invites ironic recognition that
there are in fact things that Jesus would not do. He would not cast the first
stone, nor, more importantly, would he sidestep his destiny. He even anticipated the mockery of those who would say to him, on the very cross, *cura te
ipsum*, heal thyself. He would not. He did not.

Here one discerns the rationale behind making Victor Mancini, like his
mother before him, a failed medical student. His running symptomatolo-
gies ("[t]he way to remember the symptoms of melanoma is . . ." [100], "a
bruise means cirrhosis of the liver" [104]) coalesce to signal a Kierkegaard-
ian spiritual disease. Unable to heal himself, the quondam medical student begins actually to embrace the absurd identification with Christ. His
mother, declares the highly unreliable Dr. Paige Marshall (whose mental
instability Victor discovers belatedly), "truly believes" that he represents the
long-awaited eschatological consummation, "the second coming of Christ"
(146). As Jesus gravitated to publicans and sinners, so does Victor prefer
the company of slackers and dopers and sex addicts, the ostensibly preter-
ite in the moral economy of his own age's Pharisees and Sadducees. In the
biblical phrase that Handel would put into the past tense and set to music,
"[h]e is despised and rejected of men; a man of sorrows, and acquainted with
grief" (Isa. 53:3). As Antonio Casado de Rocha observes, Victor "enacts his
own death and resurrection" every time he chokes.[21] He defends his nasty
little game of staging asphyxiation for attention, sympathy, and dollars as a
kind of salvation suited to the times. "You gain power by pretending to be
weak. . . . You save people by letting them save you" (50). His gloss on the
story's primal scene, when, as a child, he chokes on a corn dog (a detail in
which the reader may "smell" Mark Leyner), reframes a familiar biblical precept and provides the basic meaning for what will become one of the novel's
central conceits: "It seemed that . . . . you had to risk your life to get love. You
had to go right to the edge of death to ever be saved" (3). ("If I don't fall all
the way," says the narrator of *Fight Club*, "I can't be saved" [70].) Similarly, by
going along with her cracked notion that he is the individual who long ago
wronged or violated her, he "saves" more than one elderly, damaged patient
who, having misplaced her mind, finds herself in an institution ironically
named for the patron saint of lost things. Blithely "accepting responsibility
for every sin in the world" (274), Victor pretends contrition for things they

have brooded over all their lives. In feeding their delusions (however therapeutically), he feeds his own as well, and the reader traces the rise and fall of his fantasy, the identity he reluctantly embraces: "I'm the savior who wants you to worship him forever" (33), he says. "I want to be someone's constant savior" (118). "It sounds," observes Paige Marshall, "as if you'd like to be God" (119), and Victor, in spite of his skepticism, arrives at outlandish conviction: "I know that I'm Jesus Christ" (268). He even tries his hand at literal resurrection, "just like with Lazarus" (270). In the end, he ruefully yields up his delusion: "for a while, I really did think I was Jesus Christ" (274). The punch line to this joke, which Palahniuk tells in a variety of ways throughout his career, is that Victor may indeed be modeling the deity's irresponsibility and carelessness.

As G. Christopher Williams has pointed out, Victor Mancini is not the only Palahniuk protagonist to suffer from messianic delusions.[22] Of course, anyone who has taught English knows that just about any suffering protagonist can be seen as a Christ figure. Small wonder that certain authors—Nathanael West, for example, in *Miss Lonelyhearts*—present parodic versions of this conceit. Characters such as Miss Lonelyhearts and Victor Mancini frustrate the reader's desire for some degree of transparency on the part of a storyteller—transparency regarding the presence of irony, for example. Unable to discern some thematic emphasis or key, readers find themselves in the postmodern limbo of irony that may not be irony, suffering that may be sacramental or hugely specious. Such readers engage in an often painful and frustrating exercise in what—to borrow and modify a term from the Palahniuk novel—might be characterized as tantric hermeneutics. They must read signs that call attention to their own arbitrariness. Yet meaning, thus suspended, becomes spiritually enabling, "tantric."

Palahniuk characterizes as "Tantric Architecture" (264) the teleologically indeterminate principle behind the rock collecting and wall building to which Victor's friend Denny commits himself. The seismic destruction of the wall Denny, Victor, and their stripper friend Beth have labored over signals the need, periodically, to rebuild—for our mental blueprints are especially susceptible, at the beginning of the third millennium, to being exposed as architectural fantasy, the fanciful work of some deranged Piranesi. Together presently, like good postmodernists, they undertake to fashion a reality, "to build a world" (292). This world-building becomes a paradigm that governs reading as well, not to mention the epistemic striving of philosophy and psychology, which have grappled for centuries with the problem of perception: is it neutral and passive—or does it build a reality that, as Wordsworth says, we half perceive and half create? From Bishop Berkeley in the eighteenth century to F. H. Bradley and his pupil T. S. Eliot, the suspicion that our senses betray us recurs. In *The Crying of Lot 49*, for example, Pynchon's heroine Oedipa Maas contemplates a painting by Remedios Varo and realizes the extent to which reality is not, after all, shared. Everyone makes her own, weaves or embroiders it, a perceptual Philomela, in the cranial tower where the senses, converging, make sense. Whether in the shabby "bordello of the subconscious" or the more expansive "theater of the mind" (131), says Palahniuk, one conjures a reality tinged with prurience and inevitably histrionic.

And decidedly unstable. When Palahniuk reveals, late in the narrative, that Paige Marshall is not the resident psychotherapist at St. Anthony's— that, in fact, she is herself one of the patients—he restages and reconceptualizes a classic drama of reality's perspectival lability. Yet another "doctor" unable to heal herself, Paige Marshall burlesques the psychotherapeutic premise and reverses the conceit at the heart of Robert Wiene's celebrated exercise in expressionist horror, *Das Kabinett des Dr. Caligari* (1920). Aimed at destabilizing the viewer's sense of the real and the irreal, the sane and the insane, Wiene's film climaxes with the revelation that its narrative viewpoint is that of an institutionalized mental patient, its sinister title character the director of the asylum. Palahniuk, overturning the *Caligari* conceit, appropriates and reframes the trope that reflected an earlier generation's sense of disorientation and betrayal (which extended far beyond Weimar, as one sees in the contemporaneous Fitzgerald lines quoted previously—or their even more famous echo in the Gertrude Stein remark that became one of the epigraphs to Hemingway's *The Sun Also Rises*).

Part of the modernist project that theorists formulate as "representing the unrepresentable," expressionism was an aesthetic aimed at reifying the alienation, the *Verfremdung*, that characterized a lost generation. Making his Dr. Paige Marshall a Caligari who is one of the deranged, Palahniuk devises an exercise in what might be called postmodern expressionism, a bringing up to date of the aesthetic crafted by Robert Wiene in film, Edvard Munch on canvas, and Bertolt Brecht on the Weimar stage. Now that alienation has been revealed as part of the very weave of consciousness (not some correctable psychological or social pathology), the artist seeks to represent—the formulation is Lyotard's—"the unpresentable in presentation itself."[23] To put this another way, the expressionists and other moderns could still subscribe to metanarratives and depth models of consciousness and history and art. The postmodernists did not invent self-referential art—they invented an art answerable to what was perceived as a crisis of representation. Grappling with the exhaustion or complete evacuation of the signifier, postmodern art risks making the case for its own inconsequence. Committed to exploring a foundationless world of simulacra, in which every serious thing—history, consciousness, belief, the Good—can be engaged only as text, such art invites dismissal as intellectual self-abuse, for its logic is constantly at odds with the practical exigencies of real life. When these exigencies take on sufficient immediacy—when al Qaeda operatives fly airplanes into tall buildings, for example—an oversubtilized art finds itself unable to represent or transmute the resultant trauma. In *Choke*, however, readers see an understated but stunning anticipation of the challenge to discourse posed by the acts of terrorism that inaugurated the millennium in America.

We can, then, note an unexpected element of timeliness in Palahniuk's novel. In addition to his ludic engagement with Christology, his calculated teasing of the millenarianism so widespread at the beginning of this century, he may in some measure foresee the spirit in which American intellectuals would reflect on the horrors of 9/11 in the days and weeks after the Twin Towers came down. What is remarkable about this fiction, published less than four months before the terrorist attack, is that it anticipates one of the most striking responses to that terrible event, heralded at the time— prematurely, as it turned out—as the moment for a paradigm shift in intellectual style, a shift away from irony as a culture's discursive and ideational norm. Reflecting on the events of 9/11, Graydon Carter, editor of *Vanity Fair*, observed: "I think it's the end of the age of irony."[24] Roger Rosenblatt, in *Time*, echoed the sentiment:

> One good thing could come from this horror: it could spell the end of the age of irony. For some 30 years—roughly as long as the Twin Towers were upright—the good folks in charge of America's intellectual life have insisted that nothing was to be believed in or taken seriously. Nothing was real. With a giggle and a smirk, our chattering classes—our columnists and pop culture makers—declared that detachment and personal whimsy were the necessary tools for an oh-so-cool life.[25]

The clumsiness, incoherence, and rhetorical poverty of these remarks offer one gauge of the extent to which events so difficult to process intellectually could rattle thought. Irony was not, of course, invented in 1970—in modern times, it has been a feature of intelligent discourse since World War I exposed the full cost—fifteen million lives—of rhetorical dishonesty. But yes: on 12 September 2001 and for some months after, lots of otherwise unconnable public intellectuals imagined that sincerity might once again come into its own. Palahniuk, in a novel published scarce weeks before the Manhattan towers fell, registers a prophetic impatience with irony.

In a kind of palinode, Palahniuk disperses, like Prospero, the elements of his romance. He does so with characteristic scatology, and, recapitulating psychogenesis, his narrator brings full circle that moment when, as child, he choked on a corn dog. When he chokes for the last time (evidently wanting to kill himself or cause brain death), a policeman saves him with the usual Heimlich maneuver, but the "[p]eriabdominal pressure" (286) undoes not only the windpipe obstruction but also the intestinal logjam to which Victor has adverted with increasing urgency. The forceful evacuation reminds us—or confirms our suspicions (never really resisted by Mancini)—that the sardonic references to being "full of shit" (239) are, as it were, doubly confessional. But the clearing of the blockage, according to this scatological metaphor, takes on additional meaning of considerable importance to contemporary discourse and postmodern aesthetics. The reader is invited to think about a discourse that is not "full of it" or "bogus"—a discourse, in short, that is *not ironic*. One begins to see the significance of the narrator's plaintive iteration of "for serious" (thirteen times), "for real" (fifteen times), and "for sure" (twenty-eight times), for Palahniuk's denouement signals the prospect, at least, of a return to the rhetoric of sincerity so long occluded by the default irony of both modernism and postmodernism. "[F]or sure seriously" (227), then, the author of *Choke* grapples resourcefully with the challenge of being late to the postmodern party. His sardonic recycling of Freudian case history and millennial Christology, along with his surprisingly subtle and proleptic problematizing of modern and postmodern irony, reveals more ideational substance, in the end, than his critical disparagers might lead one to expect.

CHAPTER 8

The Aim Was Song

Ann Patchett's *Bel Canto*

The singer alone does not make a song, there has to be someone who hears:
One man opens his throat to sing, the other sings in his mind.
Only when waves fall on the shore do they make a harmonious sound;
Only when breezes shake the woods do we hear a rustling in the leaves.
Only from a marriage of two forces does music arise in the world.
Where there is no love, where listeners are dumb, there never can be song.

—RABINDRANATH TAGORE, "BROKEN SONG"[1]

Though no one would confuse the tonalities of Ann Patchett with those of Chuck Palahniuk, both authors risk academic contumely for resisting (or seeming indifferent to) the politics of race, gender, and class. Both Patchett, in *Bel Canto*, and Palahniuk, in *Choke*, build on ancient ideas of the origins and purpose of art. Published in the months before 9/11, both novels seem variously uncanny now, at more than a decade's remove. Reading or rereading these fictions after the terrible events that took place that September, one experiences the literary imagination at its most acute. Like certain animals that become restive before an earthquake, the authors seem, at least in retrospect, to sense some significant shift in cultural tectonics.

As thoughtful citizens, we strive to learn the lessons taught by history, but the past is a Delphic pedagogue. Too often, a lesson specific to time and place will be mistaken for a universal precept (thus did the nations learn from the misguided Munich Agreement of 1938 to sustain a decades-long policy of containment—even as it led to military quagmires in Southeast Asia and alliances with dubious regimes around the world). Often as not, a lesson presents itself as little more than a kernel that must germinate before it sprouts; only the passage of time brings full fruition. Thus the lessons of 9/11 seem different now than they did in the immediate aftermath of events.

Many thought, as noted in the previous chapter, that they would now see an end of irony as discursive dominant, but of course reports of that death were premature. Another of the lessons—the one realized as a vast "war on terror"—seems also to have miscarried.

One recognizes here a crucial element in the generational problem addressed in the present study. Writers in every generation strive, consciously or unconsciously, to capture their historical moment. Some writers meet this challenge by scrupulous attention to the minutiae of the cultural present, knowing that the future will reveal itself as a coalescence of the seemingly trivial. Thus does Don DeLillo, for example, explain his seeming prescience.[2] But like a Gioacchino Rossini crescendo, history seems to accelerate, to become more and more resistant to literary representation, less and less friendly to the ambitions of a modern-day Homer or Virgil or Tolstoy. With every passing year, writers face fresh challenges to their ability to hold some mirror up to an historically inflected present, "to show," as Hamlet says, "the very *age* and body of the time his *form* and *pressure*" (III.2.17–24). Nor does recognition of this or that particular event as watershed, turning point, or *kairos* simplify their task, for one catastrophe supersedes another, as 9/11 displaced the Kennedy assassination as perceived climacteric. Certain writers, however, seem still to manage actual augury and thereby to go Hamlet's desideratum one better. A writer like Ann Patchett, compelled on the eve of 9/11 to dramatize a notorious incident in the developing world's long history of strife, aims at insights that, bypassing vulgar prophecy, contrive nonetheless to challenge much of the thinking about terrorism in the aftermath of that September day.

Contemporary writers of fiction may not worry unduly about their relationship with slightly older peers. That is, rather than embracing, consolidating, or repudiating a postmodern aesthetic, many strive simply to learn from masters farther back along the great chain of writing. If classic literature merits respect, its premises may well prove immune to changes in literary fashion. Novelists in the twenty-first century have much to learn, still, from Jane Austen, George Eliot, Charles Dickens, and the Brontës; from Nathaniel Hawthorne, Herman Melville, and the naturalists; and from Joseph Conrad, Virginia Woolf, and James Joyce.

In interviews, Ann Patchett names several writers who have influenced her work—some traditional, others cautiously avant-garde. Although she studied at one time or another with Russell Banks, Allan Gurganus, Geoffrey Wolff, and Grace Paley, she learned plot, she has remarked, from Raymond Chandler, characterization from Anton Chekhov, description from Joan Didion. She also mentions Welty, Updike, and Alice Munro, and she professes particular regard for Nabokov and Thomas Mann (perhaps unaware that the one despised the other). As one might expect from the basic idea of *Bel Canto*—concentrate interesting, diverse characters under stress in a literally or figuratively carceral space—she thinks highly of Mann's *Magic Mountain* ("a book that I'm constantly trying to plagiarize"), and obviously she shares with the author of *Doktor Faustus* an interest in serious music and the moral questions that great art engages (even as its creators, like Adrian Leverkühn, prove variously compromised).[3] She names García Márquez as an influence, too, and one can profitably think of both *Bel Canto* and its successor, *State of Wonder* (2011), as edging at times into magic realism. Like the authors of *One Hundred Years of Solitude* or *The House of the Spirits*, Patchett returns perception to that "state of wonder" in which, for children, the world is indeed magical. Such flights are hardly to be despised—in a way, all literature involves some negotiation between reality and its subjunctive inflections. But fiction, however playful, recurs eventually to perception's iron standard, the reality principle, and Patchett's modulates toward perceptual and imaginative discrimination. Readers of *Bel Canto* experience what Thomas Pynchon once described as storytelling "made luminous, undeniably authentic, by having been found and taken up, always at a cost, from deeper, more shared levels of the life we all really live."[4]

Readers ought also to think of Richard Powers, whose extraordinary sensitivity to and knowledge of fiction's sister art, music, buttresses his conception of the idealizing element in his own work. Powers takes an interest, that is, in what he has called "the virtuality of fiction, fiction not as a replacement for the real world, but as a hybrid place where the real world is suspended and reconstituted into something more survivable."[5] Over and over again, he invokes music as the ideal complement to this vision. In *Galatea 2.2* (1995), a writer who calls *Doktor Faustus* "the formative storybook of my adult years" bonds with scientific colleagues who listen to Wolfgang Amadeus Mozart and John Taverner.[6] *The Time of Our Singing* (2003) is the massive chronicle of a gifted singer born to a black woman and a white man who meet at the Washington Monument on the occasion of Marian Anderson's famous concert. Powers exploits musical analogues to narrative most exhaustively in his 1991 novel *The Gold Bug Variations*, in which, as the title suggests, the spirit of Edgar Allan Poe presides over a story about early attempts to decipher the cryptography of the human genome. The structure that gradually comes to light resembles that of Bach's *Goldberg Variations*. One of the scientists grappling with the genetic code undergoes an existential metamorphosis when he hears the famous Glenn Gould recording: "The first sound of the octave, the simplicity of unfolding triad initiates a process that will mutate his insides for life." Here and in *Orfeo* (2014), Powers makes of musical allusion a foundation for his imaginative flights, "a bass line" like that of the Bach piece, "as patterned as the orbit of seasons, fueled by the inexorable self-burning at the core of stars."[7]

Sometimes influence is more dispersed: a presence like spores in the air, as opposed to something a writer might consciously embrace. I wonder whether Patchett might not have been exposed to certain of the arguments John Gardner advanced for "moral fiction." Indeed, the scene in which Roxane Coss, in *Bel Canto*, stuns the music-starved company by singing "O mio babbino caro" bears a kind of Gardner signature:

> Their eyes clouded over with tears for so many reasons it would be impossible to list them all. They cried for the beauty of the music, certainly, but also for the failure of their plans. They were thinking of the last time they had heard her sing and longed for the women who had been beside them then. All of the love and the longing a body can contain was spun into not more than two and a half minutes of song, and when she came to the highest notes it seemed that all they had been given in their lives and all they had lost came together and made a weight that was almost impossible to bear. When she was finished, the people around her stood in stunned and shivering silence. Messner leaned into the wall as if struck. He had not been invited to the party. Unlike the others, he had never heard her sing before.[8]

This scene may strike the reader as a little contrived, but it echoes the moment at which, in Gardner's *Grendel*, the monster first hears, "arresting as a voice from a hollow tree," the singing of the Shaper, which silences a loutish company and thrills the listener in the shadows. The rapt silence presently gives way to the "howling and clapping and stomping of men gone mad on art.... Men wept like children: children sat stunned" (43). Seeking as it were to blend Matthew Arnold's Hebraic and Hellenic (broadly, the moral and the sensuous), Gardner modified the ancient precept that art should delight and instruct, for he saw how the second part of that binary—truth telling— might in modern times threaten to swamp the aesthetic bark. Yes, art's first allegiance must be to truth, however painful, but Gardner saw that art must do more than simply hold a mirror up to chaos, meaninglessness, and confusion. He would have agreed with a remark made by Thea Kronborg, heroine of Willa Cather's *The Song of the Lark* (like *Bel Canto*, a novel with an opera singer at its center): "Artistic growth is, more than it is anything else, a refining of the sense of truthfulness. The stupid believe that to be truthful is easy; only the artist, the great artist, knows how difficult it is."[9] The difficulty, Gardner believed, lies in the devising of fictions undidactic yet moral, art that presents models of virtue. Gardner knew that powerful art calls into being its real-world likeness. If life imitates art, he asked, what art conjures the most comely reflection in the human heart or on the stage of the world? One recalls the distinction that Aristotle noted between two great tragedians: "Sophocles said he drew men as they ought to be; Euripides as they are."[10] In suggesting that reality can be improved, Gardner came down on the side of Sophocles. Patchett, too, enlists under that aesthetic banner.

Moral art, moral artist. Not necessarily good or virtuous in their private lives, novelists become moral artists insofar as they answer the implied Sophoclean challenge. The virtue lies in their commitment to the depiction of an imagined world worthy of reality's speculum. In *Bel Canto*, Ann Patchett brings the moral imagination to bear on the political violence of the age. Although it represents this political violence and teases with the elements of a politicized aesthetic, her story resists—I will argue—much of the ideology that seems so widespread in critical discourse about literature. *Bel Canto* seems remarkably fresh, that is, because its rhapsodic celebration of art dispenses with—or at least reframes—the expected politics and ideology. Its author candidly aspires to subordinate politics to aesthetic *jouissance*. She reaffirms art's ability, however temporarily, to dispel what E. M. Forster called panic and emptiness. Like Forster, too (not to mention the Beethoven he invokes in *Howards End*), she understands that the sublunary disorder cannot be dispelled permanently. She depicts the inevitable return of violence, moreover, with nothing less than tragic intensity. Attempts to reproach the author for false consciousness (does she not see that opera is an instrument of cultural imperialism?) strike one as decidedly misguided. Such strictures imply that one can weep for beauty wed to a political vision of one kind or another, but not for beauty alone. Patchett, whose characters literally weep when they hear the singing of Roxane Coss after several miserable days of captivity, depicts the aesthetic experience as a relief from political strife.

SOOTHING THE SAVAGE BREAST

The twentieth century rather specialized in depicting the artist as her or his own hero (Hawthorne and Robert Browning had tested these waters, but it was perhaps Ovid and Dante who really invented the *Künstlergeschichte*). The moderns, however, began to critique their own aesthetic pretensions in more obviously autobiographical self-projections. One thinks of Joyce Cary's Gulley Jimson or, again, Cather's Thea Kronborg. Poets had been at this for a long time—though commonly reserving complete approbation for selves more radically disguised (often, famously, as birds: hence John Keats's nightingale, Percy Bysshe Shelley's skylark, William Cullen Bryant's waterfowl, Thomas Hardy's thrush, Robert Frost's oven bird, the mockingbird in Walt Whitman's operatically structured "Out of the Cradle, Endlessly Rocking").

The earliest poetry was sung, and "song" remains the universal figure for "poem" in the lexicon of versifiers. Robert Frost tells a relevant parable: singing began, he declares, when the raw howling of wind in "a narrow place" seemed to call for human correction. A little of that icy north wind, warmed and converted to its austral antithesis in the mouth of some primal poet, issued forth as sound more congenial to human ears. According to that first poet's successor, "[t]he aim was song."[11] But no sooner does Frost's conceit come into focus than one recognizes in the supposedly insentient howling a figure, withal, of human misery—also processed and transformed by art. Here and in many other poems, Frost contemplates both the birth of art in suffering and the struggle to compensate for nature's often harsh indifference to human need. Thus one discerns in his farmers and orchard keepers figures of the poet who shoulders the Sisyphean task of imposing on nature (or discovering in it) a modicum of order or sense. Hence his famous remark about art as "momentary stay against confusion."[12]

In *Bel Canto*, Ann Patchett examines terrorism and its state-sponsored suppression as up-to-date examples of the confusion that art briefly—upwards of four months, in this instance—holds at bay. What succeeds for a time in defusing the desperate and all too familiar passions of the terrorists and the emotions of their hostages is vocal music of a particular sort—the operatic and art song repertoire. Shortly after the terrorists take over Mr. Hosokawa's birthday party, the authorities surround the compound, their sirens and loudspeakers reminiscent of Frost's boreal shrieking and doubtless finding their echo in every captive breast. "Through the windows, bright red strobe lights flashed across the walls accompanied by a high-pitched wailing. The sound was . . . nothing, nothing like song" (27). Days later, when one of the hostages reveals his ability to play the piano, he furnishes the desperate company with a kind of musical manna: "nothing in their lives had ever fed them so well" (127). Roxane Coss furnishes even more musical sustenance, and Patchett characterizes her singing, along with the repertoire to which she devotes her professional life, as wholly transformative. Reflecting on art as deflection, corrective, or sublimation of the violence in nature and in the hearts of human beings, the author updates an idea that made its way from Latin—"*musica delenit bestiam feram*"—into English in the opening line of William Congreve's only tragedy, *The Mourning Bride* (1697): "Musick has Charms to soothe a savage Breast." Patchett assesses this venerable precept by imagining its applicability to the heightened savagery of the millennium, in which atrocities proliferate on both sides of political legitimacy.

In doing so, she must revive in some measure a genre much degraded in the modern age. Congreve courted a muse already a bit shabby; in tatters in our own day, she survives as journalism's bitch (unable to register nuance, the reporter on the nightly news characterizes every fatal accident as a tragedy, all suffering of innocents as tragic). The literary artist, with her more discriminating moral vision, understands that tragedy resides more legitimately in the flawed heroics or misguided sacrifice of those willing to take life (or lay down their own) to advance a desperate political cause. In that the "terrorists" will be annihilated only after the reader has begun to be uncomfortable with that question-begging epithet, the story discovers a fatalism that is precisely and powerfully tragic. As the fictionalized instance of political conflict chronicled in *Bel Canto* runs its inevitable course, the author imagines the extraordinary transmutation, before the fated end, of the powerful emotions—anger, anguish, fear—generated by state-sponsored as well as terrorist violence. Invited to observe the curiously moving sense of community that emerges among and binds the hostages and terrorists, the reader feels pity and terror for both groups. Thus the wedding with which the narrative concludes hardly represents a comedic resolution. As Deborah Weisgall observes in remarks introducing her interview with Patchett, the novel "ends in no joyous *Figaro*-like finale."[13] Nor is this "epilogue," as one reviewer remarked, a "bathetic conclusion."[14] Rather, it is a calculated piece of tragic irony—the kind immune to cultural fashion.

Patchett bases her tale on real events that took place in Peru over 126 days, beginning in December 1996 and ending late the following April. Fourteen Túpac Amaru revolutionaries, led by Néstor Cerpa, interrupted a reception at the Japanese ambassadorial residence in Lima, taking over 600 hostages. After releasing all but seventy-two, they settled in for an excruciatingly long siege that ended only when Peruvian commandos, two of whom died in the assault, rescued all but one of the hostages. Trained by American and British special forces, the commandos killed all of the terrorists—even those who tried to surrender.[15]

Although she clearly shapes her story around these events, Patchett advances by two months the beginning of the siege (Mr. Hosokawa's birthday falls on 22 October). She also declines to name the country in which it takes place.[16] One may wonder at this reticence—especially when she catalogues the many specific nationalities represented among the hostages. Not that one finds the Peruvian setting and the real events hard to spot: Patchett evidently means for her *roman* to open with a *clef* in the desk drawer of any reasonably informed reader. Yet she also wants to confer an archetypal quality on her terrorist incident, to allow it to float free of particular historical circumstance. As Daniel Mendelsohn pointed out in a perspicacious review, the story becomes "allegory" or "fable."[17] Like all good allegorists, in fact, she wants to have her real cake and, at the same time, its symbolic eating. Although the two entities here—captors and hostages—naturally occupy disparate social and economic strata, one occasionally senses the presence, in spirit, of Giovanni Boccaccio or Geoffrey Chaucer, both of whom organized great literary works around the idea of individuals who, thrown together, gradually reveal themselves as a cross section of humanity. Patchett imagines, on the one hand, a band of desperate revolutionaries and, on the other, captains of industry and politics, along with diplomats, a translator, a priest, and a radiant representative of the arts. But even the revolutionaries define a spectrum—from the quondam schoolteacher General Benjamin to the illiterate peasants he and his fellow officers command. Transforming the vice president's mansion into a microcosm, Patchett joins the company of those who distill from a band of pilgrims, a crowded stagecoach, or a ship of fools an allegory of human character and destiny. In motion in these famous examples, pilgrims, travelers, or refugees make their way toward heaven, freedom, safety, the New World, or another symbolic destination. But Patchett declines to imagine any such promised land for her characters, who exist in a double prison: the captors are themselves held captive. A static microcosm, then, a *Parliament of Fowls* rather than *The Canterbury Tales*, a *Magic Mountain* rather than *Das Knarrenschiff*.

One discerns another such static microcosm (and withal a more proximate intertext) in the chapter of Thomas Pynchon's *V.* set in German
South-West Africa in 1922. Here a company of Europeans—another cross
section—embarks on a long, decadent party as rebellion against the colonizer breaks out (for the second time in as many decades). Isolated within
a villa and its walled compound, the variously corrupt Europeans parody
the League of Nations just coming into belated and impotent being. But
like Messner, the Swiss negotiator in Patchett's novel, Pynchon understands
perfectly well "how these stories usually ended" (*Bel Canto*, 137), and in fact
the slaughter of the Herero and other native populations becomes a spectacle, an entertainment, for his jaded westerners.

Patchett at once deconstructs this premise and, as will be seen, challenges assumptions about the Stockholm syndrome. She imagines rebels and
captives presently united in their humanity; unlike Pynchon, who contrasts
the decadence of his Europeans with the integrity of indigenes whose suffering becomes moral capital, she breaks down the distinction between In-
dio or mestizo or campesino and Euro-American or first-world *privilegiado*.
Thus, too, she creates her own little bicameral parliament of the nations
and classes. The hostages come from Sweden, Germany, France, Denmark,
Japan, Russia, Italy, Argentina, Greece, and the United States, as well as at
least one of the countries in which Portuguese is spoken. The terrorists include peasants, a schoolteacher, and the urban poor. Patchett has remarked
that she ought not to have called the hapless guerrilla fighters in her story
"terrorists," but I think any such error serendipitous.[18] An important part of
the author's message jells (the point bears repeating) as the reader begins to
resist that tendentious label—to recognize that it promotes only indiscriminate demonization.

All the more poignant, then, that the author feigns no illusions about
how this particular story will play out. The state will violently suppress the
little enclave of civility-fostering art. Nor does Patchett mislead the reader,
for her narrator announces the story's ending early on: "in fact it was the
terrorists who would not survive the ordeal" (13). Readers, however, come
to dread the advent of military or paramilitary deliverance. They take no
joy in the success of the commandos, for part of the integrity of this book
lies in the author's refusal to gratify expectations fostered by televisual and
cinematic conventions (those governing, for example, *Dog-Day Afternoon,
Inside Man,* and the *Die Hard* films).

One has only to recall the atavistic emotions with which the public usually greets the liberation of hostages—whether through negotiations or SWAT team heroics—to see the iconoclasm with which Patchett imagines this political drama. She understands the extent to which popular perceptions have themselves been taken hostage by the tendentious, sensationalizing rhetoric of politicians. Thus she reframes the standard narrative of terrorism, which journalism tends to represent as a kind of reality *novela* or soap opera: innocents are or are not rescued from captors characterized (in the Western press) as vicious fanatics or (in what might be called the subaltern press) as freedom fighters. But as Thibault remarks to Gen at the end of the novel, "[n]othing you read in the papers is true" (317). Few, in the heat of events, try to imagine humanity on both sides. We want our terrorists demonized, our SEAL teams nothing less than Homeric. But just as it takes daring and tactical genius to prevail against desperate and ruthless elements (at Entebbe, in the waters off Somalia, in the remote jungles where real rebels vie with narco-terrorists to hold various innocents for ransom), so does it take artistic courage to imagine hostages and their captors becoming a community in which art and love make their surprise appearance, in which violence is attenuated (at least for a while) and savage breasts soothed. Artists like Patchett compose another kind of SEAL team—one that liberates perception itself, strikes off manacles forged in the smithy of a blinkered national or tribal perspective. By means of an artful handling of point of view, the author avoids inadvertent privileging of any single vantage on events. In an interview, she mentions a long-standing aspiration "to write a book with a truly omniscient narrative voice that switched easily from character to character. It's the thing I'm most proud of in this book."[19] This formal feature proves well suited to her vision here.

One of the remarkable elements of this story is the way that it contests received thinking about the psychology of hostages—especially the curious phenomenon whereby they come to sympathize or even side with their captors. The author of *Bel Canto* imagines the sympathizing without the psychopathology: privileged individuals, representative of those whom revolutionaries and radicals despise and seek to bring low, slowly come to see the humanity of those holding them hostage. Telling a story predicated on the power of art (and shared pursuits—the chess, the soccer) to obviate the invidious and often unexamined distinctions of rank and caste and ideology, the author crafts what Tom H. Hastings, in *Nonviolent Response to Terrorism*, has called a "forgiveness narrative," a text that seeks actively to disavow the mailed fist as the only legitimate response to the world's predilection for carnage. "Will our end be love for each other, as Patchett's terrorists and hostages learned," asks Hastings, "or will it be the slaughter and shootout brought to us by the state?"[20] Hastings seems to echo sentiments expressed by Patchett in another of the interviews she has given. In a conversation with Gwen Ifill, she commented on the undertow of the only hostage psychology most people have heard of:

> I read a lot about Stockholm Syndrome. Patty Hearst was a huge childhood fascination of mine. I've always followed her story. I think that the differences, with the Stockholm Syndrome people are somehow fooled into thinking that they identify with their captors. In this book, they actually do. I don't think that it is a syndrome. I think that they have so much compassion for these people, who are mostly children who take them hostage, and they spend so much time together, they play chess together, they play soccer together. They enjoy the music together. They really do find their common humanity.[21]

Obliged to negotiate perceptions and expectations anchored in real life terrorism at its least sympathetic (at the embassy in Teheran; on the tarmac at Karachi or Beirut; in a Russian grammar school or theater), Patchett emphasizes that her terrorists belong to a faction less inclined to indiscriminate violence than the extremist Dirección Auténtica (here Patchett reproduces the actual distinction between Túpac Amaru and the truly ferocious Shining Path): "Had they been taken over by La Dirección Auténtica instead of the much more reasonable La Familia de Martin Suarez, they would never have been allowed to pray. LDA would have dragged one hostage up to the roof every day for the press to see, and then shot him in the head in an attempt to speed negotiations" (199). At such moments, the author declares herself no Pollyanna: she will not be suggesting that all terrorists really need is a warm hug.

One should not confuse Patchett's perspectivism with the misguided tolerance that leads some to resist affirming the simple superiority of certain cultural achievements (democracy, say, or the enfranchisement of women) to values that foster and validate theocratic and other totalitarian regimes. Although she depicts her terrorists with sympathy and notes the foibles of their captives, she stops short of embracing a radical politics herself and thereby avoids the version of Stockholm syndrome to which western intellectuals are especially susceptible. Her sympathetic treatment of both the hostages and their captors contrasts, in other words, with the postures struck by culture critics (and at least one critic of this novel), who too readily see an insidious racism and colonial mentality in first-world discourse. Patchett suggests, quite reasonably, that any accommodation between citizens of the developed world and their less fortunate or more oppressed fellows is not, *eo ipso*, tainted and compromised.

Because artists like to range beyond doctrine and dogma, attempts to read this novel from a postcolonial perspective can easily miscarry. The artist's square peg may have to undergo mutilation before it will fit into the critic's round hole. Thus Patchett's novel presents itself as an interesting test case for contemporary fiction—especially insofar as its critics stretch every creative hide on a frame constructed of attitudes towards race, gender, class, and postcolonial identity. Patchett, though mindful of these matters, resists the notion that political content, conscious or unconscious, determines a story's legitimacy. Even in her 1994 novel *Taft*, with its black protagonist, and her 2007 novel *Run*, which concerns a pair of African American children adopted by a white Boston politician, she seems less interested in racial issues than in family dynamics. Sidestepping ideology of the kind wished on her by academic critics, the author of *Bel Canto* risks their disapprobation.

One can profitably compare this novel to Werner Herzog's 1982 film *Fitzcarraldo*, another meditation on bringing opera to Peru, by another creative artist of great musical sensitivity. Perhaps because he had in *Aguirre, der Zorn Gottes* (1972) presented a political parable of rapacious Europeans coming to grief in the New World, Herzog can in *Fitzcarraldo* dispense with the earnest postcolonial attitudinizing to imagine a story whose delight lies in its occasions for memorable cinematic tableaux. The Quixotic attempt to portage an enormous riverboat from one Amazonian tributary to another is a conceit that vies for strangeness with that of terrorists turned opera buffs. Herzog, like Patchett, juxtaposes western or civilized purpose with topographical and cultural otherness. The daunting terrain of Peru's interior wholly frustrates Fitzcarraldo's elaborate plans for a remote rubber plantation. That enterprise, however, is not condemned as colonial exploitation. Fitzcarraldo wants a rubber plantation so that he can finance the building of his opera house. Both the epic portage and the (realized) aspiration to stage opera in the jungle town of Iquitos become, as it were, metonyms for the ambition of an artist who strives to achieve the sublime (and perhaps, in the sphere of impossible dreams, Herzog attempts to bring art cinema to—and thereby "colonize"—the multiplex).

The point, finally, is that Herzog and Patchett are alike interested in something other than reproaches to colonial predation.

Which is not to say that Patchett is oblivious to political history—indeed, she seems mindful of its complexity and untidiness. Her setting—a Latin American nation struggling to suppress a bloody insurgency (bloodier, in fact, than what one glimpses here)—lends itself to reflections on the unsteady course of empire and revolution and vestigial colonialism. For Peru has been, since the sixteenth century, a colonial entity of one kind or another. Nor were Francisco Pizarro's Spaniards the first to conquer Peru's indigenes: displaced and enslaved by the Spanish invader, the Incas experienced a version of the subjugation to which they had subjected their weaker neighbors. The empire of Atahualpa gave way to another, more ruthless order that would prevail for three hundred years—until, in the nineteenth century, along with many others in Latin America, the Peruvians threw off the Iberian yoke. But like the citizens of every other former colony, the Peruvians wrestled with an invidious legacy, a population in which economic advantage remained with those of European descent, who enjoyed what they perceived as their god-given racial superiority. In time, Peru would follow the unshining path of dictatorship and a disastrous war with neighboring Chile (1879–83). From Augusto B. Leguía to Juan Velasco Alvarado and Francisco Morales Bermúdez (with a couple of reasonably progressive five-year stretches under Fernando Belaúnde), Peru suffered under one dictator after another.[22] During the period of this novel—the mid-1990s—a president with the unlikely name of Alberto Fujimori (his parents were Japanese immigrants) was well on his way to being recognized as among the most corrupt of Peru's politicians (ironically, he had been more or less democratically elected in 1990, defeating none other than future Nobel laureate Mario Vargas Llosa). Eventually forced out of office, driven into exile, repatriated, tried, and sentenced to prison for embezzlement of government funds and crimes against humanity (he had, among other things, unleashed the Grupo Colina death squad), Fujimori becomes, in the novel, the soap opera-loving President Masuda, who never appears "onstage."

OPERA AND THE "OPERATIC"

The Peruvian hostage crisis of 1996–97 was pervaded, from its beginning, by an air of absurdity. Patchett recalls thinking the situation "operatic," and when she came to write her novel, the word offered itself as ideational plinth, a kind of foundation for conceptual originality. Ostensibly patronizing and dismissive, the word prompted recognition of an unusual artistic opportunity. One could fictionalize the events in Peru as "operatic" in the fullest sense and across the whole spectrum: from the "soap" variety to bedroom farce to the tragic heights of Giuseppe Verdi and Richard Wagner and Alban Berg. As she told Sarah Johnson, "I wanted to structure the novel like an opera, by which I mean that it took on the larger-than-life qualities of opera: passion, melodrama, death."[23]

Knowing nothing about opera when she began thinking about the novel that would become *Bel Canto*, Patchett undertook rather a large-scale self-education. As she has explained in interviews, she immersed herself in a twenty-eight-hour lecture series, *The History of Opera*, started listening to recordings, read Fred Plotkin's *Opera 101*, and attended performances when possible. She modeled the personality of Roxane Coss on that of singer Karol Bennett, with whom she had become friends at the Bunting Institute at Radcliffe College in 1990–91. The voice, however, she imagined as that of Renée Fleming.[24] As will be seen, Fleming would return the gesture.

One cannot miss the story's dramatic affinities with opera. Anyone looking closely at the genre discovers a kind of built-in paradox: the operatic mythos lends itself to both absurdity and sublimity. If an element of outlandishness often figures in standard opera plots (as Gilbert and Sullivan delighted in showing), sophisticated audiences nevertheless manage still to be transported by their moments—now comedic, now tragic—of lyric intensity. Patchett invokes this intensity in a novel replete, like opera itself, with powerful drama, passages of heart-stopping lyricism, and, yes, a plot that challenges credulity.

One can, in any event, trace nearly every detail in Patchett's story to an operatic antecedent—sometimes to several. Patchett's plot, characters, and dramatic situations echo operatic topoi at every turn, and readers in the know enjoy spotting the allusions, parallels, and outright quotations. Patchett has remarked that she imagined her hostages and their captors as two choruses. Perhaps she was thinking of the men's and women's choruses that sing to each other in Pietro Mascagni's *Cavalleria Rusticana*—or of the "Chorus of Exiled Palestinians" and the "Chorus of Exiled Jews" in the prologue to John Adams's *Death of Klinghoffer* (based on the 1985 incident in which four operatives of the Palestine Liberation Front took over a cruise vessel, the *Achille Lauro*, and murdered an elderly American passenger). Patchett recapitulates one of opera's most moving scenes, the prisoners' chorus in Beethoven's *Fidelio*, when the hostages, after weeks of incarceration within the vice presidential mansion, are allowed to go outdoors. Beethoven's opera turns on the efforts of its heroine, who has disguised herself as the Fidelio of the title, to deliver her husband Florestan (a political prisoner like General Benjamin's brother Luis) from the chains of an oppressor.

Opera sometimes features a reflexive touch: characters who are themselves singers, often of the operatic repertoire. Examples include Stella and Antonia in Jacques Offenbach's *Tales of Hoffmann* and the eponymous heroines of Leoš Janáček's *The Makroupolos Affair* and Giacomo Puccini's *Tosca*. The Puccini character inspires Coss to outface present danger: "Wasn't she Tosca?" (33), she asks herself, reflecting not only on the character's strength but on the fortitude required of the singer who must fling herself from the battlements of the Castel Sant'Angelo in performance after performance. Premiered in 1900, *Tosca* features depictions of secret-police tactics that would, on the stage of the twentieth century, reify themselves many times over. Its heroine desperately—and unsuccessfully—attempts to deliver a lover, Cavaradossi, from the clutches of Scarpia, the vicious head of Rome's security apparatus. Although Patchett includes no Scarpia in *Bel Canto*, her readers glimpse the Peruvian jackboot in the unhappy histories of Ishmael and General Benjamin. Ishmael's "father had been taken from the house one night by a group of men and no one saw him again" (189); General Benjamin's brother has been jailed for passing out pamphlets (he is executed after the commandos rescue the hostages). Unlike Puccini's Tosca, Roxane will survive, but Mr. Hosokawa will suffer a version of Cavaradossi's fate.

Other parallels abound—even with Peruvian history (*La Forza del Destino* concerns the doomed love of its Spanish heroine, Leonora, for Don Alvaro, a descendant of Inca royalty). Esmeralda, the governess in the vice president's home, calls to mind the central character in *Turn of the Screw*, which Benjamin Britten reframed as an opera. The idea of a plot against the government figures in *Un Ballo in Maschera* (which turns on the assassination of a king). Indeed, from *Giulio Cesare* to *I Puritani*, *Don Carlo*, and *Il Trovatore*, such political struggle often figures in opera. In Francis Poulenc's *Les Dialogues des Carmélites*, set during the French Revolution, political violence invades a nunnery. In the finale, the doomed nuns form a dwindling chorus as, one after another, they mount the scaffold.

The great singer at the heart of this story takes her name from the Bactrian princess who married Alexander the Great (in Persian, Roxana means "luminous beauty" or, more simply, "dawn"). She figures in George Frideric Handel's 1726 opera *Alessandro* and would have figured in *Alexandre et Roxane* if Mozart had gotten around to writing it. Patchett names her two women terrorists, Carmen and Beatriz, for more familiar operatic heroines. Beatriz shares a name (and an acerbic personality) with the title character of Hector Berlioz's opera *Béatrice et Bénédict*, based on Shakespeare's *Much Ado About Nothing*. Carmen shares the name of the dark-skinned seductress immortalized by Georges Bizet. Gen, reflecting on the unpredictability of love (here it brings together a guerrilla fighter and a hostage), recalls the words of a famous aria: *"l'amour est un oiseau rebelle que nul ne peut apprivoiser, et c'est bien en vain qu'on l'appelle, s'il lui convient de refuser"* (249–50). The assignations of lovers such as Carmen and Gen, not to mention the perils of paramours smuggled into bedrooms, are classic features of drama operatic and otherwise—notably Richard Strauss's *Der Rosenkavalier* and Mozart's *The Marriage of Figaro*. Unlike the heroine of *La Sonnambula* (compromised when discovered in the bed of Count Rodolpho), Roxane and Mr. Hosokawa manage to avoid exposure.[25]

Patchett has remarked that she does not think her novel would make a good film—but "I would . . . love to see this book made into an opera."[26] For a while, one imagined that some Anthony Brandt, Jake Hegi, John Harbison, Jennifer Higdon, or even Osvaldo Golijov might one day gratify that desire. But Renée Fleming, as Creative Consultant to the Chicago Lyric Opera, ended such speculation when she commissioned Peruvian composer Jimmy López (a teenager living in Lima at the time of the hostage crisis) to create for the 2015–16 season an opera based on the novel, with a libretto by the Cuban American playwright Nilo Cruz. Any expectation that Fleming herself would sing the role of Roxane Coss was dashed when Danielle de Niese was invited to create the part. Nor did the company cast the celebrated Peruvian tenor Juan Diego Flóres, who specializes, as it happens, in bel canto roles. Born in Lima in 1973, he was twenty-four (and just arriving at international stardom) when the incident on which this story is based took place. Flóres is the singer that the doomed Cesar, in the novel, might have become.

López and Cruz had to meet a challenge or two. Because "bel canto" refers to a particular phase of operatic history (and, more specifically, to a compositional style), it may be thought a little misleading as the title of a twenty-first-century work. A greater difficulty will be to marry a contemporary musical idiom to the operatic set pieces named in Patchett's text. These would threaten to charm the ears more than the framing music—or the music that must convey the important dramatic moments. Will the fated passion of Gen and Carmen—or Roxane and Mr. Hosokawa—transport an audience as readily as the grand moments between Rodolpho and Mimi, Manon and Des Grieux, Pinkerton and Butterfly, or Giovanni and Zerlina? Composers have, however, faced such difficulties before. Richard Strauss introduces into his highly Teutonic and chromatic score for *Der Rosenkavalier* a brief scene for an Italian singer and his faux-Puccini aria. Such musical code-switching may in fact be especially congenial to postmodern audiences.

Because she depicts opera finding a ready audience in a South American backwater, Patchett has been accused of indifference to or lack of respect for indigenous culture. The juggernaut of operatic imperialism announces itself in Mr. Hosokawa, who "believed that life, true life, was something . . . stored in music" (5). But Patchett merely notes that this character—himself a nonwesterner—dislikes Andean ensembles, "bands playing high-pitched pipes and crude drums. The music gave Mr. Hosokawa a headache" (133). One irony to this remark is that it reverses the disdain often expressed by philistines who claim that operatic singing causes them cranial anguish. Yet the attentive reader may notice that the Andean music is something that the vice president and General Benjamin have in common. Asserting that the novelist unwittingly recapitulates unexamined assumptions about the superiority of "civilization" over "barbarism" (superiority manifest in invidious comparisons between Western high culture and the artistic productions of a "primitive" third world), critics miss these subtle ironies.

One of the first scholars to analyze this novel attacks its allegedly unexamined politics. Jane Marcus-Delgado points out details that confirm the Peruvian milieu (references to pisco sours [50], the *garúa* [105–6], and certain terms in Peruvian Spanish, e.g., *requetebueno* [108], slang for "terrif," "super-fine"), but she reproaches the author—unfairly, I think—for depicting a first-world art form as the vehicle of the characters' spiritual deliverance. The critic makes statements about opera, however, to which one strongly objects. She claims, for example, that "opera . . . became the vehicle through which cultural hegemony could be conveyed, as its words delivered messages charged with political, ethnic, racial and gender-biased content."[27] Thus, too, the critic sees the female characters as stereotypes: the light skinned, blue-eyed, and lovely Roxane vs. the dark-skinned, uneducated temptress, Carmen (who shares with the operatic character of that name a kind of gypsy eroticism). She adduces Malinche and Pocahontas, enablers of colonial purpose, as this Carmen's prototypes (one wonders at her omitting Sacagawea). "Although at first glance the novel appears sympathetic in portraying the relationships and love interests that develop among its diverse cast of characters, it ultimately reinforces the age-old stereotypes of the good, innocent European/Americans versus the bad, unwashed Primitives, saviors versus sinners, and the triumph of civilization over barbarism."[28]

One quite resists these assertions and the argument they serve. What "triumphs" here is inflexible state power. But it does not completely deny the other, spiritual triumph shared by "unwashed" guerrilla fighter and Euro-American sophisticate alike. The critic interrogates phantom binaries:

> As the novel purports a normative hierarchy within music, privileging Western art, it goes further and glorifies opera as an even higher form of expression. Thus it is not only the musical form that the civilized must appreciate, but they necessarily must learn to understand the language in which it is written, and to *accept* the values and norms it conveys. This is the crux of the civilization and barbarism distinction: the dominant powers devalue, eliminate and replace the pre-existing culture—language, traditions, values, notions of beauty, religion, music, and art—and install one they deem superior. It is an abhorrent practice when carried out militarily, but perhaps even more insidious when conducted in the name of love. It is a tradition that is repeated endlessly in dynamics between wealthier, more powerful societies against their poorer counterparts.[29]

These, alas, are the observations of someone uninformed about this art form, "the American," as Willa Cather says, "proverbially bored by opera."[30] In the first place, one need not "understand the language in which it is written." Many, in fact, experience the language as itself musical, its denotative meanings available, if needed, in synopses (or, nowadays, in supertitles). [31] Thus Mr. Hosokawa's pleasure remains keen despite his inability to master Italian; by the same token, few outside of Antonín Dvořák's homeland understand the language of *Rusalka*, an especially beautiful aria from which Roxane finishes singing just before the novel opens. Those beside themselves with delight on that occasion include the hitherto indifferent or hostile, the guests formerly convinced "that opera was a collection of nonsensical cat screeching, that they would much rather pass three hours in a dentist's chair. These were the ones who wept openly now, the ones who had been so mistaken" (2). Whether or not one knows the language or cavils at absurdities in the plot, opera offers aesthetic transport at once complex and simple— transport achieved through an extraordinary combination of music, drama, dance, spectacle, and the human voice in its full glory. In short, it levels at sublimity, the aesthetic experience that, as Longinus observes, trumps every other form of persuasion, including what Richard Powers once called "logic's arctic crystal."[32]

If Patchett had depicted movies and fast food and rock music corrupting the innocent taste of her less sophisticated Peruvians, or if she had shown conquistadors stealing Inca gold for the treasuries of Spain, one might ac- cept assertions such as those of critics who monitor "hegemonic" erosions of subaltern cultures. But even to mention such things is to be reminded of how absurd it is to deplore classical music as a nefarious means to im- perial ends. Itself a popular form in much of the Old World through the nineteenth century and into the twentieth, opera does not appeal to mod- ern tastes enough to compromise them. Again, one has only to contemplate *real* imperialism, as when enslaved artisans are set to building the fanes and carving the holy figures of an alien religion, to see hyperbole at work. (Nor, for what it is worth, does any of the slave art rise to the aesthetic level of Inca architecture or the codices, friezes, and feather-work of the Aztecs). After any contact between civilizations—whether through peaceful trade or conquest—there is a mutual exchange of art, often the art of the conquered taking on special value (thus the Romans particularly prized that of the an- cient Greeks). This novel's exaltation of opera, then, has little to do with any recognizably imperial ends. No doubt there are people in the third world (as in the first) who embrace "culture" for its cachet—but most poor people (again, in either sphere) seek only economic opportunity (as the Peruvians seek Japanese investment during the height of Asian-tiger economics). The objection here seems to be that the art of one culture is alleged to be su- perior to that of another, but the indictment seems out of proportion to a passing remark about Andean music (best known, incidentally, in perfor- mances of "El Cóndor Pasa," which originates, interestingly enough, in a 1913 *zarzuela*—a popular opera—by Peruvian composer Daniel Alomía Robles).

Some critics, like Wagner's captious Beckmesser, refuse to accept art that does not adhere to the rules. Others, like church censors, insist on doctrinal purity without consideration of the other ways in which an original work of art achieves legitimacy or validity. Those who disparage this novel for its supposed blindness to a colonial agenda and its allegedly unwitting endorse- ment of cultural imperialism fail to see that the author directs her attention to other, more substantive abuses. Patchett's politics are not patriarchal or ethnocentric, nor are they unexamined. They are, however, presented obliquely (to do otherwise would be to risk allowing art to become propaganda). Critics who fail to see the good judgment in Patchett's understatement of political themes would dispense with the indirection so important to the framing of artistic insight.

Patchett's story features, as it happens, more than one challenge to masculine prerogative (especially the machismo widespread in Hispanic culture). The word *diva* means *goddess*, and readers should not miss the divine attributes of Patchett's heroine, who undermines and breaks the authority of those who subscribe, consciously or unconsciously, to patriarchal imperative. Roxane Coss gradually emerges as the wielder of a power—her art—that subverts and transforms the rude male energy of the generals and sustains the spirits of the besieged. Like the goddess celebrated by literary mythographers from Henry Adams and Robert Graves to Mary Renault and Gloria Naylor, she even acquires a noble but doomed consort, Mr. Hosokawa, whose fate bears out that of the archetype: the king must die. Born in October, he is a tragic figure, subject to what Northrop Frye called the Mythos of Autumn. He perishes in March, on the eve of the vernal equinox—a little more than four and a half months, that is, after the October 22nd birthday party (nor does the dating of his death become less significant if, from the perspective of the Southern Hemisphere, it is seen as occurring close to the autumnal equinox). Roxane's marriage to a youthful successor, Gen, may please casual readers, but the more thoughtful may, like Ruben Iglesias, wonder at so hasty a consummation (it resembles that of Gertrude and Claudius, for whom "the funeral bak'd-meats / Did coldly furnish forth the marriage tables"). Other readers will recognize in Gen another solar hero, whose season of fulfillment with the White Goddess in Lucca and Milan must also have its end. This marriage, as noted previously, seems almost a parody of the traditional "happy ending."

The artfully submerged feminism also dictates Patchett's sly mockery of banana republic dictators and their lieutenants. She anchors contumely in the same ancient prophecy invoked by T. S. Eliot toward the end of *The Waste Land*: "Shall I at least set my house in order?"[33] Eliot, one recalls, invites biblical contextualization of that fragment: "Set thine house in order," says the prophet to Hezekiah, "for thou shalt die, and not live" (Isaiah 38:1). Thus is it for benighted Peru, violently pursuing the elusive grail of a just political order—whether through the atrocities of the Shining Path or the counterviolence of the scarcely more respectable Fujimori regime. Fujimori would in fact come to an end worse than that of King Hezekiah (whom God reprieves). But Patchett's fictional vice president, chastened by experience, may be redeemed after all. Like Celie's abusive husband in Alice Walker's *The Color Purple*, he comes to embrace a redemptive domesticity. Initially a kind of junior patriarch, hungry for more political power and eying the toothsome governess, Ruben Iglesias reveals a remarkable aptitude for, of all things, housework. Cleaning, scrubbing and polishing floors, picking up, serving food, presiding over the laundry, he amplifies, as it were, the implied effeminacy of his superior, President Masuda (so devoted to soap opera, that traditional diversion of the homebound distaff, that he cannot preside over his country's desperate bid for foreign investment). Yet Iglesias succeeds, literally and figuratively, in "putting his house in order."

Patchett does, then, demonstrate sensitivity to issues of politics and ideology. Despite her privileging of an art form cherished by the first world, she is hardly oblivious to oppressive politics, whether encountered in national or personal struggles for freedom. But these are secondary to her interest in an idea of great art as a source of apolitical joy. Patchett keeps "correctness" at bay, knowing it as an adulterant of true art.

In that she follows her instincts for the aesthetic sublime, Patchett risks alienating academic criticism, which has forgotten Nabokov's dictum: "mediocrity thrives on 'ideas.' Beware of the modish message."[34] As judge of literary quality, the most important part of the brain is its caudal stem, the spine.[35] The brilliant and charismatic ten year old who narrates Adam Levin's *The Instructions* (2010) iterates this sentiment: "books with lessons are bad books."[36] Thus Patchett, on record as admiring Nabokov, offers up a kind of crescendo of delight in her evocations of music and love. She reflects in this novel, without didacticism, on the aesthetic principle, something rather compromised in the contemporary criticism that describes and assesses it. We ask relentlessly political questions of texts and have almost forgotten the aesthetic criteria proposed by Longinus, Thomas Aquinas, Immanuel Kant, Georg Wilhelm Friedrich Hegel, the Schlegels, Friedrich Nietzsche, and Oscar Wilde. Among the wonders of Patchett's novel is its ability to communicate the supernal beauty and pure ecstasy of the musical art it foregrounds as splendid alternative to violence and brutality.

I have sought to show here that Patchett's attention to what has turned the oppressed into terrorists (the author includes understated glimpses of their backgrounds and the complacency and corruption of the privileged classes) is necessarily of secondary importance. The author reveals as her chief priority the vision of music's power to liberate the heart. It is no small thing that the reader laments the deaths of the accompanist and Mr. Hosokawa no more than those of Cesar, Ishmael, Carmen, Beatriz, General Benjamin, and their comrades. If one imagines being asked to sympathize with the terrorists responsible for Munich in 1972, Lockerbie in 1988, and the manifold enormities of 9/11, one sees the alchemy brought off by Patchett (albeit by dramatizing a terrorist incident fairly remote in time and space, an incident in which little or no innocent blood is shed—unless it be that of the terrorists themselves). Her achievement involves something more than a simple reversal of perspective—as happens when the occasional think tank researcher samples Muslim sentiment around the world regarding this or that terrorist action carried out against the Great Satan. Rather, she seeks emotional, affective synthesis in the music she evokes—and thereby reminds us of what art really is, what it can really do. It deals with the human heart in conflict with itself, as Faulkner famously declared, but it also imagines and constructs the space in which opposing passions can seek resolution.

CHAPTER 9

The Sorrows of Young Icarus
Mark Z. Danielewski's *House of Leaves*

> I think it . . . arguable that our daily life, our psychic experience, our cultural languages, are today dominated by categories of space rather than by categories of time.
>
> —FREDRIC JAMESON, *POSTMODERNISM, OR THE CULTURAL LOGIC OF LATE CAPITALISM*

> Our Coach is a late invention of the Jesuits, being, to speak bluntly, a Conveyance, wherein the inside is quite noticeably larger than the outside, though the fact cannot be appreciated until one is inside.
>
> —THOMAS PYNCHON, *MASON & DIXON*

Literary critics characterize as "encyclopedic" those fictions—by Miguel de Cervantes, François Rabelais, James Joyce, Thomas Pynchon—that seem to contain their whole culture. Like the last named of these authors, Mark Z. Danielewski embraces the encyclopedic in its postmodern guise. In his 2000 novel *House of Leaves*, he aims at the representation of a multiplicity resistant to the undertow of any single perspective. Here the three central figures (Navidson, Zampanò, Johnny Truant), the many voices, the flow of language, the proliferating footnotes, the index (at once absurdly inclusive and frustratingly selective)—all rehearse the Topsy-like growth of information, data, factoid, rumor, and subjunctive possibility that have come to characterize postmodern knowing. More to the point, *House of Leaves* incorporates forms of postmodern knowing peculiar to literature: its author takes as his subject the culture's millennia-thick accumulation of stories that purport to explain the phenomena of human experience, whether in a pre-scientific manner (a god's chariot hauls the sun across the sky every day) or in the modern sense in which myth distills instinctive truth. Modern li-

146

terati founded a "mythic method" on this premise, but postmodern artists, incredulous toward metanarratives, prefer their myths without pretensions to universality, if not frankly factitious. Where "the various avant-gardes," as Lyotard remarks, "humbled and disqualified reality by examining the pictorial techniques which are so many devices to make us believe in it," postmodernists participate in yet larger delegitimizations.[1] Postmodernists of the second or third generation go further than their predecessors, discrediting the mythopoeic impulse by allowing it to operate unchecked. In indiscriminate, self-canceling plenitude, myth enters the limbo of collective opinion or urban legend. Neil Gaiman's *American Gods* (2001), for example, features a host of superannuated deities who have gone to earth in the New World. In *House of Leaves*, published a year earlier, Danielewski contrives with more subtlety to deny myth its cultural cachet. Interrogating mythography, Danielewski further instantiates the "depthlessness" (of history, of consciousness, of language) that Jameson sees as the chief characteristic of postmodernism.[2]

This chapter will unfold in three parts. In the first, I will play the author's language games and consider the ways in which a disorderly bundle of written material might inspire what Derrida calls "archive fever." In the second, I will review Danielewski's refinements of a literary convention, the catalogue, with particular reference to another great compendium of lists, Walt Whitman's *Leaves of Grass*. In the third, I will consider *House of Leaves* as a test case in the dynamics of literary originality (a concept explicitly disavowed by its author). Arguing against critics who have pronounced postmodernism dead, I explore the strategies whereby Danielewski differentiates himself from proximate literary fathers and mothers (the Pynchons, the DeLillos, the Toni Morrisons, the Joan Didions) without repudiating the aesthetic they crafted. *House of Leaves*, I suggest, demonstrates the continuing viability of fiction that decenters the subject, doubts the transparency of language, and treats metanarratives with thoroughgoing skepticism.

Like T. S. Eliot and Federico Fellini (possible source of the name Zampanò), Danielewski seems to know the *Satyricon* of Petronius Arbiter—a work often invoked when identifying Pynchon's *oeuvre* as Menippean satire.[3] Like Petronius and Eliot, Danielewski includes a brief reference to the Cumaean Sibyl, that strangely cursed votary of Apollo, as part of a larger program of allusion. In Eliot or Joyce, however, allusions serve a vision of cultural fragmentation that readers are implicitly invited to correct: as they assemble the fragments, they reassemble an orderly world. In the work of

Danielewski and his peers, such material at once proliferates and becomes less and less susceptible to reassembly or holistic recuperation. It also becomes self-referring: allusion, pastiche, and the Menippean proliferation of mythoi shift toward a kind of hodgepodge encyclopedism of literature itself.

Danielewski's suggestive yet riddling title echoes and subsumes a number of conceits. Coming across allusions to *Beowulf*, "The Seafarer," and *The Battle of Maldon* here, one wonders whether somewhere in Old English literature, alongside "swan road," "sky candle," "weaver of peace," and so on, one might not happen upon Danielewski's titular phrase. Like William Goyen's title *The House of Breath*, Danielewski's sounds like an Anglo-Saxon kenning that somehow never got written down. Kennings, however, are one-dimensional metaphors in which, in the terms devised by I. A. Richards, vehicle ("whale road") and tenor (the sea) are neatly joined, transparent, unambiguous. "House of Leaves" is by contrast a metaphor with no defined tenor—only, like a koan, a great stock of figurative, brain-teasing possibility. Kenning or koan, it invites unpacking. Certainly the novel so titled abounds in foliate figures. Insofar as one can call a tree a "house of leaves," Danielewski's title gestures toward Yggdrasil, the great-rooted blossomer described on the last page of this vast dendritic text—the world ash of Norse mythology, under and within which all living things subsist. Other referents are less grandiose: Johnny Truant, for example, characterizes personal letters as "leaves of feeling."[4] Leaves crown the victorious warrior or athlete (as in the Wallace Stevens line among the "Various Quotes": "There are not leaves enough to crown . . . The actor that will at last declaim our end" [647]). The leaves are *feuilles* in a French prose piece (564) and in a chaotic script produced by Pelafina, Johnny Truant's mad but multilingual mother (633), who elsewhere characterizes her tattered "leaves of memory" as the forage of "some marauding rabbit" (617). An insistent atheist (616, 624), she nonetheless offers a simile of strained spirituality: "as leaves are to limbs, so are your words to your soul" (601). According to a Zampanò poem, finally, "this great blue world of ours / seems a house of leaves" (563).

Like Wallace Stevens's ideal poem, which should "resist the intelligence / Almost successfully," *House of Leaves* risks a perfect opacity.[5] It resists being mastered or intellectually encapsulated. The often literal turning and twisting needed to read (always with the danger that one will lose a prior thread or threads) mimics the this-way, that-way of a labyrinth, especially the Borgesian variety, which figures the vast, interlinking systems of human consciousness and pattern-making—all that strives to define itself against circumambient chaos and meaningless. A labyrinth of a book, *House of Leaves* constantly calls attention to its pathlessness—or, rather, to the superfluity of paths offered to its courageous readers, many of whom realize belatedly that for every triumphant Theseus a hundred must perish in the great Daedalian maze, some starving, some falling prey to the Minotaur of exhaustion, confusion, intellectual intimidation—or boredom. Others, consciously or unconsciously identifying with Will Navidson and his team, forge ahead, damned if they will be daunted or defeated by the maze. Ironically, one thinks Navidson foolhardy for going back into the dark depths, over and over, yet many readers embrace a similar folly, sacrificing their daylight world for the challenges of an obscure and bizarre narrative and the endless "ashen walls" (123, 399) of its fictive "passages." These readers include a few literary critics who, scholiasts themselves, identify as well with Johnny Truant, post-Nabokovian Kinbote, "popomo" Icarus (4).

ARCHIVE AND DEATH INSTINCT

The story concerns an enigmatic manuscript, *House of Leaves*, ostensibly a work of amateur scholarship by a blind octogenarian, "Zampanò," who has undertaken the exhaustive analysis of an imaginary film, *The Navidson Record*, which chronicles the heroic attempts of a famous photojournalist to plumb the mystery of the house he and his family have moved into: its interior dimensions exceed those of its exterior. Measurement with increasingly sophisticated instruments confirms and reconfirms what initially presents itself as merely a quarter-inch anomaly, but presently, off the living room, the inhabitants discover a hall that seems to have no terminus—it leads literally nowhere. Repeatedly explored, it reveals a lightless, terrifying maze of corridors and levels that shrink and expand. When Zampanò dies in strange circumstances (the floor beside his body is scored as if by the claws of some Minotaur conjured in the labyrinth he has imagined), his papers fall into the unready hands of a troubled young man, Johnny Truant. At first indifferent, Johnny becomes obsessed with the manuscript, which he undertakes to edit, to annotate, and to augment—mostly by adding endless, looping footnotes in which he tells his own story of loss, abuse, and despair.

Despite the difference in scale, one notes parallels between *House of Leaves* and Palahniuk's *Choke*. In each novel a troubled individual, attempting to come to terms with fosterage, falls prey to family romance. A traumatic memory of choking figures in both. Both authors invoke Pliny's *Natural History*. A visit to Colonial Williamsburg by Danielewski's Johnny Truant (500–501) will find its sardonic echo in Victor Mancini's workplace, Colonial Dunsboro. Both novels feature an erudite, multilingual mother in a mental institution presided over by a kind of Caligari. Victor Mancini's elaborate Christ complex finds a brief reflection in Johnny Truant's being addressed on one occasion as "darling J" by the mother who styles herself "your only Mary" (611).

Danielewski, like Palahniuk, goes to considerable lengths to undermine reason, logic, order, and other values dear to Enlightenment thinkers. In *House of Leaves*, the natural order of events and their recording undergo baffling reversals. At one point, for example, a struck-through Zampanò note refers to "*The PXXXXXXX Poems*" (138n177). In a note to the note (138n178), Johnny Truant identifies the work as his own Pelican Poems, which appear in appendix II (573–80). Never mind that Zampanò could hardly know the juvenilia of his posthumous editor (all but one of the Pelican Poems were written before Johnny turned eighteen). If such a detail were more prominent, and repeated, one would take it as an intimation that Zampanò and Johnny Truant are in fact the same person. Though I will glance at that possibility presently, I am more comfortable with the idea that it buttresses a small pattern of significant paradoxes, deliberate departures from linear, logical storytelling logistics. The novel ends, to take an obvious instance, with a paradoxical vision of the world tree, which one cannot conceptualize logically: "ten thousand feet high," Yggdrasil "doesn't reach the ground. . . . Its roots must hold the sky" (709). If the great black dot or period above this verse represents the earth (as does the similar figure at the end of the "Ithaca" chapter of Joyce's *Ulysses*), the paradox is compounded: the roots cannot reach what never lay beneath them.[6] The large "O" at the bottom of the page is not, as one might think, the terrestrial orb. The last symbol on the last page, it denotes the infinite nothingness over which existence arches.

Certain of these paradoxical features contribute to the novel's approximations of a digital environment. Though it originates in analog technologies, notably the footage and still photographs from Will Navidson's many cameras, the evidently more shapely film *The Navidson Record*, and the disorderly pile of pages left behind by Zampanò, *House of Leaves* seems to prevent itself as digital simulacrum. The analog features (the novel was actually drafted entirely in pencil) are overlain by innumerable forking paths and abundant narrational simultaneities that replicate hypertext.[7] Thus

House of Leaves feigns a digital identity: the reader interacts with it as with a computer. Subsuming and recycling text, photograph, film, sound, and so on, the novel offers itself as an exercise in the mediation and remediation theorized by Richard Grusin and Jay David Bolter: "Our culture wants both to multiply its media and to erase all traces of mediation," they observe; "it wants to erase its media in the very act of multiplying technologies of mediation."[8] Thus N. Katherine Hayles, who succinctly defines remediation as "the re-presentation of material that has already been represented in another medium," characterizes mediation itself as a kind of food chain, with digital technology at the top, aspiring to the status of an "ultimate medium" that "can incorporate every other medium within itself. As if learning about omnivorous appetite from the computer, *House of Leaves*, in a frenzy of remediation, attempts to eat all the other media."[9] In other words, the novel's faux hypertextual elements ironically "remediate" that which purports to be mediation's digital apotheosis. *House of Leaves* comes full circle, giving the lie to all notions of caudal or conclusive or definitive remediation.

Danielewski's vast chronicle was supposedly encountered—*even by certain of its characters*—on the Internet before its completion (513). In a sop to the empiricists, this detail appears in the fevered fantasia of chapter 21, said to be omitted from a "first edition" that "was privately distributed" (vii)—hence the appearance of "2nd Edition" on the title page and the lining through of the phrase "First Edition" on the copyright page.[10] Mischievously described on the jacket flap as consisting of "a badly bundled heap of paper, parts of which would occasionally surface on the Internet," the putative edition zero may or may not have included any of the material missing from—yet noted in—the printed text (the only one available to real-life readers): the citation for a Dr. Haugeland's research (165n201); parts of words and sentences in the analysis of "Holloway's madness" (323, 327–338), the result of "some kind of ash" having "landed on the . . . pages" (323n276); lengthy portions of the geological report on fragments from the subterranean walls (372–76), as well as part of Zampanò's footnote 349 and "seventeen more pages of text" (376n349, 377); Exhibit Three and its "Zero Folder" (379, 532); Exhibit Four, said to include the Reston Interview and The Last Interview (533); Navidson's "terrifying *Dream #3*" (402); and appendix E, said to include *The Song of Quesada and Molino*, a poem about the Magellan mutineers (xx, 135, 137, 543, 546). One of Danielewski's earliest critics, Will Slocombe, sees such gaps and omissions as part of a larger demonstration that the novel's central construct, the Navidson house, is in a continual process of "unmaking," seeking to evacuate the language in which it has its being or even to "unwrite" itself.[11] But perhaps this feature could be described more simply: the text's many aporiai hint at or adumbrate some kind of progressive degradation, some analog to the house's mysterious despoliation of the explorers' markers and caches. Rereading the novel, one half expects to find it riddled with additional, unremembered lacunae.

Logic goes begging again when Zampanò reports that Will Navidson, embarking on Exploration #5, carries with him reading material eventually revealed to be a 736-page copy of *House of Leaves* (424, 438, 465, 467). The Danielewski volume in one's hands, however, runs to only 709 pages—until one adds the color frontispiece and the twenty-six pages of the introduction and front matter. More curious still, Navidson tries to read the book, after exhausting his supply of matches, by setting fire to each finished page and reading its successor by the dwindling flames. Mark B. N. Hansen, who analyzes this novel's numerous "epistemic logjams" resourcefully, reads this scene as "an inversion of the postmodern topos of the *mise en abyme*: stripped of its epistemologically debilitating impact, this episode of Navidson reading the very text in which he figures as a fictional character functions to foreground the equivalence between the two forms of consumption—reading and material destruction—here thematized."[12] One might also discern in this sequence the representation of what Stanley Fish calls a "self-consuming artifact"—a literary work of art that functions dialectically to confront readers with the inadequacy of their belief systems. Such a work, says Fish, "succeeds at its own expense; for by conveying those who experience it to a point where they are beyond the aid that discursive or rational forms can offer, it becomes the vehicle of its own abandonment."[13] In short, there are more things in heaven and earth than are dreamt of in Navidson's philosophy.

These details compound the challenge to a reader's understanding. Yet one expects a labyrinth, however disorienting, to bear traces of the genius who created it. In a specifically literary labyrinth (one devised by Borges, for example), one expects verbal structures that replicate complexity both artificial—that of a garden, say, no matter the number of its forking paths— and natural, for example, that of the giant, luminous snail shell Navidson explores in a dream (399ff). One also expects the play of wit, even at moments ostensibly uncongenial to humor of any kind. Thus is it with the plight— and fate—of Johnny Truant's mother.

In a letter she tries to have privately delivered, Pelafina advises her correspondent, Johnny, that she will presently communicate by a simple cipher:

the first letter of each successive word will spell out a secret message. In her next letter, interestingly dated May 8, 1987 (Thomas Pynchon's fiftieth birthday), the phrase "rape a fifty-six year old bag of bones" (620) leaps out at the decoder. So far as one knows, her sensational claims of regular sexual violation originate in the same mental extremity that lands her in the Three Attics Whalestoe Institute in the first place (the letters after this one are the most wildly disordered of all). One does not want to make light of such matters, but the coded messages here are erratic, to say the least. "Her" cipher has previously figured in an authorial signature: the spelling out of "Mark Z. Danielewski" via the first letter of the first word of footnotes 27 to 42 (22–37). Also curious: Pelafina (or Someone else) has in an earlier letter encoded a message—"my dear Zampano who did you lose" (615)—that toys with the reader's desire to discern what N. Katherine Hayles calls "ontological priority" among the narrators in this novel.[14]

The acrostic play pays homage to the Nabokov of "The Vane Sisters," in which a ghostly message is spelled out by the first letter in the successive words of the last paragraph. The message is from the deceased Sibyl Vane, whose name recalls the ancient seer who communicated her prophecies in acrostics. When Pelafina, in a last letter to her son, calls herself "this old Sibyl of Cumae" (642), her immediate reference is to the Petronius story that Eliot quotes in the epigraph to *The Waste Land*. (Ironically, according to Tacitus, Petronius himself would die at Cumae.) Pelafina may recall as well the Cumaean Sibyl's directing Aeneas to the golden bough that enables passage to the underworld concurrently dared by Odysseus and presently entered by Navidson (who like his heroic predecessors performs the journey literally), by Zampanò (the blind man who dwells in an underworld of darkness), and by Johnny Truant (who descends into a dark text and a darker self). Petronius's Sybil wastes away until, like Echo, only her voice remains; Pelafina, too, wastes away, leaving only the handful of letters in which her voice rehearses its melancholy echoes. Her son, meanwhile, follows Zampanò—and Navidson—into depths that shelter no sage Tiresias.

When the Whalestoe director notifies Johnny Truant that his mother has hanged herself, her surname appears in two ways: "Pelafina Heather Lièvre" and "Ms. Livre" (643). This carelessness, a familiar technique for signaling the indifference that lies beneath the pro forma condolences of officialdom (one thinks of Colonel Cathcart's form letters to the bereaved in *Catch-22*), teases with the possibility that one of these spellings, accidentally unredacted, might reveal the true surname of "Johnny Truant." The curious wording of the editors' disclaimer seems also to leave an onomastic window open: "though some names here [in Pelafina's letters] were not deleted many were changed" (586). Like a flawed syllogism, the odd phrasing invites rec-ognition of an undistributed middle: some of the names must be undeleted and unchanged (including the name, perhaps, of Pelafina's late husband, Donnie—the Johnny-Donnie rhyme, however, should make the reader skeptical). But like so much else in this text the names given Johnny's moth-er dissolve in ludic lability. Both given name and the two versions of the sur-name hint at paronomasic play. Pelafina suggests *piel fina*, thin-skinned, one who lacks the tough hide (*piel gruesa*) that enables the sane to survive the world's slings and arrows. *Pelo fino* is Spanish for "fine hair," and Johnny has recalled, much earlier in the text, his mother's "amazing hair, like sunlight, extremely fine and whisked with silver" (380). The surname, too, is unstable: it first appears as *Lièvre*, French for "hare," a creature whose erratic behavior generates a familiar phrase for any brevity of the intellectual attention span. One "hares after" this or that ideational will o' the wisp—and who can read *House of Leaves* without thus pursuing one likely interpretative scent after another? She is as mad, in short, as the proverbial March hare.

The director's variant spelling—he repeats the surname as "Livre"—extends this game of names. A *livre* is also a "pound," and one thinks of an-other erudite but unhinged encyclopedist, the poet who also languished for years in a mental hospital, the poet whose "Canto I" depicts, in Odysseus's descent into the underworld, the archetype foregrounded here in Navid-son's explorations. But of course the most obvious meaning of *livre* is "book," and to call Pelafina "Ms. Livre" is to hint that this woman (so complex, her malady so mysterious) is yet another approximation of the *livre*—the book—entitled *House of Leaves*, which is, after all, a house of *livres*. Like the discourse of the madwoman in the institution's eponymous three attics, this *livre* is at once crazed and preternaturally learned, playful and serious. All of its important figures (Navidson, Zampanò, Johnny Truant, Pelafina) are brilliant obsessives; the author signals at every turn that his is a tale told by one or more lunatics.

The book's reflexive play on the question "what is a book?" concludes with a reference (in the "Various Quotes" that follow the Pelafina correspon-dence) to Proust's conceit of a *"livre"* as "a vast cemetery where for the most part one can no longer read the faded names on the tombstones" (646n437). The quotation comes from *Le temps retrouvé* (1184) and seems the very prolepsis of later ideas—also French—about intertextuality and authorial death. Roland Barthes, one recalls, saw in literary expression a kind of sustained echo (if not a tomb) of prior discourse—that of no longer remembered speakers and writers, often as not. Proust's *mot* invites reflection, again, on the many literary, cultural, and philosophical antecedents of Danielewski's imaginative flights—those announced (Dante, Ovid, the Anglo-Saxon poets, and so on) and those deeper in the diegetic strata that *House of Leaves* comprises. Among the Gothic echoes in this particular textual *cimetière*, this resting place for the imagined, the literal, and the literary dead, one discerns the recurrence to catabasis, the descent into the underworld, that standard—indeed, primal—feature of mythographic letters. Heroes from Hercules to Odysseus and from Beowulf to Leopold Bloom perform this archetypal descent into the nether regions in search of some interview, some boon or triumph, which they must carry back out of the depths. These antecedents confer resonance, if not totalized meaning, on the subterranean explorations of Will Navidson, not to mention the descents into darkness— literal or figurative blindness—of Zampanò and Johnny Truant. That surname, which derives from the Welsh *truan* or Gaelic *truaghan* ("wretch" or "wretched"), suggests an affinity, once more, with the Man of Sorrows, whose harrowing of hell (another example of catabasis) he replicates in his own fashion.

When Pound rewrote the Homeric *Nekuia* or Book of the Dead as "Canto I," he was under the impression that, as the oldest part of our oldest book, it was older, even, than Homer himself.[15] That is, he strove to get back to a cultural genesis, back to literary seed corn. He involved himself in that *arkhē* around which Derrida circles in his 1995 study *Archive Fever: A Freudian Impression*. An archive always poses the same question, says Derrida: "What comes first?"[16] The question occupies Danielewski as well: his Johnny Truant, reluctant scholiast, inherits an archive in the form of "reams and reams" of pages left by Zampanò (xvii). Navidson's house is an archive within this archive, at least in the broad sense that Derrida perpends, and Danielewski's novel, like Zampanò's study of *The Navidson Record*, may be said to archive humanity's investigations, whether realized in heroic exploits or in literary and cinematic works of the imagination.

As its subtitle makes clear, *Archive Fever* is a Freudian meditation on (and, yes, deconstruction of) the dream of comprehensive depositories for the information that serves (or will serve) a variety of historiographical ends. Derrida explains that his term *mal d'archive* or "archive fever" derives from or plays with the French idiom "*en mal de,*" meaning not only "to suf-

ce of Zampanò, the ostensibly tormented fabulist whom Johnny Truant never actually meets. For Johnny, his reluctant literary executor, Zampanò exists *only* as text. Zampanò's work would not, in its original form, include the annotations of Johnny Truant. Or would it? To raise this issue is to be beset by questions of textual integrity and anteriority: is the whole the product of two separate hands—or one hand in two complementary guises? Does "graphomaniac" (xxii) Zampanò invent his own annotator? Does he, like Carlo Collodi's artisan Geppetto, craft a puppet who turns into a "real boy"? ("Perhaps in the margins of darkness, I could create a son" [543]). Or does Johnny Truant annotate a text that he has authored himself under a false flag? Does a third party (not necessarily Danielewski) conjure Zampanò, Johnny Truant, and their complementary texts? Like certain Nabokov characters who glimpse their own fictional status, Johnny Truant airs at one point "the most terrible suspicion of all, that all of this has just been made up and what's worse, not made up by me or even for that matter Zampanò" (326). The question of authorial identity and responsibility must sooner or later force a reader, especially an academic seeking to analyze or interpret, to reflect on the extent to which she or he becomes yet another collaborator. Indeed, the very definition of a *scriptible* or ergodic text, whose meaning depends on the minds that engage it, presumes such collaboration. Thus does one understand the observation that "Prometheus ... must have been a book" (546)—a book bringing fire, the spark of enlightenment and illumination, a book that "creates" the very readers with whom it shares light.

Some books, however, share darkness, and as the original Prometheus created in human beings a race afflicted by mortality and its attendant ills, so do certain Promethean fictions dwell on the more tenebrous aspects of life and history. Devoted to needful corrections to the sunny optimism of Pangloss and his Enlightenment brethren, such books historically constellate the literary Gothic, and *House of Leaves* takes an honored place beside such classics of the late eighteenth and early nineteenth centuries as Horace Walpole's *Castle of Otranto*, Matthew Lewis's *The Monk*, and Mary Shelley's *Frankenstein; or, The Modern Prometheus*. The last, indeed, offers itself to the neurasthenic Johnny Truant as an analogue to his obsessive labors as editor: he describes Zampanò's "papers" as a "body, spread out across the table," and he imagines himself the Frankenstein "necessary to animate it all." Unless, that is, "Zampanò's work . . . has created me" (326).

Haunted by Zampanò's manuscript, his rest destroyed, Johnny Truant reads and edits as if in a mirror: his anguish, his sleeplessness, his flirtations with some final breakdown—all find reflection in the horror-world that Zampanò creates, a world that more or less naturally accommodates, as rambling annotation, the personal story told by its troubled editor. Thus Truant's scholia do little, really, to clarify or enhance Zampanò's analysis of *The Navidson Record*; rather, they become the vehicle of a parallel story of personal anguish that distorts an already phantasmagorical narrative. Johnny's vast disquiet stems, then, only partly from the real-seeming horror of the story Zampanò tells. Distressed at the dredging up of the manifold miseries of his own past, Johnny reflects, at one point, on the unredemptive death by water of a friend swept overboard in Alaska's Kachemak Bay. When he likens the "freezing meadows" of the sea to "a million blue pages" (608), he comments prophetically on the icy ocean of the pages that will one day murder sleep. As Kafka says, "a book should be the axe for the frozen sea within us," and Johnny learns that the resultant abreaction, the unfreezing of that sea, will not come about painlessly.[18]

One recognizes in the passing of Zampanò, Danielewski's Ur-scribbler, a suggestive "death of the author." An interrogation of originality as a feature of literary art, *House of Leaves* mocks the critic's desire to "claim first source" (to echo a phrase of Zora Neale Hurston's regarding Shakespeare as *fons et origo* of the ideas he gave life to on the stage), to get at some kind of imaginative genesis, whether an Ur-document or the primal artist who can claim to be "sole owner and proprietor" of this or that imaginative Yoknapatawpha.[19] Zampanò and Johnny Truant are strange mirror-images of each other, but which, if either, might be the eidolon remains a scholarly riddle. When Mc-Caffery and Gregory asked him to comment on this enigmatic feature, the author turned coy:

> The real issue we're circling around has to do with the question of wheth-er or not the novel can be seen as having a single dominant voice creating all the others, and if so, identifying that voice. In short: who really is the originator of this book? ... But I'm not going to answer because for me to move further and further into the narrative details would require me to begin to deprive readers of the private joys of making such a discovery on their own.[20]

The implied encouragement to keep digging is, one suspects, the author's joke. Although the previously noted discovery of Pelafina's coded naming of Zampanò (615) is momentarily exhilarating, it hardly resolves the conun-drum of nested narrators. "Such a discovery" may generate more frustration than "private joy"—those attempting to demonstrate the "ontological priori-ty" of Zampanò, Johnny Truant, or Pelafina (or, more ambitiously, to resolve what Nick Lord calls the "metaleptic collision of ontologies" in the novel) will manage only to tie their hermeneutical shoelaces together.[21]

The symbiotic relationship of Zampanò and Johnny Truant seems to replicate that of Shade and Kinbote in Nabokov's *Pale Fire*. Although Dan-ielewski had not read that fiction at the time he composed *House of Leaves*, he admits to an awareness of Nabokovian precedent.[22] Certainly both novels feature an elaborate scholarly apparatus that mocks the "academic onanism" (467) of critics striving to interpret a complex piece of literary artifice. Both feature an accomplished work of literature, its author, and an annotator or editor given to self-indulgent digression.[23] The works diverge, on the other hand, in their tone: one is comedic, the other Gothic. A reader laughs at the completely nutty Kinbote but not at the genuinely tormented Johnny Truant.

With regard to the question of twinned narrators, however, one gets readings that reveal in this mine other, finer veins of Nabokovian ore. Who can read such an annotational extravaganza without thinking of the Nabo-kov who leads his reader a merry chase—a "cryptographic paper chase," to be precise, in *Lolita*? In the realm of real-world scholarship, one thinks, too, of *The Annotated* Lolita (prepared by Nabokov's onetime student Alfred Ap-pel). A Nabokovian Doppelgänger conceit may lurk, then, in the complementarity of Zampanò and Johnny Truant. Like Humbert Humbert and Clare Quilty, they share an obsession. Their voices echo each other, even as they seem most strikingly different. Casually appropriating conceits from the Navidson narrative, Johnny even refers to "my own dark hallway" (516) and to "those five and a half minutes" (517) in which, at age seven, he is pried from the loving yet filicidal arms of his mother (she has burned his arms and now attempts to choke him).

But rather than grapple with the enigma of a "single dominant voice," one may find that accepting what seems to be the case does not violate the metafictional spirit of the text before us. One does so "under erasure"—a concept that operates, as will be seen, in more than one way in Danielewski's pages. Mindful, then, of the ultimately irresolvable argument for the primacy of any single voice here, I submit that a provisional acceptance of what purports to be the case—that Zampanò is a writer who, having labored in obscurity, leaves behind a work of genius and that Johnny Truant is his perturbed literary executor—will sustain analysis more readily than endlessly circling the question of whether Zampanò or Johnny, Shade or Kinbote, is "real." In fact, Johnny Truant offers an instructive insight on a parallel problem: "it makes no difference that the documentary at the heart of the book is fiction. Zampanò knew from the get go that what's real or isn't real doesn't matter here" (xx). As those who read a lot of postmodernist fiction know, such questions are epistemological: they represent the dead ends one must expect in a labyrinth. They serve only the dubious project of attempting to force metafictional pegs into mimetic holes, and Danielewski, like Nabokov, takes little interest in mimesis per se. The artifice of a book by either is self-referring, ontological. Whether "orbicle of jasp" (as John Shade would say) or the dark, terrifying labyrinth devised by Zampanò, such a book is a world unto itself, the house of its own telling.

PERMUTATIONS OF THE CATALOGUE: DANIELEWSKI AND WHITMAN

Before undertaking a more detailed discussion of Danielewski's place on the postmodern (or post-postmodern) spectrum, I should like to compare *House of Leaves* with an earlier work noted for its catalogues and the encyclopedic ambitions of its author. By such a retrospect, I mean to show that the genius of another century poses less of a challenge to today's writer than her or his more proximate predecessors. Whatever a writer's relationship to the literary parent or parents—resentful, jealous, intimidated, falsely adulatory—the grandparents and other ancestors can assume their place in a temporally distant pantheon of greatness one need not directly challenge. Thus can Danielewski, nervous about his relation to older postmodernists, treat as tutelary spirits his great Gothic predecessors, from Matthew Lewis to Mary Shelley and from Charles Brockden Brown to Edgar Allan Poe. Another such honored ancestor, Walt Whitman, might be said to offer the postmodern encyclopedist valuable lessons in listing. A comparison of these two writers may be helpful in my larger project of reading the work of a young postmodernist against that of his immediate predecessors—for Whitman had also to come to terms with artistic belatedness: in a career bisected by the illusion-dispelling carnage of the Civil War, he had to negotiate a relationship with poets and thinkers whose transcendental philosophy was as it were artistically fresh and untrammeled by the intrusion of post-Romantic reality.

Given the encyclopedic scope and expansive form of Danielewski's novel (like the Navidson house, it features penetralia that seem perpetually to metastasize), the reader must think, sooner or later, of a certain well-known Whitman title, itself mysterious and resonant. How ironic, then, that *House of Leaves* contains no explicit reference to *Leaves of Grass*, the book of poems worked over, arranged, and rearranged over Whitman's lifetime. One thinks of the ten years in which Danielewski labored over *House of Leaves* as, under the postmodern dispensation, a comparable stretch. Both titles invite reflection. Whitman, observes F. O. Matthiessen, exploits the affinity between the "leaves" of a book and those of the grass, at once "the smallest . . . sign of nature's fertility" and the "most universal."[24] Early and late in the sequence, the poet recurs to this humble emblem. Whitman intimates that the phenomenal world, figured in blades of grass, is itself a great volume to be read (an idea traceable back to Ralph Waldo Emerson and to the Puritan belief in nature as the book of God—an "encyclopedic" fiction indeed). Whitman's title translates simply as "the Book (leaves) of Nature (grass)," but Danielewski manages a yet more Delphic suggestiveness. As he appropriates the leaves-as-pages conceit, the novelist allows it to hint at a number of additional referents. He also, paradoxically, straitens it: the title of his Promethean book is, as he writes, *Book*. (As such, it calls to mind a conceit elaborated by Nabokov's novelist hero in a mirror, Sebastian Knight, who contrives a story literally coterminous with the dying man who is its central character: "The man is the book; the book itself is heaving and dying, and drawing up a ghostly knee.")[25] But *House of Leaves* remains a book of nature—though no longer one to read with the piety of a Puritan or even the Emersonian latitudinarianism. In Danielewski's novel, the reader contemplates, among other things, the raveling of Whitman's late-romantic metaphysics. The divine book of nature reverts to the Shakespearean tale told by an idiot.

Thus the affinities of Whitman and Danielewski go beyond their titles. Poet and novelist are both energetic encyclopedists, world-class cataloguers. Both Whitman's poem and Danielewski's novel chronicle the mental ingestion and transformation of a world—its things, its people, its ideas. Not only does Whitman take in everything in his environment, he synthesizes and becomes that environment in an act of pantheistic identification. Though most memorably a catalogue of the poet's America, a holding of the mirror up to all the strengths and weaknesses, beauty and vulgarity, of the nation in its rude, nineteenth-century vigor, the poem features, withal, abundant cosmic referents. *House of Leaves* offers the same geminate vision—now sending its unhappy scholiast back and forth across the American continent like a later Kerouac, now entangling characters and readers alike in depths of metaphysical and cosmic speculation.

But neither crowded canvas is more impressive than the artist who paints it. Like Whitman, Danielewski can say, "I am large, I contain multitudes."[26] The poet, a great egoist, refers to himself on every page; the novelist waxes "self-referential" in another, more current sense. The inclusiveness and breadth of Whitman's poem make it especially powerful, but these features—they subsume the full American spectrum—are contained, incredibly, within one person's rich mind and experience. As an account of Walt Whitman himself, "a Person . . . freely, fully and truly on record," it is an extraordinary exercise in self-study and self-revelation. Whitman makes a virtue of inconsistency and famously admits to self-contradiction, but his is a unified personality, an identity equal to the variety it beholds and celebrates. Danielewski, by contrast, remains veiled, his voice unlikely to be that of either Zampanò or Johnny Truant. A Whitmanesque Poe, as it were, he catalogues sublime terrors, a plenum of Gothic affect. Both writers aim at and achieve a meaningful repletion.

The centerpiece of *Leaves of Grass* is the 52-poem sequence entitled "Song of Myself," a wonderfully generous, liberal, and positive series of lyrics in which the author ranges over and integrates an immense body of material. The reader experiences a bardic voice, a powerful personality, announcing in various ways its transcendental union with a continent and its people, with nature and cosmos. Among the first lists in this great catalogue of phenomena is an enumeration of answers to a central question:

A child said *What is the grass?* fetching it to me with full hands. . . .

The poet runs through several conceits, from the fanciful to the sublime: he likens grass to the handkerchief dropped by a deity who sounds like a flirtatious camerado, yet it "seems," too, "the beautiful uncut hair of graves." In the closing poems, he recurs to that conflation of grass and grave; as a final variation on the figure announced in the title, the poet declares a truth to be realized on the morrow of his life: he will presently revive as the grass about which the child asked:

I bequeath myself to the dirt, to grow from the grass I love;
If you want me again, look for me under your boot-soles.

Thus does he reaffirm his sense of divinity in all things, his sense that God suspires in every object and every face. It is a pantheistic revision of the scriptural precept that "all flesh *is* as grass, and all the glory of man as the flower of grass. The grass withereth, and the flower thereof falleth away: But the word of the Lord endureth for ever (1 Peter 24–25, itself a reframing of verses from Isaiah).

Wordsworth's *The Prelude,* another vast work of many years' accretion, bears the subtitle *Growth of a Poet's Mind,* and this formulation seems as well to characterize the *opera magna* of Whitman and Danielewski. But perhaps one ought to speak here of the growth of a *subject*—for Danielewski's, like Whitman's, keeps proliferating and extending. Although both bring immense energy to their catalogues, Danielewski seems the more manic, punctuating his text with lists that spread like verbal kudzu. In this extravagance, he seems at once to subvert an ancient convention and to make it new. Traditionally, the catalogue—the list of Gatsby's guests one summer, for example—represents plenitude, though in fact it may only feign or gesture toward exhaustiveness. Readers are charmed by Homer's list of ships; lists of trees in Chaucer and Spenser; lists of funereal flowers in the great pastoral elegies of Milton, Keats, and Matthew Arnold; even the multipage list, in two languages, of synonyms for "hooker" in Barth's *The Sot-Weed Factor.* Danielewski treats this conceit with deconstructive verve. All relegated to multipage footnotes and mostly featured in chapter IX ("The Labyrinth"), his lists overwhelm the reader with their staggering inclusiveness. One encounters a list of "literary hauntings" (131–135n167) compiled by "Candida Hayashi" (a fictional but botanically witty name), a long, undifferentiated catalogue of photographers (64–67n75), and another of documentary filmmakers (139–141n182), seeming complete except for Kirby Dick and Amy Ziering, whose 2002 film on Derrida Danielewski would work on shortly after publication of *House of Leaves*. Also missing from the list is the author's father, Tad Danielewski (IMDB.com lists him as a director with four titles to his credit). The documentary filmmakers include many that one could swear made only feature films. Investigation, however, is facilitated by the footnote that, appended to the list, lists in turn the titles of the directors' documentaries (140–144n183). The only problem is that this note on a note is printed backwards, so that to read it one must hold it up to a mirror.

For the most part placed into the abyss of footnotes, the endless lists rehearse and reduce to the absurd this novel's larger cataloguing project. The lists feature just enough interest to detain the really dogged reader or critic, who finds, for example, that the index entry for "Raymond" includes not only references to Johnny's abusive stepfather but also a couple of names in the catalogue of photographers (65, 67). More ingeniously, the author includes a list of building and construction features (119–142n144) that tunnels through the text in a box, each succeeding page the reverse image of its predecessor. When Zampanò characterizes the "layout" of the Navidson house as "in no way reminiscent of any modern floorplans let alone historical experiments in design" (120), he adds a footnote that, paused over, proves to be a one-sentence, fourteen-page catalogue of notable examples of architecture from his end-of-millennium present back through the centuries to prehistoric times (120–134n146). This note is itself footnoted with the names of the architects responsible for the edifices previously listed—all the way back to Daedalus. *This* note, however, is printed upside down and runs fourteen pages *backward* (135–121). Each of these formal catalogues is a *mise en abyme* of the larger catalogue that strives to exhaust the meaning of the house occupied by the Navidsons.

A much more concise catalogue presents itself to Johnny Truant when his friend Lude summons him to the scene of Zampanò's death. In his introduction to the sprawling, many-layered work he edits and augments, Johnny briefly glimpses a unifying principle: he senses it in the olfactory character of Zampanò's room, freighted with "the scent of human history—a composite of sweat, urine, shit, blood, flesh and semen, as well as joy, sorrow, jealousy, rage, vengeance, fear, love, hope and a whole lot more" (xvi). Brief but complete, the catalogue subsumes every human substance, every human emotion. It will be fleshed, as it were, in a narrative that seems to incorporate all the mythoi of human storytelling.

Which does not make it any easier to understand. The book's depiction of vast, mysterious depths and what they might figure intimates one configuration of its subject: the ways in which we grapple with the unknown or, perhaps more accurately, the ways in which we conceptualize, read, construct, and represent the unknown. An island of life that subsists over seemingly infinite lifelessness, the strange dwelling on Ash Tree Lane seems to invite allegorical interpretation. Certain of its investigators see the Navidson house as, first and foremost, a grave. (Though he does not mention the gravedigger in *Hamlet*, Danielewski recurs to the old riddle about the artisan who builds for eternity [260, 319].) Others (rightly, no doubt) reject the idea of a master trope. "[L]ike Melville's behemoth," observes Zampanò, "the house . . . remains resistant to summation" (3). Danielewski imagines the real-life illusionist David Copperfield reflecting on *The Navidson Record* as "a trick that constantly convinces you it's not a trick. A levitation without wires. A hall of mirrors without mirrors" (364). A fictitious British playwright, Byron Baleworth, declares "You've created a semiotic dilemma. Just as a nasty virus resists the body's immune system so your symbol—the house—resists interpretation" (356). As the house resists being known or parsed, so does the book in which it figures. As Navidson and company discover the uselessness of compass and altimeter (90, 94), so do readers and critics find—to reverse Auden's line—that all of their instruments disagree. The house and its story are many things—none, in the end, definitive. Although Harold Bloom, conjured for the occasion, declares the house "pointedly against symbol," he delivers some fairly trenchant symbolic interpretations: "A bit like Dante's house after a bit of spring cleaning. It's a. . . . lifeless objectless soulless place. Godless too. Milton's abyss pre-god or in a Nietzschean universe post-god" (359). *Pace* Bloom, in fact, the novel relentlessly inventories the symbolic meanings of the Navidson house until, like Hegel's sphinx, it becomes a symbol of symbolism.[27]

Thus one incurs no ridicule to see in the house a figure of life itself, that "brief crack of light," as Nabokov says, "between two eternities of darkness."[28] Hovering abandoned in gelid, indifferent space, it also resembles planet Earth. What lies beneath this house or beyond this Earth, what brackets consciousness, is a terrible nothingness that human beings keep trying to plumb or explore or map—only to discover the disturbing isolation of sentience, the fate of the islanded cardplayer-self who holds, as it were, anything but a winning hand. "Yeah well, sometimes," as the Paul Newman character observes, "nothing can be a real cool hand" (656), and in fact Danielewski deals cards at least as legitimate as those of Eliot's Madame Sosostris. Among other things, Danielewski brilliantly renders what early theorizers of the postmodern (Ihab Hassan, Fredric Jameson) understood to be the radical superficiality, under the postmodern dispensation, of history, consciousness, language itself. Only surface—the Navidson house—subsists. Beneath it, where one once might have imagined fabled depths, a whole underworld to which heroes might descend to prove themselves, nothingness yawns, an endless, mocking, ferocious vacuity.

"INFLUENCE" AND ITS DISCONTENTS

Literary artists from Ovid to Apollodorus, from Shelley to Auden, and from Joyce to Borges have seen in the story of Daedalus and the Cretan labyrinth a parable of their calling. The great Daedalus devises a labyrinth to hide the Minotaur, the monstrous son whose very existence shames King Minos. Presently imprisoned there with his own son, Icarus, Daedalus devises wings in a yet greater demonstration of cunning artifice, and the two escape. When Icarus disregards his father's cautions about flying too close to the sun, the wax in his wings melts, and he plummets to his death, the victim, supposedly, of his own pride, narcissism, and presumption. But flying is from antiquity the figure for artistic performance (as in Keats's "viewless wings of poesy"), and the failure to manage his wings successfully suggests an additional symbolic dimension to the story of Icarus, who falls because he is an inferior artist, content to dare the heavens with equipment he himself did not design. The parable, that is, comes with a dark corollary: a judgment on any son who confuses his abilities with those of the father. The filial state, according to the tendentious logic here, carries inferiority with it, and so Icarus, taking wing, manages only to literalize what Alexander Pope, in *Peri Bathous*, called "the art of sinking."

The travail of Danielewski's Johnny Truant resembles that of Stephen Dedalus, whose creator saw in the fate of Icarus no discontinuity, no change of subject, in the ancient allegory of artifice and artificers. In condemning his

autobiographical alter ego to an Icarian fall (remembered in *Ulysses*), Joyce
sought to inoculate himself against a similar fate.[29] Indeed, the presentation
of a flawed version of the authorial self—Lawrence's Paul Morel, Eliot's Pru-
frock, Pound's Mauberley, perhaps the Great War protagonists of Cather,
Hemingway, and Dos Passos—seems to be a kind of generational signature
among the modernists. Whether or not he is a negative projection of his
creator, Danielewski's Johnny Truant experiences his own portentous Icarian "dream where I was soaring far above the clouds, bathed in light, flying
higher and higher, until finally I fell." (514). Like Stephen Dedalus, he finds
himself enmeshed in an elaborate family romance involving the belated discovery of a father somehow truer than the ones known in childhood. Like
Stephen, too, Johnny mourns a mother who is, as Joyce's Buck Mulligan
says, "*beastly dead*."[30] Joyce's young Telemachus unites at last with the humane Leopold Bloom, but to whom can Johnny Truant turn after the deaths
of his biological father, Donnie (a passionate airman, he is, ironically, a true
Daedalian figure), and the appalling foster parent, "Marine Man Raymond"
(593, 595, 596, 604)? The father he presently recognizes, Zampanò, is the
cunning artificer who has devised a great labyrinth, *House of Leaves*, which
he bequeaths to an Icarus he has never known, an Icarus whose indepen-
dent flight remains decidedly problematic, fraught with the possibility of
failure. Seeking to understand the inherited manuscript, this Icarus seems
to mistake his role for that of Theseus. If so, one must consider first whether
Danielewski's young hero, stumbling upon—and into—a vast and terrible
maze, undertakes to slay a Minotaur—or a literary father.

As will be seen, the mythology here sounds less than coherent for a reason.

Sharing a name with the "strong man" of Fellini's 1954 film *La Strada*,
Zampanò is not only an artistic father, he is a version of the "strong poet" that
Harold Bloom—who appears here in cameo—describes in his 1973 study
The Anxiety of Influence. The novel includes references—threads in the great
tapestry—to a couple of the terms Bloom proposes to characterize the ways
in which unfledged literati ("ephebes") struggle against influence: *kenosis*, or
"movement towards discontinuity with the precursor," and *clinamen*, or the
"swerve" away from the direction taken by the literary parent, seem both to
come into play as one attempts to conceptualize Johnny Truant's relationship with Zampanò.[31] Bloom quotes himself on the first in the transcript
of Karen Green's *What Some Have Thought* (359), and Zampanò refers to
the second—and quotes Bloom—in a partly struck through journal entry
(547) that becomes one of "his" footnotes (137n171), its crossed-out phrases

restored by Johnny Truant. The explicit references to Bloom prompt one to suspect the presence of at least two more of the strategies whereby, according to his typology, literary neophytes wrest distinction from their elders. Surely one sees a mighty instance of *tessera*, in which the younger poet seems to complete the work of the predecessor, and *apophrades*, in which the later writer seems, like Borges's Pierre Menard, to have written the work of the precursor. *Kenosis, clinamen, tessera, apophrades*—at one time or another, Johnny Truant tries them all. So does Danielewski.

Bloom's thesis lends itself to succinct expression: "*Poetic influence—when it involves two strong, authentic poets,—always proceeds by a misreading of the prior poet, an act of creative correction that is actually and necessarily a misinterpretation.*"[32] What is staged in *House of Leaves*, I suggest, is the subversion of one such "strong poet's" work by a jealous successor. Ostensibly an apprentice tattoo artist (he evidently lacks talent), Johnny is really a budding storyteller, as his friend Lude understands: Johnny's stories break the ice with the women they meet in bars. Pelafina rhapsodizes on Johnny's Orphic "tale-telling [that] stilled wind and bird" (605). The Pelican Poems also testify to literary aspirations that anticipate the life-changing encounter with Zampanò's manuscript. Though he alternates between deference to and pity for the author of the work he edits, Johnny Truant becomes a better, more promising apprentice to this master. As the ephebe in this relationship, however, Johnny is troubled by the literary anteriority of the powerful and tragic original. (Spelled without the accent mark, "Zampano" is German slang for a braggart or four flusher—another appropriate appellation for the literary master an aspirant writer might resent.[33]) The task of this literary second-comer is to bring order to and thereby complete Zampanò's inchoate masterpiece, but Johnny Truant undertakes something closer to wholesale appropriation. A Buck Mulligan-like usurper of another's artistic redoubt, the demotic-voiced Johnny seems to arrogate to himself a distinction denied Zampanò—at least if the dead father can be pigeonholed as yesterday's writer, a mere modernist, shoring literary ruins. If successful with his daring and unconventional paratextual apparatus, Johnny could be recognized as the truly innovative literary performer, a real postmodernist. But in fact Zampanò is not, like the character in Fellini's *La Strada*, a mere street performer; nor is he some modernist dinosaur like the Eliot Johnny echoes or burlesques at various points. ("I can't connect any of it," he wails [498], "that['s] not it at all" [516], "This is the way the world ends / Not with a bang but an alarm clock" [575].) As one sees in miniature in the note citing a study by "Clarence Sweeney," published by "Apeneck Press" (350), Zampanò, too, parodies the modernist enterprise—notably Eliot's appending of notes to his own labyrinthine work of the imagination, *The Waste Land*. It is Zampanò, in fact, who interrogates and subverts the mythic method, he that depicts, in the story's central conceit (a house perched over endless corridors of nothing), a rhizomatic superficiality. The very disorder of his literary leavings reveals him as the already postmodern predecessor, the artistic first-comer whose achievement at once breaks with tradition and threatens to preclude or forestall fresh creation.

As should be obvious, Johnny's position vis-à-vis Zampanò is also Danielewski's vis-à-vis the older generation of postmodern innovators. As Josh Toth observes, "the work of a still emergent generation of American writers . . . often appears, at least superficially, indistinguishable from the mass of high postmodernism it follows." But one resists Toth's argument that *House of Leaves* "marks a clear move away from the no longer efficacious (or relevant) narrative gestures of postmodernism."[34] Rather, the challenge to Danielewski's generation is to see that the postmodern diadem lacks, still, its full complement of gems.

One must bear in mind, in discussing "postmodern generations," that younger writers, however comfortable with the epistemic conditions within which they strive to create, must still negotiate a relationship with the daunting fathers and mothers who, dismantling modernism, met the challenge of their own day and enjoyed the cachet of artistic pioneers. Bloom would say that in Zampanò's death Danielewski disguises a kind of wish-fulfillment, a complex gesture of homage to and resentment of the real-life Zampanòs whose cerebral, encyclopedic fictions ushered in post-Joycean literary aesthetics. Even as they enjoy *House of Leaves*, in fact, readers familiar with post–World War II literature see that none of its powerful conceits is new. The DeLillo of *Libra* imagines a disorderly archive that somehow structures the story he has to tell. Morrison's flying African (in *Song of Solomon*) unhitches the Icarus myth from its putative Joycean universality. Updike and Pynchon conceive of fictions (*Rabbit, Run, Gravity's Rainbow*) that are really movies (one notes again that a film, *The Navidson Record*, furnishes the conceptual centerpiece of Danielewski's novel). Pynchon also beats Danielewski to the idea of an interior greater than its exterior: the author of *Mason & Dixon* (1997) imagines a disquieting vehicle: "Our Coach is a late invention of the Jesuits, being, to speak bluntly, a Conveyance, wherein the inside is quite noticeably larger than the outside, though the fact cannot be appreciated until one is inside."[35] This volumetric uncanny figures in *Inherent Vice* (2009) as well: "The place was turning out to be bigger inside than out," declares the narrator. "Inside was ... more space, judging from the outside, than there could possibly be in here."[36]

To inoculate himself against accusations of authorial anxiety, then, the author of *House of Leaves* stages a cleverly disguised instance of it, Bloom's influence model becoming less persuasive when anticipated and mocked. In presenting his reader with a dead author and his curiously motivated successor/annotator/literary executor, that is, Danielewski at once feigns and wards off the anxiety supposedly inevitable for artists coming to terms with the greatness of their predecessors. Here, too, ironically, Danielewski is a second- or even third-comer, for he replicates the very tactic deployed when Joyce, competing with Homer (and Ovid), stages something like his own Icarian failure. Thus, too, does Nabokov, in *Pnin*, rewrite Joyce's rewriting of the *Odyssey*. These antecedents compound the challenge to a writer such as Danielewski: how to tell stories under a postmodern dispensation that might seem to require no additional artistic modeling?

One can shed more light on this challenge by comparing myths of aesthetic genesis in *House of Leaves* with similar material in the work of Danielewski's contemporaries. All of these latter-day postmodernists seem to take a special interest in the aesthetic impulse at degree zero. Thus Richard Powers grapples with the strange tendency of stories to sanitize calamity over time—to turn the disappearance of a generation of children, for example, into a fairy tale that requires considerable probing if the vast horror that it papers over is to be discerned. Chuck Palahniuk, in *Choke*, takes his readers back to Butades, the primal potter of Pliny's parable. Steve Erickson, one recalls, disguises himself as Etcher, "history's file clerk," to imagine an intervention in the archive of national memory and myth.

To some degree, this feature (Foucault would call it "archaeological," Derrida "archontic") recapitulates what earlier poets, from Ovid to Eliot, do with the Philomela myth, which allegorizes the origin of art in suffering (I have previously considered its relevance to the Palahniuk novel). In *House of Leaves*, however, Philomela gives way to Perilaus, whose horrific legend cloaks an even darker parable of primal art. Perilaus designed for the tyrant Phalaris a hollow, life-sized, brazen bull, an especially nasty instrument of torture under which a fire would roast whatever hapless victim or victims had been shut up inside. Tubes within the bull converted the screams of the condemned into "music" congenial to a despot's ears—into art, that is, unmediated by retrospect, not recollected in tranquility before some loom or canvas or page. How disturbing the reflection that aesthetic beauty, distilled from suffering, must perforce link the tastes of art lovers with those of a tyrant. However grim, the myth of Perilaus affirms that pain underlies all art (even, perhaps especially, in those versions of the story in which Phalaris consigns Perilaus himself to the bull [337n301]). Thus does Johnny Truant imagine "pipes" in the head of Zampanò and in his own, from which emerge their tormented voices, heard by readers as literary art (337, 338).

Yet Zampanò has crossed out his references to this material. The postmodern—or post-postmodern—writer contests every myth's pretensions to universality, to "explaining" art, history, and the human heart. After the high-water mark of the "mythic method," literary artists began to reframe as multiplicity what their predecessors perceived and presented as a unified field theory of culture—revealing the enterprise of the moderns as always already mocked by the failure of George Eliot's pathetic Mr. Casaubon to find "the key to all mythologies." This repudiation of mythography explains (in part, at least) Zampanò's crossing out of all lines of text concerning Minos and Minotaur, Daedalus and the labyrinth, Phalaris and Perilaus (109–11, 335–36n295, 337n301). "Zampanò tried to get rid of" this material, but Johnny Truant has "managed to resurrect" it (111n123). He does so—the point bears repeating—to impugn Zampanò's postmodernity. Ostensibly making an editorial decision to restore allusions that might make Zampanò's meanings clearer, he attempts to force his predecessor to look like a myth-bandying modern but succeeds only in showing Zampanò's thoroughly postmodern distrust of the strategy that served Eliot and Joyce so well. In the end, the crossed-out references and allusions survive here *sous rature*, as Derrida would say: "under erasure," thus not to be credited as any kind of definitive, mythic grounding or explaining of Zampanò's story—or Johnny Truant's, or Danielewski's.[37]

The Jonah allusions further instantiate myth as "Vandal" (335)—to be interrogated and resisted, not served up as cultural *Urstoff*. The sequence of letters from Johnny Truant's mother, Pelafina, tantalizes again with the prospect of mythic reaffirmation. Jonah-like, "swallowed by the Whale" (517), she writes from the very "belly of the beast" (545)—from the institution that literalizes the carceral labyrinth of her mind, her durance a commentary on the freely chosen journeys into darkness and sensory privation of those who, like Navidson, explore nether regions. They, too, are "swallowed" (465). But no one in this story manages real deliverance from the cetacean maw. No one returns intact from the night sea journey. Pelafina's death cancels the prospect that she might, emerging one day from "the Whale" (48, 380, 503), make it back from the dark labyrinth of insanity, and Navidson hardly returns in triumph from Exploration #5. The fetal posture in which he is discovered by Karen only mocks expectation of an archetypal rebirth.

Though Navidson survives his harrowing experiences in the House of Leaves, he loses his right hand and left eye (523)—rather like Charlotte Brontë's Rochester, who also presides over a rambling Gothic edifice with a terrible secret (Danielewski even jokes about the Madwoman in the Attic in the interview with McCaffery and Gregory).[38] One can read Rochester's maiming as a condign punishment for his moral dereliction, a kind of quid pro quo for his present fulfillment (Jane Eyre becomes his bride), but Navidson's harrowing experience eventuates in no happy ending. A professional photographer surely requires two hands (to hold or focus a camera) and two eyes (to see stereoscopically and to compose shots). When last glimpsed in this narrative, Navidson is an Othello with his occupation gone, shooting only "home movies" at their most banal.

But perhaps he gains valuable insight. To lose one eye, after all, is to advance halfway to the complete blindness often represented, in the Western imaginary, as a condition that accompanies "second sight" or enables artistic vision. The blind, like Tiresias, are sometimes compensated with another kind of sight (even the self-blinding of Oedipus ironically complements his "seeing," at last, a terrible reality). Zampanò may intend disparagement when he characterizes Hollywood as "land of the blind" (546), but the author who imagines him, sometime film technician or actor himself (he appeared in the 1993 film *Gettysburg*) and the son of filmmaker Tad Danielewski, may well affirm artistic vision among the supposedly sightless of cinema's capital city. By the same token, the younger Danielewski's narrative abounds in references to blind literati—Homer, Milton, Borges—and to the blind of story and myth from Thamyris to Shakespeare's Gloucester. Zampanò is literally blind, Johnny Truant figuratively so (117). Blindness figures in the Pelican Poems as well (574, 576).

In the fate of Will Navidson, however, Danielewski declines to affirm the myth of blindness that empowers. Navidson's passion transpires in a house situated on a street named for the World Ash of Nordic mythology. This tree, Yggdrasil, appears as the final image in *House of Leaves*, as if (but only as if) to endorse the perennial dream of some *omphalos*, some "Circle Round a Stone," some version of what St. John of the Cross (echoed by Eliot in "Burnt Norton") called the still point of the turning world. On Yggdrasil, for the boon of esoteric knowledge, the god Wotan hung self-crucified for nine days. Another place for the getting of wisdom, Mimir's spring, lies at the root of the world tree, and here Wotan gave up an eye for a single drink. The god's willing sacrifice suggests that introspection complements vision, that self-knowledge frames and completes external truth. The Norse story represents wisdom, in other words, as a looking out and a looking in. But Navidson, chastened and one-eyed, bears no more resemblance to Wotan than to the fulfilled Rochester. Even if the great mystery of Danielewski's novel accommodates the idea that the house "on the corner of Ash Tree Lane and Succoth" (18) is an *axis mundi* (113), the story gives the lie to archetype. The world axis is not unique to Norse mythology. Heroic travail leads to neither triumph nor rebirth. Maimed, Wotan's would-be avatar retreats to rural Vermont. The reader sees again the universal truth of myth—that modernist pretense—localized, atomized, postmodernized.

Succoth, the street that crosses Ash Tree Lane at the Navidson house, hints at additional meanings and participates in the larger mythographic tease. The Jewish festival of Sukkot (as it is more commonly spelled) commemorates shelter at its most rudimentary—its name derives from the temporary dwellings of woven branches (etymologically, the name remembers the weave) constructed by the Israelites during the forty years in the wilderness. Every Sukkot booth is a "house of leaves," a temporary edifice commemorating temporary shelter. As a dwelling for the displaced, such booths also commemorate an older and evidently different Succoth—the place in which Jacob, after parting from Esau, built stalls or "booths" for his cattle (Gen. 33:17). So: nonce locus meets *omphalos*, tenuous weave meets world axis, Hebraic meets Nordic, all approximating the twin axes—call them the notionally numinous and the nugatory—of Danielewski's great enterprise.

The pattern holds throughout: the author (or his surrogate) introduces a myth or archetype, then undercuts it. Zampanò devotes several pages to the moral resemblance of Will and Tom to Jacob and Esau (246ff), then discards the idea, just as he crosses out his references to Minos, Daedalus, and the rest of Cretan mythology (not to mention those to Phalaris and Perilaus). The point lies, again, in the postmodern repudiation of mythic universality, realized continuously in the text's figures of erasure. Over and over, in a variety of ways, it performs a kind of tease, a dance of the seven veils of Meaning. Suggestive instances abound. Details keep trying to assume or signal significance: having concluded his narrative, that is, the story of the Navidsons, on 25 December 1996, for example (528), Zampanò dies on 6 January 1997 (xix). Is it significant that these dates represent the span from Nativity to Epiphany? If so, they hardly affirm or endorse the spiritual saga of Christianity—and 6 January is also Twelfth Night, an occasion for irreverence and general misrule. Indeed, it resembles April Fools' Day, the date on which Navidson begins his fateful Exploration #5 (424). Gaspar de Quesada and two of his fellow captains mutinied against Ferdinand Magellan on the first of April as well—which in 1520 coincided with Easter (135). (Readers of Pynchon's great novel of World War II and its aftermath, *Gravity's Rainbow*, know that the year 1945 saw another such calendric concurrence of sacred and profane.) Johnny Truant's birthday, similarly, falls on 21 June (503), making him a quasi-Druidical child of the solstice. Appropriately enough for the prolegomenon to such a Gothic extravaganza, he completes and signs the introduction to *House of Leaves* on 31 October, All Hallows' Eve or Halloween (xxiii)—which the ancient Celts observed as Samhain. The text introduced—Zampanò's—will itself end (not counting the appended material) with an evocation of the chastened Will Navidson observing and filming trick-or-treaters (527–28) in, oddly enough, Dorset, Vermont (birthplace of Johnny Truant's father, Donnie [585]). All a tease, invitation after invitation to the innocent reader or the less innocent critic to take this stranger's candy.

House of Leaves, then, will make sense only if the reader understands the provisionality of its mythic material, its phenomenology, its economies of knowing and of representation. *Rature* rules. "[T]he perfect pantheon of absence" (423) beneath the Navidsons' house finds its mirror in the myth-canceling narrational strategies of Danielewski's novel. These sustain a perpetual postponement of closure, a relentless deflection of meaning or signification. Indeed, the novel's form mimics the way language itself, in the eyes of theorists from Ferdinand de Saussure to Jacques Lacan, cocoons its referents, postpones indefinitely the marriage of signifier to signified, and endlessly rehearses what Derrida, echoed by Johnny and Pelafina (515, 637, possibly 48), called *différance* (a term describing semantic instability: words always differ from—and defer—what they ostensibly name). Hence, too, the appearance here of material "under erasure"—as signaled by the struck-through words that repeat the strategy Derrida indulges as a way to work with language without conceding or affirming its referential transparency.

In the end, the author of *House of Leaves* insists on the textuality of myth and the elusiveness, in texts, of truth. A younger artist disguises himself in the literal (and littoral) margins of work by an older artist with whom he discovers an unexpected affinity. Although the host text—Zampanò's—is disturbing in its subject matter, its first reader—our own surrogate—experiences horror and distress in excess of what the tale might be expected to generate. The real life reader of Danielewski's novel, while fascinated and often spooked, probably goes on with her or his life without the extreme, disabling credulity of Johnny Truant. The strange bond between Zampanò and Johnny Truant more plausibly invites recognition as a suitably "Gothic" representation of the problem—and, yes, the anxiety—of literary belatedness. The younger storyteller, at once Eliot's "individual talent" and Bloom's ephebe, writes in the shadow of uncomfortably proximate genius—genius that has seemingly exhausted the storytelling techniques best suited to the age. Zampanò is a first-generation postmodernist, Johnny Truant a successor who may end up, as Donald Barthelme would say, sucking the mop. Behind both Zampanò and Johnny Truant, of course, stands Mark Z. Danielewski, a Nabokovian enchanter whose genius shines in his ability to think and represent across his own generation and that of the writers who first shaped a postmodern aesthetic. An acute awareness of literary practice going back to antiquity further enriches ideation in this book about darkness, this extraordinary exercise in the Promethean sublime.

CHAPTER 10

Thirteen Ways of Looking
Jennifer Egan's *A Visit from the Goon Squad*

Le temps est un grand maître. Le malheur, c'est qu'il tue ses élèves.
—HECTOR BERLIOZ

In the thirteen intricately related chapters of her remarkable 2010 novel *A Visit from the Goon Squad,* Jennifer Egan stages and restages the doomed battle of youth with time, the "goon" of her title. Egan's characters—variously involved in the making, packaging, marketing, and promoting of rock music—embrace an ethos notoriously uncongenial to the examined life. Immersed in the now, in what Richard Powers calls "this flickering, specious present," they awaken, one after another, like children in the Irish tale who dance all night with the fairies, only to find that years and years have passed.[1] The fairy tale might seem routinely cautionary anent the dangers of dallying with the pagan supernatural, but one can also read it as a darker parable: every youth dances with those illusory emissaries of timeless delight before awakening with an adult's temporal hangover.

Not that dancing with the fairies is limited to unwise or unwary individuals. Whole cultures participate in those revels and suffer, in time, the shocking, universal fate of unexpected superannuation. Early in the twenty-first century, some would say, Americans awoke to the possibility that the nation itself had been overtaken by history. The more fatalistic may have pondered the date of a millennial climacteric, 11 September 2001, and wondered at its persistence in the popular memory as "9/11," a pair of numbers like those of a biblical verse. How apropos, in fact, chapter 9, verse 11 of Ecclesiastes: "I returned, and saw under the sun, that the race is not to the swift, nor the battle to the strong, neither yet bread to the wise, nor yet riches to men of understanding, nor yet favour to men of skill; but time and chance happeneth to them all." Time and chance—purblind Doomsters, Hardy called them—take their toll on human beings, on their institutions, on nations, and on the earth itself. Set at Ground Zero, the conclusion to Egan's novel offers readers a prophetic and disturbing glimpse of the future augured by 9/11.

Pausing over that famous verse in Ecclesiastes, one realizes that time has long exercised the literary and spiritual imagination. "Time which antiquates Antiquities," says Sir Thomas Browne, "hath an art to make dust of all things." Others insist that art—in a sonnet, in a Greek vase, in ancient sculptural reliefs—confounds such temporal entropy. When not perpending the *ars longa* theme, poets urge seizing of the day, even as they admit that, seized or not, the moments make toward death's fated shore. "And Time that gave doth now his gift confound," laments Shakespeare. "Time doth transfix the flourish set on youth / And delves the parallels in beauty's brow." An American poet, nearly three centuries later, is less troubled. In "Crossing Brooklyn Ferry" (originally called "Sun-Down Poem"), Walt Whitman reflects on time and eternity as he makes a crepuscular transit of the East River. Suggestive of a traditional symbolism of life's journey toward death and afterlife or rebirth, this crossing of water prompts thoughts of the temporal continuum defined by human generations. Hurried by wind and current, the poet remains stationary at the rail, confident that his sojourn on the river of time can issue in nothing evil. Nor will imminent sunset.

Later literati would recur to such visions of stasis in flux, though seldom with Whitman's sanguine outlook. One thinks of the elusive, hovering trout whose shadow Quentin Compson, in Faulkner's *The Sound and the Fury*, studies in the moving water. "[O]nly when the clock stops," observes Quentin's father, "does time ever come to life."[2] Robert Frost, in "West-Running Brook," balances the grim recognition that "[o]ur life runs down in sending up the clock" with contemplation of a permanent ripple or standing wave that embodies an ideal of immutability.[3] The wave resembles the gull breasting the blast in Eliot's "Gerontion"—the Eliot who in "Burnt Norton" risks tautological absurdity in striving to capture the temporal enigma:

> Time present and time past
> Are both perhaps present in time future
> And time future contained in time past.[4]

Fitzgerald's Nick Carraway offers the most familiar of these observations: "So we beat on, boats against the current, borne back ceaselessly into the past."

Replete with such memorable evocations, modern literature becomes a sustained meditation on what Sir Arthur Eddington called time's arrow. Literary artists of the early twentieth century, looking for ways to make an old subject new, discovered in contemporaneous science and philosophy much to stimulate their thinking. From Max Planck, Albert Einstein, and Werner Heisenberg, they learned the relativity of temporal mensuration; from Freud and William James, they learned to differentiate linear or clock time from mental or durational time (what Henri Bergson called *durée*). The moderns discovered in time an aspect of consciousness, which psychologist, philosopher, and artist alike sought to comprehend and parse.

The question of temporal reality exercises postmodern literary artists as well. Ursula Heise, in her brilliant 1997 study *Chronoschisms*, credits new conceptualizations of temporality for "striking developments in the transition from the modernist to the postmodernist novel." She observes "that the time of the individual mind no longer functions as an alternative to social time. Neither is social time any longer perceived as a threat to psychological *durée*, memory and the flow of consciousness. . . . The weakening of individual as well as social and historical time as parameters for organizing narrative is the most crucial problem the postmodern novel articulates in its multiple formal experiments as well as many of its thematic concerns."[5] In other words, as a character in Pynchon's *Inherent Vice* (2009) observes, "there is no avoiding time, the sea of time, the sea of memory and forgetfulness, the years of promise, gone and unrecoverable."[6] Toni Morrison, conjuring the temporal uncanny in *Beloved* (1987), frees a baleful spirit, a vengeful ghost, from its oubliette in the African American psyche. In effect, she reframes Octavia Butler's 1979 novel *Kindred*, in which a modern-day black woman travels back in time to rescue the white rapist who is her own ancestor. Other novelists—Heller, Vonnegut, García Márquez—present their chapters out of temporal order: one recalls the challenge of assembling a time line for the plot of *Catch-22* (1961)—and what did it mean that Billy Pilgrim, in *Slaughterhouse–Five* (1969), repeatedly becomes "unstuck in time"? Other fictions—*Gravity's Rainbow* (1973), for example, or Updike's *Rabbit, Run* (1960)—unfold in a relentless present tense. Lauren Hartke, in DeLillo's *The Body Artist* (2001), recognizes time as "the thing you know nothing about"; she calls it "the thing no one understands."[7] Initially, such fictions seemed merely to compound the modernist fragmentation of time, but as the dislocations became more radical, readers began to see them as part of an epistemic rupture and its new aesthetic. However resourcefully readers worked out scrambled chronologies (not to mention larger formal incoherence), they arrived at no transcendent temporal vision such as Whitman or Yeats tried to affirm. History, time's deranged offspring, proved especially chaotic and twice resistant to eschatological expectation. Thus the reader of Pynchon's *V.* (1963) labors to assemble a linear chronology for the eponymous heroine—only to discover that her career distills the factitiousness of all historiographical metanarrative.

EGAN'S DIALOGUE WITH PROUST AND ELIOT

Born in 1962, Jennifer Egan was one year old when *V.* appeared. A quarter of a century younger than the first-wave postmodernists, she might be expected to break with them, to repudiate the aesthetic they crafted as outmoded or unfresh. But in fact she takes her place in their ranks and augments their exhilarating formal and ideational deconstructions of such vestigial metanarratives (of language, of history, of the unconscious) as continued to shelter in the shadow of that great rock, modernism. Her later situation in literary history, however, makes a difference, for she can treat the moderns as ancestral figures—as much to be venerated as rebelled against. A kind of epistemic amphibium, she is by turns Proustian and Calvinoesque. Like the author of *To the Lighthouse*, *Mrs. Dalloway*, and *The Waves*, she grapples with the strange imbrication of time and consciousness (the one striving endlessly to integrate the other). Like the Don DeLillo of *Cosmopolis* or *The Body Artist*, she perceives temporality and sentience as inseparable from the language games in which they figure. But chiefly she reframes the insights of Proust and Eliot at a century's remove; from the epistemic vantage of her second-generation postmodernism, she re-conceptualizes their themes of time lost and problematically recaptured.

Indeed, Egan's novel, though spare, shares something of the architectonic quality of Proust's great roman fleuve, *À la recherche du temps perdu*. The author has remarked that she worked on *Goon Squad* concurrently with reading, thinking about, and discussing Proust, and one discovers, as expected, a good deal of Proustian matter here—correspondences and parallel features that modulate toward postmodern pastiche.[8] But unlike Proust, she embraces an aesthetic of radical economy. Elevating fifty years of rock and roll history to significance, she also dismantles—or seems to dismantle—the Proustian distinction between serious art and vulgar entertainment or (what would Proust's Marcel, who dismisses as mere popular piffle the wonderful music of Pietro Mascagni, make of the Ramones?).

In all else, however, Egan seems to have found inspiration in Proust—in his pursuit of the real in consciousness and time, his lapidary prose, his difficulty, his formal architecture. Thus Egan's characters, like Proust's Bergotte, Elstir, Vinteuil, Swann, Madame Verdurin, and Baron Charlus, undergo various reversals of social standing: whether overnight or in prolonged free fall, they plunge from the heights of rock and roll stardom (Bosco) or managerial success (Bennie Salazar) or public relations clout (La Doll/Dolly) to the depths of has-beenism. Not that Fortune's Wheel limits itself to the casting down of the once mighty and successful. Several characters—Bennie, Sasha, Jules, Bosco, as well, perhaps, as Dolly, Kitty, and the General—pass out of and back into social and professional distinction. The musical redemption of Scotty Hausmann (the grade-school janitor and near derelict who emerges as bearer of the rock and roll torch) resembles the transformation of the scheming Madame Verdurin, via a third marriage, into the Duchesse de Guermantes. Other characters fit the Proustian mold more neatly: Egan includes a less elegant Swann in Sasha's Uncle Ted, another anchorless aesthete. Like Odette de Crécy, Sasha herself spends time in the "demimonde" before becoming respectable as college student, rock amanuensis, and surgeon's wife.[9] Her collegiate psychidion, the unhappy and divided Rob, resembles Proust's narrator Marcel, a lover by turns besotted and confused. Indeed, as Proust disguised his own preferences in Marcel's pursuit of Gilberte and Albertine, Rob hesitates between an emotional need for Sasha and a physical desire for her boyfriend (and later husband), Drew Blake. Significantly, Egan's artist characters bear less resemblance to those of Proust: one sees little of Proust's writer, Bergotte, in *Goon Squad's* bipolar "celebrity reporter" (88), Jules Jones; nor does one see in Scotty Hausmann a musician and composer of Vinteuil's gifts. To be sure, the French author tends to differentiate art from its unprepossessing creator (it comes as a surprise that the colorless Vinteuil is a composer of genius), but one credits the recognition that comes to Proust's musician more readily than one accepts Scotty's rigged triumph.

The author of *Goon Squad* undertakes to amplify, in terms of time and character, the insight articulated in one of the passages from Proust that furnish her epigraphs: "The unknown in the lives of other people is like that of nature, which each fresh scientific discovery merely reduces but does not abolish."[10] Like the author of *À la recherche du temps perdu*, Egan interrogates fictions of identity and subjective continuity among characters visited and revisited at various moments in their intertwined histories. Like the creator of Swann and the Guermanteses, she conceptualizes and represents the quantum mechanics of psychology itself: the self proves at the same time continuous and serial. Deft, subtle, and original, her representation of this *aperçu* is conveyed, in intricate counterpoint, in surprising—at times exhilarating—linkages among characters and among chapters.

At the same time, again like Proust and many others, she valorizes art as that which outbraves time. Proust affirms, in the summing up of Edmund Wilson, that "only in artistic creation may we hope to find our compensation for the anarchy, the perversity, the sterility and the frustrations of the world."[11] But Egan does not, I think, present rock music as great art—however faithfully or fondly she chronicles its energy from the late seventies into an imagined third decade of the third millennium. She understands that the punk repertoire will not be remembered as the Elgin Marbles of its era. Nor does this author seem particularly invested in her reproaches to the music industry, whose vitality-vitiating commodification of the product has become something of a cliché (along with a complementary—and ironic—development: the obsolescing of once-lucrative distribution models). If, as Fredric Jameson points out, "aesthetic production today has been integrated into commodity production generally," why should rock be any different?[12]

Like DeLillo in his 1973 novel *Great Jones Street*, Egan sees in the foregrounded musical idiom a convenient vehicle for ideas about authenticity, decadence, and aesthetic legitimacy. Rock's popularity, however, poses a challenge to aesthetic discrimination; it reflects contemporary American life much less perspicuously than does serious fiction, the work of a literary artist who hews to a more exacting aesthetic standard. Whether in *Great Jones Street* or *A Visit from the Goon Squad*, in other words, one cannot take the music evoked as seriously as the art of the novel itself. Nor does one perceive DeLillo's Bucky Wunderlick or the musicians in Egan's novel as real artistic heroes: none emerges as a creative figure comparable to Mann's Adrian Leverkühn—or Proust's Marcel. Like Proust, Egan assembles a large cast whose actions and social intercourse she searches for value and meaning. Like Proust, too, she thematizes "lost time." But where Proust makes the work of his fellow artists—Bergotte the writer, Vinteuil the composer, Elstir the painter—part of his aesthetic weave, Egan offers only the dubious talents of the Stop/Go Sisters, the Pinheads, Bosco and the Conduits, Chronos and the Mad Hatters, and the once and future Flaming Dildo Scotty Hausmann, this musical wasteland's shabby Fisher King.

A downsized, epistemically chastened Proust for the twenty-first century, Egan sees the self as an imago; she sees, too, that the world retreats behind the signifiers that ostensibly represent it. (As Germaine Brée and Margaret Guiton have observed, the creator of the scene with the madeleine never, for all his attention to consciousness, impugns "objective reality.")[13] Thus Egan's perspectivism—emphasized in the thirteen takes on person-alities in time—transforms that of the cubists or Wallace Stevens (who fa-mously presents "Thirteen Ways of Looking at a Blackbird"). From Virginia Woolf to Pablo Picasso, modern art factors in the perspectival uncertainty of current science and philosophy, but always with the promise—after shor-ing the ruins or looking at the cubist image or the blackbird from the requi-site number of angles—of some more integral mimesis. For all its difficulty, for all its jagged edges, *The Waste Land* is one of the most coherent poems ever written. Its fragments, like the battered books and broken statues of Pound's "Hugh Selwyn Mauberley," invite reassembly into the civilization shattered by modernity and late war. But its aesthetic, predicated on the same "mythic method" that anchors the Yeatsian unity or the shapely artifice of Joyce's quasi-divine artist, depends for its efficacy on the survival of cul-tural metanarratives unacceptable to postmodern mathesis.

Later artists, representing a more absolute fragmentation, do not pre-tend that their jigsaw puzzle can be put together in such a way as to be mimetic in any traditional sense. Their structures are as intricate as those of their predecessors, but to different, self-referring ends (one can, after all, date and reassemble Egan's chapters in chronological order, and reviewers marveled at how it all "hangs together").[14] Given to what Lyotard calls "in-credulity toward metanarratives," artists now deny or dispense with "the sol-ace of good forms."[15] They contend with fragments no longer recuperable to wholeness—at least not into a dream of Fisher King healed and Waste Land restored to fertility in a *quondam et futurus* cultural order.

Even as she miniaturizes Proust's masterpiece, then, Egan parodies *The Waste Land*, and those familiar with its features—the fragmentation, the den-sity of allusion, the exploitation of myth—will recognize them in *Goon Squad*. The last two offer abundant scope for Egan's reframing of the Eliot poem for an audience nearly a hundred years on. Like Eliot, the author of *Goon Squad* presents a tapestry of myths and allusions that signal an elaborate concep-tual counterpoint. In her fragmented narrative, with its complicated character relationships and tangled chronology, Egan parodies, withal, the "difficulty" that Eliot demanded of (or saw as inescapable for) "poets in our civilization."[16] Postmodern practitioners rise like their predecessors to that challenge (for the homely word "difficult," however, one now favors *scriptible*).

In "Goodbye, My Love," the *Goon Squad* chapter in which Ted Hollander halfheartedly searches squalid Naples for his niece, Sasha Grady, the author deploys allusive and mythic features that, by design, never quite jell. The title and *cherchez la femme* action promise strangely to conflate Raymond Chandler's *Farewell, My Lovely* with the story of Orpheus, the archetypal musician doomed to sorrow. Like Chandler's Philip Marlowe, the searcher for Sasha stumbles into a dangerous milieu with a complex, devious woman at its center. Uncle Ted admires a famous Roman relief depicting Orpheus and Eurydice but fails to see that he and his niece are reenacting their story (nor does he note the proximity of Naples to Avernus, entrance to the realm of Hades). The artwork is, significantly, a copy, and Ted is, as it were, the copy of a copy, a mythic simulacrum, a counterfeit Orpheus. In the original story, the rescue miscarries tragically, but here, ironically and more or less accidentally, it succeeds. Though he manages to bring his niece up out of the seedy underworld that has claimed her, his success yields little, strangely, in the way of comfort or reassurance. Sasha's deliverance remains, now and in future years, problematic.

A final irony: Ted rescues the wrong Eurydice. The real one, Susan, the wife he can no longer tolerate, will presently slip from his life altogether. With a twinge, he remembers a romantic idyll of many years ago, a Whitmanesque ferry crossing during which "the passage of time" unexpectedly asserted itself as an aspect of the circumambient flux: "the leaping brown water, the scudding boats and wind—motion, chaos everywhere." Buoyed by their own united hearts, husband and wife affirm that "[i]t will always be like this," little realizing that only the flux, not the passion, is permanent (174). "Time," as Auden says, "watches from the shadow / And coughs when you would kiss."[17] Years later, Egan's bemused, vodka-swilling Orpheus denies the most basic element of what he has unwittingly undertaken, the archetypal quest to deliver a beloved from her own mortality: "life would be terrible, Ted supposed, without death to give it gravitas and shape" (159). Perhaps he has been reading the poet who observed: "Death is the mother of beauty."[18]

As an expression of instinctive truth, myth embodies coherence that, although anchored in spiritual thinking, functions perfectly well in a postreligious context. But claims to "mythic" universality make postmodernists squirm, they are disinclined to invoke myth uncritically. Thus the myths in *Goon Squad* remain incoherent or inchoate. The references to the Orpheus story are notably attenuated, inconclusive. The Orphic myth of universal harmony and the power of art to gainsay death suffers much the same diminution as the once-powerful words that, in the studies of an academic mentioned in a later chapter (Alex's wife Rebecca), devolve into mere "word casings." Those studies concern what might be called irony creep, a phenomenon much noted in postmodern discourse, especially in

> words that no longer had meaning outside quotation marks. English was full of these empty words—"friend" and "real" and "story" and "change"— words that had been shucked of their meanings and reduced to husks. Some, like "identity," "search," and "cloud," had clearly been drained of life by their Web usage. With others, the reasons were more complex; how had "American" become an ironic term? How had "democracy" come to be used in an arch, mocking way? (262)

These once valorizing words, along with their referents, enter the penumbra of irony or simple desuetude, as do the culture's myths. Like Eurydice, they are banished to an underworld of empty or outmoded or irreparably damaged signifiers.

Orpheus, like the other sacrificial archetypes in *The Waste Land*, suffers *sparagmos*, dismembered (in his case) by Maenads, the frenzied worshippers of the deity said to preside over or inspire passionate and rhapsodic art. Nietzsche famously differentiates such "Dionysian" art from the more measured, "Apollonian" variety. In a novel consecrated to popular music at its most Dionysian (i.e., rock and roll), one does not expect to see Orpheus, who recognized only Apollo as divine, accorded much status. Thus Egan presents her Orpheus, the hapless Uncle Ted, as something of a mediocrity, his sterile aestheticism rather like that of Cecil Vyse in Forster's *A Room with a View* (1908). Nor does he undergo the sacrifice that might confer dignity, if not redemption. Gone, in fact, is the sacred element in the Orpheus story, leaving only the "casing" of marital passion or spiritualized aesthetic ecstasy.

Egan's Orpheus may come from any of a number of classical sources. One can more easily trace the provenance of other allusive material. Egan has, for example, appropriated at least one significant element from Chaucer— another great pioneer in the depiction of diverse personalities interacting. Bennie's ingesting of supposedly medicinal gold dust (admittedly a detail that could come from anywhere) may strike the reader as one of the things remembered by someone properly introduced to Chaucer, whose Doctour of Phisik "lovede gold in special" (l. 443).[19] More plausibly, one hears The

Parson's Prologue in the novel's closing pages, as the characters "were hurry-
ing west, trying to reach the river before sunset. The warming-related 'adjust-
ments' to Earth's orbit had shortened the winter days, so that now, in January, sunset was taking place at 4:23" (261). Much along the lines of a world
valedictory is intimated here, as it is in the Chaucer passage in which the
pilgrims ("Wel nyne and twenty in a compaignye" [l. 24]) discover that time
is running out.[20] The pilgrimage—symbolic of our life's journey—seems to
be coming to a close portentously imagined as coinciding with sunset:

> The sonne fro the south lyne was descended
> So lowe that he nas nat, to my sighte,
> Degreës nyne and twenty as in highte.
> Foure of the clokke it was tho, as I gesse. (ll. 2–5)[21]

Twenty-nine degrees, twenty-nine pilgrims. Bringing to a close one of the
"hazardous pilgrimages" evoked in the Proust epigraph, Egan replaces me-
dieval eschatology with something more up to date: the climate change that
annunciates a whole planet's journey into night. (In her penultimate chapter, Egan includes her own little numerical nudge: the graphing by Sasha's
daughter Alison of thirteen songs with notoriously long pauses replicates, in
miniature, the novel's thirteen chapters.)

But the allusions to Chaucer, to the Orpheus story, to Raymond Chandler, even, are decidedly subordinate to those evoking *The Waste Land*, a
poem itself famous for its overdetermined intertextuality. In forty-four-
year-old Bennie Salazar's libidinal exhaustion, for example, one discerns
the symptom described in the biblical passage that Eliot quotes, when "the
grasshopper shall be a burden, and desire shall fail" (Eccles. 12:5). The major allusions, however, are more structural and thematic. The closeted Rob
Freeman, who drowns at nineteen (the same age as Kitty Jackson when she
became a star), resembles "Mr. Eugenides," whom Eliot conflates with "the
drowned Phoenician Sailor" tarot card and with Phlebas the Phoenician.
Mr. Eugenides, who invites the speaker of the poem to spend a weekend at
the Metropole, represents not only the theme of Waste Land sterility but
also Eliot's own disquiet about sexuality. Rob, too, suffers a "death by water" and so contributes to Egan's thorough rewriting of *The Waste Land*,
which recurs to figures of sacrificial death that retain nothing of the sacramental. By the same token, the figurative death and resurrection of various characters here—Sasha, Scotty, Bosco, maybe Kitty, maybe the rocker

Chronos (casualty and survivor of Lou Kline's Henderson the Rain King adventure)—play out in terms emptied of spiritual significance.

Egan subverts Eliot's mythography most obviously in the story's unsavory Amfortas, Scotty Hausmann, whose fishing in the polluted East River comes in for repeated notice (71, 153, 269). The fish he catches and presents to Bennie is the ancient symbol of fertility under—as it were—some kind of late-punk dispensation. Here it becomes the symbol, too, of invidious memory, compacted and more noisome by the hour.[22] One takes the "healing" of this spiritual invalid, years hence, as emphatically ironic. His publicists, guileless Alex and knowing Lulu, make an unimpressive Parsifal and Kundry; the triumph they effect, ostensibly grounded in some vestigial artistic purity on Scotty's part, is vitiated by its circumstances. The sun of dawning celebrity will set shortly after it rises; Scotty's fame, secured by Lulu and Alex's manipulation of social media, will hardly extend beyond the statutory fifteen minutes.

Scotty's Footprint concert takes place in the novel's last chapter, set "more than twenty years" (267) after the destruction of the World Trade Center in 2001. If the concert takes place in the January in which Bennie is "pushing sixty" (253), the novel would seem to culminate in the year of the *Waste Land* centennial, 2022. Certainly Egan in her closing chapters plays sibyl with a deft, understated touch. She conjures a future in which Americans look back on "two generations of war and surveillance" (271). She presents the redoubtable Lulu as the half-frightening, half-amusing embodiment of a generation that has rejected the manners characteristic of young people in the recent past (the reader's present): the young of Egan's future eschew "piercings, tattoos," and "scarifications" (258). That they even abjure profanity suggests one meaning of this chapter's title, "Pure Language." But the chapter problematizes "purity" in a number of senses: purity of sound, purity of motive, purity of language as sign system. All such purity, the reader learns, is false, nor will the future accommodate millennial dreams of human immaculation. ("Man," says Faulkner, "[a] problem of impure properties carried tediously to an unvarying nil: stalemate of dust and desire.")[23] Alex realizes the impurity of his shilling for Bennie Salazar's scheme to sell the dubious Scotty Hausmann to music lovers of the cultural twilight. Lulu, last seen as a nine year old in chapter 8, has grown up and replaced Sasha as Bennie's person Friday. She has her own perceptions of language and lectures Alex on the obsolescence of metaphor. Like Eric Michael Packer in DeLillo's *Cosmopolis*, Lulu waxes impatient over words—"viral," "transmit," "connect"—that embalm outdated technology: "those old mechanical metaphors that have nothing to do with how information travels." Because it travels "faster than the speed of light" (257), students of marketing must now apply themselves to the particle physics about which Jules Jones speculates (127n1). This conceit (itself, ironically, metaphorical) mirrors contemporary perceptions of the speed with which information spreads. In actual physics, of course, such acceleration would create a perceptual slowing down of time. *Exceeding* the speed of light (if that were possible) would reverse time's arrow, as in F. Scott Fitzgerald's "The Curious Case of Benjamin Button," the film of which came out in 2008, as Egan was publishing chapters from this novel as self-contained stories ("Found Objects" appeared in the *New Yorker* late in 2007). Yet however swiftly information travels, time's goon squad will continue its roughing up of those guilty of being young and heedless.

Purity of language, insofar as it involves something more than the avoidance of profanity, means different things at different moments in literary history. Modern literary artists aspired to restore precision and purity to "the words of the tribe" (the phrase, a favorite of Eliot's, comes from Mallarmé). Motivated by this ideal of "pure language," Hemingway repudiates the corrupt abstractions ("honor," "glory," "sacrifice," "in vain") and Frost clears out the pasture spring (at once his homely New Hampshire Hippocrene and the "clear fount" of Pound's Sextus Propertius: "Now if ever it is time to cleanse Helicon").[24] These writers believed in the possibilities of restoring language's integrity, but their successors have come to recognize that words can never be simple enough or concrete enough to close the signifying gap. They think of language as a tissue of signifiers that screens rather than represents reality. They respect the medium, and in their hands it remains an instrument of precision—but they sharpen it to ends other than those of earlier literary practitioners. If their prose is as pellucid as Orwell's windowpane, it is the better to see through to the words beneath the words.

L'OBJET TROUVÉ

When one teaches Shakespeare's Sonnet 116 ("Let me not to the marriage of true minds"), the better students notice how the poet composes a great affirmation of love's constancy wholly out of negative diction, negative constructions, and negative sentiments. A similar ab hi my figures in *A Visit from the Goon Squad*. Egan's novel, which foregrounds a temporal thematic as old as Ecclesiastes, invites its readers to assemble a complete chronology, but however willingly, even enthusiastically, they carry out this task, they arrive at no larger meanings such as they might work out in a novel by Woolf or Joyce, a poem by Pound or Stevens or William Carlos Williams. The floating associations with *The Waste Land* do not knit together as do similarly random-seeming juxtapositions in the actual Eliot poem. The novel offers no solution to the central mystery of time's arrow—or to the meaning of life in thrall to time. No "supreme fiction" of time and consciousness presents itself. Egan's characters merely struggle to remember the past—and to reconcile themselves to the disappearance of their youth. The "story" written by Sasha and her therapist (5, 7, 13) moves toward no meaningful resolution: its aimless unspooling mocks any larger metanarrative as well. Readers may assemble, order, and recapitulate the novel's component parts, but they discover no mythic, valorizing narrative of the type that structures and conveys meaning in, say, Yeats's "Leda and the Swan" or Hardy's *The Mayor of Casterbridge* (which reframes the story of Saul and David) or Bernard Malamud's 1952 novel *The Natural* (which reconfigures the wasteland myth as baseball saga). Nor, as Bennie and Alex make their way to Sasha's old apartment in the novel's closing paragraphs, is the past recaptured. Yet all of these negatives, as in the Shakespeare sonnet, add up to an altogether fresh aesthetic experience. As the novel comes full circle, as Alex stands before the building on Forsyth Street, readers find that Egan has included them in one of those "hazardous pilgrimages" described in the epigraph from *The Guermantes Way*. She expects us to see the genuine complexity of Proust's proposed corrective: "It is in ourselves that we should rather seek to find those fixed places, contemporaneous with different years."

Many of Proust's contemporaries (most notoriously the Dadaists) embraced the idea that the validity of their art could be gauged, at least in part, by the degree of bafflement or outrage it generated. The arts were not always so swift to alienate a prospective audience. But as the nineteenth century gave way to the twentieth, the idea that art should offend the unimaginative came to seem axiomatic. The bourgeois were to be *épatés* on any and every occasion. Oscar Wilde saw in "[t]he nineteenth-century dislike of realism . . . the rage of Caliban seeing his own face in a glass." In the same era's "dislike of romanticism," he saw "the rage of Caliban not seeing his own face in a glass." Within a generation, however, artists would themselves become Calibans, raging at every species of audience complacency. Caliban's contumely would, moreover, enjoy its own unique cachet, prelude to the man-monster's recognition, late in the twentieth century, as postcolonial hero. Yet the latter part of the twentieth century also saw the erosion of traditional distinctions between popular and serious art. The once-universal outrage of the bourgeois came to be more sporadic—and politicized, insofar as daring or irreverent artists sometimes received government support. The commodification of the avant-garde also posed problems for those seeking to shock. All of these developments lie behind rock and roll's inheriting the mantle of bourgeois-shocking outrageousness—and laying claim to artistic legitimacy. Hence Egan's depiction of Bennie Salazar's anger at the corporate suits to whom he becomes answerable. He feeds them "cow pies," literalizing the "shit" he has been forced to purvey to those who purchase the commodified dreck produced by Sow's Ear Records after its absorption by the multinationals (253). One glimpses the world of marketplace morality that is as much a part of postmodernity as the ideational and formal features of the art it fosters—pastiche, reflexivity, repudiation of metanarratives, and so on. In the precession of late capitalist simulacra, only the image of musical purity survives, and Egan intimates that Bennie is too late to rescue the kind of authenticity he tries to affirm in a resurrected Scotty Hausmann. The fate of these characters remains bleak, clearly linked now to that of a benighted economic order and its planet-pithing energies.

From Elvis Presley's gyrations forward to the Sex Pistols and beyond, rock and roll has been at pains to live up to its own reputation for Dionysian excess. In many ways, this feature reaches an apogee in the punk aesthetic that shapes the musical sensibilities of Bennie Salazar and company. From internal evidence, the reader can determine that Bennie was born in 1962. The reader first encounters him and his classmates (Scotty, Rhea, Jocelyn, Alice) as seventeen year olds in San Francisco, deeply enamored of the late-seventies music scene—the era of Iggy Pop, the Ramones, the Clash. That scene more or less naturally makes its way into the fiction of authors themselves born in or circa 1962: Cristina García and David Foster Wallace, for example, as well as Jennifer Egan. The heroine of García's 1992 novel *Dreaming in Cuban*, a disaffected young immigrant, embraces punk subversion when she paints the Statue of Liberty, most sacred of American icons, with a safety pin through the nose and the caption I'M A MESS.[25] Similarly, Wallace's 1989 *Girl with Curious Hair* collection features, in its title story, ᴛᴇᴇɴ ᴀ similar to those in the chapter in which Egan introduces the predatory Lou Kline, and more than one reviewer has suggested that Egan parodies the Wallace style in the chapter devoted to Jules Jones's account, written in prison, of attempting to rape a starlet.[26]

The author of *Goon Squad* has characterized herself as keenly interested in literary theory—even though she finds, experientially, that action and character in her novels eventually slip the bonds of the theoretical thinking that supposedly underpins them.[27] Egan may be aware of British culture critic Dick Hebdige's analyses of the punk ethos in the 1979 study *Subculture*. Whatever its merits as music, late-seventies punk seemed to revive the possibilities of shocking the middle class. One can read its outré regalia as alienation's imaginary. The dog collars and swastikas and multicolored, spiked hair and Mohawks and chains and safety pins through the nose "become signs of forbidden identity, sources of value," Hebdige explains. They "take on a symbolic dimension, becoming a form of stigmata, tokens of self-imposed exile."[28]

One also recognizes in punk the flamboyant, defiant creation of performers (and their audience) who had missed the sixties. Hunter S. Thompson was, as it were, their prophet, his violent, performative prose an augury of aural transgressions to come. In 1971, at the beginning of the low, dishonest decade that would see the extinction of all the excitement of "San Francisco in the middle sixties," the gonzo journalist rhapsodized about a generation's "riding the crest of a high and beautiful wave," only to see it spend itself on an indifferent shore. Now "you can go up on a steep hill in Las Vegas and look West, and with the right kind of eyes you can almost *see* the high-water mark—that place where the wave finally broke and rolled back."[29] Egan herself has commented on life in the shadow of an era so politically and musically dynamic:

> I grew up in the 1970s, and my friends and I felt very keenly that we had missed the 60s. We were bummed out about it. I grew up feeling like I wanted to grow up ten years earlier, and I wanted to reconstruct every sense of what that moment was like. I made a study of what the counterculture consisted of, and it led me into other queries, like the impact of mass media on people's inner lives, the longing for transcendence as a basic human yearning, the human tendency to wish ourselves in other times and places.[30]

One can compare Egan's after-the-fact perceptions of the sixties with those of Thomas Pynchon, himself slightly too old (having taken a belated college degree in 1959) to be truly a part of the fabulous decade. Both writers—the one a little too young, the other not quite young enough—see and value a particular kind of energy, there then gone. Both imagine a record producer, himself a little too mature for the scene in which he immerses himself, as the embodiment of an older generation's attempt to hijack the party (and with it what a Pynchon character calls the "young stuff").[31] Egan's Lou Kline is last seen in extremis, dying after a second stroke, visited by former Maenads Rhea and Jocelyn, now in their absurd forties; Pynchon's Mucho Maas, introduced in *The Crying of Lot 49* (1966), reappears in *Vineland* (1990) as record czar and recovering cocaine addict. Sex, drugs, and rock and roll take their toll on both.

A century's artistic practice flows together and into Egan's modest yet accomplished novel. Its author shows herself a sympathetic reader of modernism, yet she clearly inhabits the postmodern universe in which realities are largely created by the sign systems that purport to represent them. To understand the postmodern text, readers must become comfortable with fresh levels of paradox: intricate structures prove self-referring, not mimetic, or they discover multiple, contingent realities that elbow each other at the service counter of validity. Propositions that common sense would recognize as mutually exclusive prove, however illogically, to be simultaneously true. The primitive theologian in John Gardner's *Grendel* has it conspicuously wrong when he declares that "alternatives exclude."[32]

This element of simultaneity recurs, early and late, in postmodernist fiction. Ursula Heise points it out in Jorge Luis Borges's "Garden of Forking Paths" (1941), in the title story in John Barth's *Lost in the Funhouse* (1968), and in Clarence Major's *Reflex and Bone Structure* (1975).[33] In the work of late twentieth- and early twenty-first-century writers, the conceit becomes almost commonplace. One thinks of the parallel worlds in Philip Pullman's *Dark Materials* trilogy (1995–2000), which, like Egan's *Goon Squad*, anticipates such 2013 novels as Eleanor Catton's *The Luminaries* (with its twelve interleaved, overlapping, and frequently contradictory narratives) and Kate Atkinson's *Life after Life* (with its spinning out of the conceit of life as some infinitely branching rail yard). At each successive moment of death in the Atkinson fiction, the narrator transitions to another version of the life, with its different paths and outcomes. In effect, Atkinson develops Pynchon's recurrent figure of the demiurge or "pointsman" who shunts the train of one's destiny from one set of tracks to another.

The title of Egan's first chapter ("Found Objects"), along with the seemingly gratuitous element of Sasha's kleptomania, hints at the history of art itself as a chronicle of the appropriations or thefts that enable each succeeding generation to achieve a paradoxical originality. In *Olympia*, Édouard

Manet repaints a Titian Venus; Marcel Duchamp repaints the *Mona Lisa.* "Immature poets imitate," declares Eliot, "mature poets steal."[34] The found object, *l'objet trouvé*, becomes by the same token the legitimate ravin of the artistic kleptomaniac. Isolated and exhibited, it can demand recognition as art, as the painters and sculptors of Eliot's generation discovered. Belatedly embracing the legacy of Duchamp and Kurt Schwitters, an older Sasha alternately "collages" (206) "'found objects'" that "[s]he glues . . . onto boards and shellacs" (207) or assembles "sculptures . . . out of trash and . . . old toys" (184). Artistic "theft," then, neither begins or ends with the moderns— but in the work of their successors the thievery becomes more and more transparent, up to and including the pastiche so heartily embraced by the postmoderns. From "Pierre Menard, Author of the Quixote" to Francis Bacon's execution-like version of Diego Velásquez's *Pope Innocent X* or Larry Rivers's *Washington Crossing the Delaware* (not to mention all of those commercial images appropriated by Andy Warhol), the cultural audience has grown accustomed to the aesthetics of ironic replication.

Egan's enigmatic conflation of art and kleptomania seems the perfect note on which to conclude these reflections on the manner in which one contemporary writer negotiates the perennial challenge of artistic originality. The author of *Goon Squad* faces that challenge with perspicacity, erudition, and wit. From the punk supernova and its *disjecta membra*, she crafts an allegory of the artistic belatedness that troubles every new generation. Readers of her novel come to see in the life and half-life of a popular musical genre something like a *mise en abyme* of postmodernity itself. The music here figures as part of a cautionary parable not so different from the one about dancing with the fairies: artistic style is as subject as other things to time's goon squad. Contemporary writers, like contemporary musicians, must be mindful of the perils of an aesthetic too much at pains to sever all ties with the art of a proximate past. Egan is exemplary in that she finds inspiration in the work of literary parents and grandparents alike. Like her generational fellows, she seems to think father (or mother) killing premature. Thus she meets the parental postmoderns on their own ground; by the same token, she venerates the grandparental moderns even as she places their mythography under erasure and dismantles their supreme fictions.

Conclusion

The Emperor Writes Back

> We shall not cease from exploration
> And the end of all our exploring
> Will be to arrive where we started
> And know the place for the first time.
>
> —T. S. ELIOT, "LITTLE GIDDING"

My study has engaged a question that recurs in cultural critique: what are the relations between one artistic generation and the next? I began with a survey of the historians and sociologists who attempted, over the course of several decades at the end of the nineteenth century and beginning of the twentieth, to define generational parameters. The efforts of Dilthey, Mannheim, Ortega y Gasset, and the rest proved inconclusive: unable to wrestle this protean question to the ground, they left to their successors the task of tracing its modulation, over the years, into the related problems of intertextuality, canonicity, and periodization. As a modest participant in this scholarly discussion, I have focused on literary filiation at the end of the second millennium and the beginning of the third. I have attempted to determine whether younger writers, at this particular juncture, admire and emulate and continue the work of their immediate predecessors or seek to demonstrate, by fresh example, its superannuation.

"In every era," observes Walter Benjamin, "the attempt must be made to wrest tradition away from a conformism that is about to overpower it."[1] More sibylline than may at first appear, this statement suggests that tradition, like quilt-making in that Alice Walker story, must perennially renew itself—often in the face of forces purporting to give it the lie. Yet Benjamin's verbs—"to wrest," "to overpower"—may overstate the agonistic element; younger writers may prefer creation more collaborative than combative. In each of the fictions analyzed in the preceding pages, to be sure, an author has amplified, subverted, negotiated with, or Signified on prior texts of notable temporal propinquity—often while proclaiming their respect for predecessors safely remote in time and space (the names Tolstoy, Chekhov, Stendhal, the Brontës, for example, recur in interviews when the inevitable question about influences comes up). Yet even as they labor in the shadow—the glare, sometimes—of predecessors more proximate, these writers candidly expressed their admiration for Pynchon (Powers, Erickson), DeLillo (Franzen, Wallace), O'Connor (Walker), or Morrison (Naylor). Danielewski rewrites Nabokov without, he says, having read *Pale Fire*. Though all continue the subversion or reframing of modernist aesthetics begun by writers as much as forty or fifty years older than themselves, one or two (Egan, Patchett) have contrived, without invalidating their postmodern credentials, to think of the moderns (Proust, Eliot, Mann) as honored ancestors rather than oppressive parents. More to the point: such writers do not in fact seem to feel oppressed by the actual parents, those first-generation postmoderns.

Critics of contemporary literature must also negotiate a generational dynamic. Older critics may be partial to work that was young when they were; younger critics may gravitate to work by their own contemporaries. I myself (to speak candidly) have at times required a bit of goading to include in my syllabi work by the new writers who share the generational perspective of my students. In the present study, by the same token, I have frequently had to restrain the urge to overfreight my discussions of the younger postmodernists with references to the work of their illustrious elders, especially DeLillo and Pynchon (the danger of a gold standard is that the currency it backs up is never thought "real"). But now perhaps I need no longer, like that Victorian ascetic in Robert Louis Stevenson, mortify a taste for vintages. Thus I mean to consider, by way of valedictory, a point only touched on heretofore, to wit, that influence, unlike water, need not flow exclusively downhill. Older writers can and do learn from—or at least converse with—the younger generation. Samuel Johnson found the company of those younger than himself especially stimulating:

> Sir, I love the acquaintance of *young* people; because, in the first place, I don't like to think myself growing old. In the next place, young acquaintances must last longest, if they do last; and then, Sir, young men have more virtue than old men; they have more generous sentiments in every

respect. I love the young dogs of this age: they have more wit and humour and knowledge of life than we had.[2]

Yeats, by the same token, cheerfully submitted to lessons in up-to-date prosody from Ezra Pound, twenty years his junior. He did so, interestingly enough, exactly one hundred years ago, early in a new century. "During the winters of 1913–1914, 1914–1915, and 1915–1916," writes Richard Ellmann, "Pound set himself the task of converting Yeats to the modern movement."[3] The great Irish poet proved an apt pupil.

Thomas Pynchon, as I have previously intimated, seems here and there in his later work to signal awareness of younger writers, especially those who have articulated their respect and admiration for (and, occasionally, their resentment of) this literary father—the David Foster Wallace who, as a senior at Amherst, hung a picture of the great man over his desk, the Richard Powers who iterates his regard for the master in novels and interviews, the Jonathan Franzen who, departing for Germany on a Fulbright, carried with him a copy of *Gravity's Rainbow*.[4] The last came to see Pynchon, early on, as a threat to his artistic autonomy. Though he "was simultaneously reading Bloom's *Anxiety of Influence*," Franzen credits his fiancée, to whom he confided the distressing sense of being the moth to Pynchon's flame, for nudging him toward repudiation. In letters written to her, recalled and quoted in the unorthodox notes to his 2013 edition of Karl Kraus's essays, Franzen describes the style of his great predecessor as a dangerous vortex into which he might easily slip: "I recognize Pynchon as my major precursor," writes the twenty-two year old. "The better he is the more I want to hate him but the less I can."[5] He had previously recapitulated this correspondence (and its upshot) in the 2010 *Paris Review* interview: "I think it's significant that she hated those letters and made her hatred of them known, and that I steered away from that voice."[6] Thus Richard Katz, the unsavory musician in Franzen's novel *Freedom*, appears at one point "wearing a black T-shirt and reading a paperback novel with a big V on the cover."[7]

The success of these younger writers—especially those easily recuperable to Tribe of Pyn kinship structures—misleads at least one reviewer of Pynchon's 2013 novel *Bleeding Edge*. Michael Robbins (the poet who wrote "Do the rich have inner lives, / Like little lambs and Antigone?") declares in the *Chicago Tribune* that "Pynchon has been lapped by his own epigones Richard Powers and William Gibson."[8] One could almost believe that Robbins, whose verse features an exhilarating mix of high and low, remains unaware of his own debt to an aesthetic pioneered by Pynchon. Certainly he seems to contradict himself when he characterizes as epigones (artists lacking originality, mere imitators) the younger writers paradoxically said to have outdone ("lapped") the master. One might more accurately say that the drive for autonomy and for their own place in the literary spotlight has at times led whilom acolytes of the Pynchon mysterium to test the waters of postmodern apostasy—to hold Pynchon and Company responsible for what they perceive as some unnaturally diminished latitude for a rhetoric of sincerity. Injudiciously, they wish for irony-free discourse and so commit—or risk committing—literary *lèse majesté*, the treason of the intellectuals. At the end of the twentieth century, the tormented David Foster Wallace gave memorable expression to this disquiet:

> The next real literary "rebels" in this country might well emerge as some weird bunch of anti-rebels, born oglers who dare somehow to back away from ironic watching, who have the childish gall actually to endorse and instantiate single-entendre principles. Who treat of plain old untrendy human troubles and emotions in U.S. life with reverence and conviction. Who eschew self-consciousness and hip fatigue. These anti-rebels would be outdated, of course, before they even started. Dead on the page. Too sincere. Clearly repressed. Backward, quaint, naive, anachronistic. Maybe that'll be the point. Maybe that's why they'll be the next real rebels. Real rebels, as far as I can see, risk disapproval. The old postmodern insurgents risked the gasp and squeal: shock, disgust, outrage, censorship, accusations of socialism, anarchism, nihilism. Today's risks are different. The new rebels might be artists willing to risk the yawn, the rolled eyes, the cool smile, the nudged ribs, the parody of gifted ironists, the "Oh how banal." To risk accusations of sentimentality, melodrama. Of overcredulity. Of softness. Of willingness to be suckered by a world of lurkers and starers who fear gaze and ridicule above imprisonment without law. Who knows.[9]

But the arch-ironists of the older generation have co-opted even this vision. The desiderated suspension of irony in fact figures in certain moving passages in DeLillo's *Underworld*, not to mention the celebrated Evensong scene in *Gravity's Rainbow*. A kelson of honest feeling, real loathing of war and injustice, lies beneath even the whimsies and wry disclaimers ("poo-tee-weet," "so it goes") of Kurt Vonnegut. Far from the vehicle of "self-consciousness

and hip fatigue," irony functions as falsehood's judge and jury. Like a flens-
ing knife, irony cuts away the blubber of hypocrisy. Like the chest saw of
a thoracic surgeon, it lays open the diseased heart of truth. Paradoxically,
irony serves the very principles Wallace invokes: sober affirmation, legitimate "single-entendre" advocacy.

To their credit, postmodernism's elders eschew the *quos ego* of patriarchs
and alpha males and queen bees throughout the animal kingdom. DeLillo
corresponds with and encourages Franzen and Wallace. Pynchon generous-
ly endorses the work of younger writers from Rick Moody, Steve Erickson,
Donald Antrim, and George Saunders to Matt Ruff, Howard A. Rodman,
Emily Barton, Phil Patton, Magnus Mills, and Jim Knipfel (he wrote an
especially generous—and perspicacious—introduction to the 1997 reissue
of Jim Dodge's 1990 novel *Stone Junction*).[10] One doubts that he gives much
thought to being "lapped" by Richard Powers, William Gibson, or—the likelier candidate in terms of sheer energy, sheer quantity of output—William
Vollmann. Pynchon sympathizes as much, I think, with the Wallaces and
the Franzens as with more deferential successors. He sees them as serious
writers, unsuperficial thinkers, soldiers—like Bunyan's Greatheart—in the
only army the humanities can field.

When Wallace's posthumous novel *The Pale King* came out in 2011,
Open Salon (Salon.com's open blogging forum) published what purported
to be Pynchon's witty appreciation of the late author. The title, "Pale Kings:
Thomas Pynchon on David Foster Wallace," discouraged a reader's notic-
ing the byline of a clever literary ventriloquist, Robert Brenner. The ersatz
Pynchon sounded plausibly unbuttoned as he aired wry—and acute—
observations about himself as literary Laius and Wallace as the assertive son
at the crossroads:

> Throughout his career, he was compared with me: his first novel,
> *The Broom of The System*, was juxtaposed favorably with my first, *V.*; we
> were both lumped together under the rubric of "post-modern literature,"
> whatever that means (as the insightful critic Clive James once said, "post-
> anything is bullshit," or words to that effect); even in his obituaries, my
> name was bandied about by lazy journalists eager to make a quick allu-
> sion, then get on to the sports pages (e.g., the *New York Times* called him
> a "heir to modern virtuosos like [me]" in the very first sentence).
> Like most literary fathers and sons, our relationship was fraught (cf.
> Kingsley and Martin Amis): in one interview David called himself "the

patricide to [my] patriarch"; in another he said "don't mention the P-word to me." I understood and accepted, even approved of, his Oedipal impulse to murder his forebear and claim sweet Calliope for his own; I myself snuffed Papa Hemingway, taking a lead pipe in the study to his short, clean, well-lit sentences; but I was filled with admiration for David's work, even if he did come to resemble Axl Rose towards the end, both in physical appearance and obsessive perfectionism (although not, mercifully, in egomania, and lord knows, *The Pale King* is worth a helluva lot more, wait-wise, than *Chinese Democracy*).[11]

And so on. The actual author of these words (a ventriloquist's dummy appears in lieu of his photograph) would seem to know his business. He captures Pynchon's offhand manner (opinionation regarding rock music lends color to the impersonation) and the voice in which, in essays, introductions, and reviews, the author occasionally speaks (or presents himself as speaking) in propria persona. The ventriloquist articulates what many readers of Pynchon and Wallace have thought: that the one was literary emperor, eagle in the dovecote of contemporary letters, the other the dashing but tragic heir apparent, dead by his own hand like Crown Prince Rudolph of Austria. The sock puppet expressed sentiments approximating those a respected literary figure might properly feel toward a fellow genius, regardless of the younger writer's occasional forays into Pynchon-doubting postmodern iconoclasm.

Brenner's ventriloquial performance proved prophetic, for one can read Pynchon's next major fiction, *Bleeding Edge*, as a kind of homage to Wallace. In this novel, published exactly five years after that author's September 2008 suicide, Pynchon pays tribute to a gifted but doomed junior partner in the great enterprise of letters. One recognizes the introduction into the narrative of a Quebec operative, Felix Boïngeaux, as the fond gesture of an admirer of *Infinite Jest* (which features the outrageous—indeed, Pynchonian—conceit of wheelchair-bound Québécois terrorists, *Les Assassins des Fauteuils Rollents*). When *Jeopardy* host Alex Trebek is invoked at one point, the reader may recall his role in Wallace's "Little Expressionless Animals." But one discerns the larger project of *Bleeding Edge* in the rewriting—or rather say "completing"—of *The Pale King* (2011), the novel Wallace left unfinished at his death. Thus does Pynchon make his protagonist, Maxine Tarnow, a professional fraud examiner with considerable knowledge of accounting principles. In other words, even as she amalgamates a couple of the protagonists in Pynchon's earlier novels (Oedipa Maas, Doc Sportello), she channels "David

Foster Wallace," the IRS functionary at the heart of *The Pale King*. Pynchon demonstrates his familiarity with such accounting arcana as Luhn checks, Benford's Law, Beneish models, Altman-Z workups, and the 1-x multiple not to outdo Wallace but to salute a comrade fallen in the endless struggle of the humanities against Mammon and Moloch, the despotic deities of American life. He also engages in a good-humored (if now, alas, one-sided) dialogue about the very subject that exercised that writer and some of his fellows: the possibility that irony has become a kind of discursive default that precludes "saying what you meant" (as Wallace biographer D. T. Max paraphrases the famous remark about "single-entendre principles").[12]

Pynchon affirms that irony remains the most efficacious weapon in the struggle with what one might call (borrowing a figure from *The Crying of Lot 49*) the humorless vice presidents of state-sanctioned reality. In *Bleeding Edge*, a sharp-tongued friend of Maxine's reacts with scorn to the notion that the immense and real horror of 9/11 should send irony to its corner, a whipped cur. But diffidence about irony, she avers, fosters only the crescive ubiquity of "'reality' programming" ("suddenly all over the cable, like dog shit"). Not for Pynchon or his favored characters the argument

> that irony, assumed to be a key element of urban gay humor and popular through the nineties, has now become another collateral casualty of 11 September because somehow it did not keep the tragedy from happening. "As if somehow irony," she recaps for Maxine, "as practiced by a giggling mincing fifth column, actually brought on the events of 11 September, by keeping the country insufficiently serious—weakening its grip on 'reality.' So all kinds of make-believe—forget the delusional state the country's in already—must suffer as well. Everything has to be literal now."[13]

Behind this mini-philippic lies an awareness, I think, of irony's full pedigree. Too often spoken of as something invented toward the end of the twentieth century ("popular through the nineties"), it is in fact one of the points of continuity between postmodern, modern, and prior eras from the eighteenth century back to antiquity. Literary discourse that is *not* ironic is almost an anomaly, the special province, perhaps, of Romantic-era discourse (Lord Byron excepted, of course). Even the Bible (one thinks of Job) has its moments of irony, and even theologians (one thinks of Søren Kierkegaard) say one thing to mean another.

Challenges to irony's legitimacy as rhetorical dominant, deadliest arrow in the postmodern quiver complement (and complicate) arguments for the demise of an aesthetic often misperceived as supremely cynical, if not radically nihilistic. But critics manage little concinnity with regard to the continuing viability (or sclerosis) of postmodernism. Some, looking for an altogether new paradigm, have begun to deploy the term "post-postmodern" with increasing boldness. Others, notably Mary K. Holland, have argued that postmodernity has by no means run its course, that the aesthetic made in its image continues answerable to the age. The punning title of Holland's important 2013 study, *Succeeding Postmodernism*, teases with the intimation that she will describe what comes after—"succeeds"—that which succeeded modernism. But her actual thesis concerns postmodernity's rediscovery of humanism. "Ultimately," she observes, "*Succeeding Postmodernism* suggests, unlike the proliferation of 'after postmodernism' criticism of recent years, that we are seeing not the end of postmodernism, but its belated success."[14] Resistant to premature periodization, such critics (I include myself) discern intergenerational continuities that augur postmodernism's longevity. Unless some emergent aesthetic can be shown clearly to repudiate both the stylistic and epistemic features of postmodern fiction (the proclivity to pastiche, the ironic self-referentiality and recursive structures, the problematizing of representation, the "incredulity towards metanarratives"), pronouncements regarding its superannuation, like those on the death of the novel or the end of history, risk inviting some variant on Mark Twain's famous quip: "reports of my death have been greatly exaggerated."

I conclude with a brief recapitulation. This book began with a question: have writers coming to prominence from the 1970s to the present embraced an established postmodern aesthetic, or have they struck out into new literary territory? In looking closely at their work, I have come to think of postmodernism as a house of many mansions or, more simply, a great dwelling with many rooms yet to fill. From the vantage of the twenty-first-century's second decade, that is, one can advance the argument that younger writers have continued to "make it new" without needing to dismantle the postmodern aesthetic crafted by a parental generation. As they engage, resist, perpetuate, and redefine that aesthetic, however, these second- and third-generation postmodernists compose a rainbow spectrum of literary possibility. Born in the 1940s, 1950s, 1960s, and later, they sustain and augment the powerful art of literati born in the 1920s and 1930s—writers whose careers, however brilliant, have arrived or are arriving at the *terminus ad quem* imposed by mortality. Hardly epigones, the younger writers add fresh inflections, I have come to see, to the grammar of literary postmodernism. Unlike Pound's Mauberley, they add jewels to the muse's diadem. They seem not to labor under any disabling anxieties regarding originality as they carry forward the project begun by their immediate predecessors: defining a millennial America.

Notes

Proem

1. T. S. Eliot, preface, *For Lancelot Andrewes: Essays on Style and Order* (Garden City, NY: Doubleday, Doran and Company, 1929), vii.

2. Richard Powers, *Operation Wandering Soul* (New York: William Morrow, 1993), 73.

3. The word appears in the fifth volume of *A Study of History*. Thomas Docherty, "Postmodernism: An Introduction," in *Postmodernism: A Reader*, ed. Docherty (New York: Columbia University Press, 1993), 1.

4. McHale's *Postmodernist Fiction* (1987) and *Constructing Postmodernism* (1992), along with *The Cambridge Introduction to Postmodernism* (2015), are important contributions to the ongoing definition of postmodern literature.

5. Vladimir Nabokov, *The Real Life of Sebastian Knight* (New York: New Directions, 1941), 90.

6. Walt Whitman, *Song of Myself*, 51, in *Leaves of Grass: Comprehensive Reader's Edition*, ed. Harold W. Blodgett and Sculley Bradley (New York: New York University Press, 1963), 88.

7. Richard Powers, *Three Farmers on Their Way to a Dance* (New York: Beech Tree Books, 1985), 333.

8. Fredric Jameson, *Postmodernism, or, The Cultural Logic of Late Capitalism* (Durham: Duke University Press, 1991), 25, 18, 21.

9. As I have pointed out in the past,

> [h]istory and fiction . . . have affinities, and in many languages the words for story and history coincide. Italian *storia*, French *histoire*, Spanish *historia*, Russian *istorya*, German *Geschichte*—all demonstrate the linguistic tendency to obscure the distinction between veracious and imagined narrative. Thus the non-English writer must at times introduce a foreign word to avoid ambiguity, as for example . . . "*Die* story

als Deutung für die Geschichte." Most of these languages retain the Latin form—*historia*—more or less intact, but in Italian and English the archaic form has undergone aphaeresis, the dropping of an initial syllable. The English word *history* was originally as ambiguous as its cognates in other languages; "in early use," according to the O.E.D., the word denoted a narrative of events "either true or imaginary."

English is remarkable in retaining both the archaic and aphaeretic forms and in their evolving toward a semantically convenient distinction. Among native speakers of English, however, this circumstance may generate unconscious resistance to the idea of a family resemblance between history and fiction.

—See David Cowart, *History and the Contemporary Novel* (Carbondale: Southern Illinois University Press, 1989), 17–18.

10. Don DeLillo, *Libra* (New York: Viking, 1988), 181.

Introduction

1. Brian McHale, "What Was Postmodernism," *electronic book review*, 20 December 2007 thread, http://www.electronicbookreview.com/thread/fictionspresent/tense (accessed 29 January 2014).

2. Rachel Adams, "The Ends of America, the Ends of Postmodernism," *Twentieth-Century Literature* 53.3 (Fall 2007): 251.

3. This was the blurb Pynchon supplied for his friend Richard Fariña's 1966 novel *Been Down So Long It Looks Like Up to Me.* The blending together is likelier to take a political or ideological form; thus Kathryn Hume, in her remarkably wide-ranging *American Dream, American Nightmare Fiction since 1960* (Urbana: University of Illinois Press, 2000), argues that "American writers . . . from 1960 into the 1990s" have in common a sense that the American Dream has been betrayed. In a play on Gertrude Stein's famous label for the literary cohort of Hemingway and Fitzgerald, Hume calls her late twentieth-century writers "the Generation of the Lost Dream" (292).

4. Andreas Huyssen, *After the Great Divide: Modernism, Mass Culture, Postmodernism (Theories of Representation and Difference)* (Bloomington: Indiana University Press, 1986), 170, 173.

5. Andrew Hoberek, "Introduction: After Postmodernism," *Twentieth-Century Literature* 53.3 (Fall 2007): 237.

6. In the near-future dystopia of Chang-rae Lee's 2014 novel *On Such a Full Sea* (New York: Riverhead, 2014), a pioneer's invoking of this proverb is recalled to ironic effect: the later generation has seen the trees—literal and figurative—dying off in a seemingly irreversible ecological collapse (18). For a discussion of the important early novels of this author, see Christian Moraru, *Cosmodernism: American Narrative, Late Globalization, and the New Cultural Imaginary* (Ann Arbor: University of Michigan Press, 2011), 81–108, 134–54. See also David Cowart, *Trailing Clouds: Immigrant Fiction in Contemporary America* (Ithaca, NY: Cornell University Press, 2006), 101–25.

7. Alexis De Tocqueville, *Democracy in America*, ed. Isaac Kramnick (New York: W. W. Norton, 2007), 418.

8. José Ortega y Gasset, *Man and Crisis* (1933), trans. Mildred Adams (1933, New York: W. W. Norton, 1958), 52. Hélène Cixous, "The Laugh of the Medusa," trans. Keith Cohen and Paula Cohen, *Signs* 1 (Summer 1976): 890.

9. John Enck, "John Hawkes: An Interview," *Wisconsin Studies in Contemporary Literature* 6 (1965): 149.

10. Under the heading "Postmodern Manifestos," the *Literature since 1945* volume of *The Norton Anthology of American Literature* (eighth edition) includes only a couple of examples by fiction writers: some 1974 remarks by Ronald Sukenick and a brief excerpt from William H. Gass's 1970 *Fiction and the Figures of Life*.

11. Thus Stephen J. Burn in *Jonathan Franzen at the End of Postmodernism* (London: Continuum, 2008) sees "the 1990s" as an era "torn between the emergence of a generation of writers seeking to move beyond postmodernism and the prolonged vitality of many writers . . . associated with the rise of the movement" (9–10). Adam Kelly, who also quotes this observation, expatiates as well on "the idea that the 1990s witnessed the signs of a transition beyond postmodernism." See Kelly, *American Fiction in Transition: Observer-Hero Narrative, the 1990s, and Postmodernism* (London: Bloomsbury, 2013), 5. Burn speaks of "a genealogy of the end of postmodernism" (3), Kelly of its "eclipse" (4). Both offer valuable surveys of critics—Charles Harris, Robert McLaughlin, Linda Hutcheon, Simon Malpas, Rachel Adams, Christian Moraru, and others—pronouncing on this question. Kelly includes a quick guide to the guides, i.e., the critics who have also, from a "twenty-first-century" vantage, undertaken this survey: Tim Woods, John Frow, Michael Rosenthal, and Steven Connors (119n5).

12. Laurence Binyon, *Selected Poems of Laurence Binyon* (New York: Macmillan, 1922), 77.

13. "Each generation writes its own history of generations," observes Alan B. Spitzer, who adds that "generational studies" perennially suffer from "a vague, ambiguous, and stretchable concept" and "a slippery, ambiguous usage that blurs distinctions which should be clarified." He goes on to suggest that "clarity can be preserved and useful explanations developed if instead of asking how long a generation really is, or how many generations usually coexist, or what points in the individual's life cycle are decisive, or whether aging has more profound political consequences than early socialization, we ask whether, and in what respects, age-related differences mattered in a given historical situation" ("The Historical Problem of Generations," *American Historical Review* 78 [1973]: 1353, 1354). According to Hans Jaeger, however, the effect of Spitzer's rigorous analysis was to deal a near fatal blow to the project of defining historical (if not necessarily artistic) generations. Noting that "the idea of . . . generations is no longer thought to have the same explanatory power it did several decades ago," Jaeger nonetheless suggests that "if one renounces the ambitious goal to derive a universal, historical rhythm from a biological, generational succession, an examination of limited phenomena from a generational perspective will frequently turn out to be productive" ("Generations in History: Reflec-

tions on a Controversial Concept," *History and Theory* 24, No. 3 [October 1985]: 280, 291).

14. Azorín [José Martínez Ruiz], "Dos Generaciones," *Obras Completas*, vol. 5 (Madrid: M. Aguilar, 1954), 1139.

15. José Ortega y Gasset, *The Modern Theme*, trans. James Cleugh (New York: Harper & Brothers, 1961), 14–15.

16. Julius Petersen, "Die literarischen Generationen," in *Philosophie der literaturwissenschaft*, ed. Emil Ermatinger (Berlin: Junker und Dunnhaupt Verlag, 1930), 161–82.

17. Karl Mannheim, *Essays on the Sociology of Knowledge*, trans. Paul Kecskemeti (New York: Oxford, 1952), 298, 310.

18. Lev Grossman, "Who's the Voice of this Generation?," *Time*, 10 July 2006, 63.

19. Huyssen, *After the Great Divide*, 188.

20. Huyssen, *After the Great Divide*, 188, 194, 197.

21. Huyssen, *After the Great Divide*, 198.

22. See Jonathan Franzen, "Perchance to Dream," *Harper's Magazine*, April 1996, 50.

23. Quoted in Franzen, "Perchance to Dream," 54.

24. Thomas LeClair, "An Interview with Don DeLillo," in *Anything Can Happen: Interviews with Contemporary American Novelists*, conducted and ed. LeClair and Larry McCaffery (Urbana: University of Illinois Press, 1983), 87.

25. Richard Powers, *The Gold Bug Variations* (New York: Morrow, 1991), 468.

26. See Thomas Pynchon, *Against the Day* (New York: Penguin, 2006), 964 (for the Powers connection) and 1055 (for Erickson).

27. Tom LeClair, "The Prodigious Fiction of Richard Powers, William Vollmann, and David Foster Wallace," *Critique* 38.1 (Fall 1996): 12–13.

28. Donald J. Greiner, "'The God Itch': An Interview with Janette Turner Hospital," *Critique* 48.4 (Summer 2007): 334.

29. F. Scott Fitzgerald, *The Last Tycoon: An Unfinished Novel* (1941; New York: Scribners, 1969), 189.

30. Quoted in Franzen, "Perchance to Dream," 54.

31. Don DeLillo, *The Names* (New York: Knopf, 1982), 77.

32. Adam Begley, "Don DeLillo: *Americana, Mao II,* and *Underworld*," *Southwest Review* 82.4 (1997): 490.

33. Norman Mailer, *Advertisements for Myself* (New York: Berkley Medallion, 1959), 20, 15. DeLillo has indicated his awareness of Mailer's remarks. See David Streitfeld, "Don DeLillo's Gloomy Muse," *Washington Post*, 14 May 1992, C4, col 3.

34. Don DeLillo, *Mao II* (New York: Viking, 1991), 41, 156–57.

35. William Carlos Williams, from "Asphodel, That Greeny Flower," in *Selected Poems* (New York: New Directions, 1968), 150–51.

36. T.S. Eliot, "Ulysses, Order, and Myth" (review of *Ulysses* by James Joyce), in *Selected Prose of T. S. Eliot*, ed. Frank Kermode (New York: Harcourt, Brace & World, 1975), 177.

37. Philip Roth, "Writing American Fiction," *Commentary* 31 (March 1961): 224.

38. Viktor Shklovsky, *Literature and Cinematography* [1923], trans. Irina Masinovsky (Champaign, IL: Dalkey Archive Press, 2008), 35.

39. Jonathan Franzen, "No End to It: Rereading *Desperate Characters*," introduction to Paula Fox, *Desperate Characters* (New York: Norton, 1999), x.

40. Ralph Ellison, *Shadow and Act* (New York: Random House, 1964), 182.

Chapter 1

1. Jack Beatty, "Discovery," *Atlantic*, April 1986, 18.

2. The affinities with O'Connor and Paley were first proposed by Kevin Kelly, "Who Is Rachel Ingalls? And Why Is She Writing about Love with a Sea Monster?," *Chicago Tribune*, 11 October 1987, http://articles.chicagotribune.com/1987–10–11/features/8703180184_1_dorothy-larry-wittgenstein (accessed 29 June 2014).

3. Kathleen Hulley, "Interview with Grace Paley," *Delta: Revue du Centre d'Etude et de Recherche sur les Ecrivains du Sud aux Etats-Unis* 14 (1982): 27.

4. See the chapter on these tales in Bruno Bettelheim, *The Uses of Enchantment: The Meaning and Importance of Fairy Tales* (New York: Knopf, 1976), 277–310.

5. Rachel Ingalls, *Mrs. Caliban* (Boston: Harvard Common Press, 1983), 18. Hereafter cited parenthetically.

6. Hardin Craig, ed., *The Complete Works of Shakespeare* (Chicago: Scott, Foresman, 1961), 1248.

7. See Sandra M. Gilbert and Susan Gubar, *The Madwoman in the Attic* (New Haven: Yale University Press, 1979), 213–47.

8. For the argument that Larry's ontological status is to be understood as constructed (not, that is, to be resolved in terms of Dorothy's mental disequilibrium), see Rebecca Ann Bach, "*Mrs. Caliban*: A Feminist Postmodernist Tempest?," *Critique* 41.4 (Summer 2000): 394.

9. Linda S. Pickle, "Christa Wolf's *Cassandra*: Parallels to Feminism in the West," *Critique* 28.3 (Spring 1987): 151. Mary Carruthers, "Imagining Women: Notes Towards a Feminist Poetic." *Massachusetts Review* 20.2 (1979): 283.

10. Anne Sexton, *The Complete Poems* (Boston: Houghton Mifflin, 1981), 282.

Chapter 2

1. Henry Louis Gates, *The Signifying Monkey: A Theory of African-American Literary Criticism* (New York: Oxford University Press, 1988), xxiii.

2. Gates, *Signifying Monkey*, 59.

3. Gates, *Signifying Monkey*, xxii.

4. Margaret D. Bauer, "Alice Walker: Another Southern Writer Criticizing Codes Not Put to 'Everyday Use,'" *Studies in Short Fiction* 29 (1992): 149–50. Bauer sees some

especially intriguing similarities between O'Connor's *Wise Blood* and Walker's "Entertaining God" (another of the stories in *In Love and Trouble*). She also notes some similarities of "plot line and character type" (150) between "Everyday Use" and O'Connor's short fiction.

5. Walker, *In Search of Our Mothers' Gardens* (San Diego: Harcourt Brace Jovanovich, 1983), 42, 57, 58.

6. Alice Walker, *In Love and Trouble: Stories of Black Women* (New York: Harcourt Brace Jovanovich, 1973), 54, 53. Hereafter cited parenthetically.

7. This rediscovery is itself evidence of a limited cultural horizon: Pan-Africanism had in fact been around since the turn of the century. Readers who know Walker's novels will recognize in this thematic element one of the foundational gestures of a career-long effort to construct or discover an idea of Africa that would not violate the geographical and historical reality. It is a struggle shared by all who seek to recover a suppressed history. The poet Derek Walcott speaks for many when he asks, "How can I turn from Africa and live?" Thus Walker spins a romantic fantasy about the Olinka in *The Color Purple*, imagines an Afro-feminist mythology of Africa in *The Temple of My Familiar*, and strives to achieve utter, unsparing candor regarding Africa's most abhorrent cultural practice—female circumcision—in *Possessing the Secret of Joy*. Africa is a complex place in the psyche of Alice Walker. If in this essay I suggest that it is a less complex place in the psyche of Wangero, I would not like to be seen as arguing that her creator is insensitive to the hunger to know Africa.

8. Walker, *In Search of Our Mothers' Gardens*, 58.

9. For the remarks about photographs, see Alice Walker, *Living By the Word: Selected Writings 1973–1987* (San Diego: Harcourt Brace Jovanovich, 1988), 63.

10. Donna Haisty Winchell, *Alice Walker* (Boston: Twayne, 1990), 81.

11. For the ingenious suggestion that the yard, in its tended state, becomes "ritual ground . . . prepared for the arrival of a goddess" (311), see Houston Baker and Charlotte Pierce-Baker, "Patches: Quilts and Community in Alice Walker's 'Everyday Use,'" in *Alice Walker: Critical Perspectives Past and Present*, ed. Henry Louis Gates and K. A. Appiah (New York: Amistad, 1993), 311.

12. Alice Hall Petry, in "Alice Walker: The Achievement of the Short Fiction," *Modern Language Studies* 19 (Winter 1989), documents "autobiographical dimensions" (19) in a number of Walker stories, notably those in *You Can't Keep a Good Woman Down* (1981). Petry sees only a kind of narcissism in Walker's autobiographical characters. I argue here that "Everyday Use" is exceptional in the sophistication with which it exploits the self-regarding impulse.

13. Marianne Hirsch, "Clytemnestra's Anger: Writing (Out) the Mother's Anger," in *Alice Walker*, ed. Harold Bloom (New York: Chelsea House, 1989), 207.

14. Walker, *In Search of Our Mothers' Gardens*, 269–70.

15. Walker, *Living by the Word*, 63, 62. Though she offers documentation to the effect that such words are authentically African in origin, Walker may have it wrong about

"pickaninny," which surely derives from the vocabulary of Portuguese slavers, whose wares included children, *pequeninos.*

16. I am indebted to a former colleague, Carol Myers Scotton, for identifying the language.

17. Gilles Deleuze and Felix Guattari, *Kafka: Toward a Minor Literature* (Minneapolis: University of Minnesota Press, 1986), 17.

18. Ellen Pifer, "Toni Morrison's *Beloved*: Twain's Mississippi Recollected and Rewritten," *Le Fleuve et Ses Métamorphoses: Actes du Colloque International*, ed. François Piquet (Paris: Didier, 1993), 511.

19. Walker, *In Search of Our Mothers' Gardens*, 262, 257.

20. Ellison, *Shadow and Act*, 17.

21. Elaine Showalter, "Piecing and Writing," in *The Poetics of Gender*, ed. Nancy K. Miller (New York: Columbia University Press, 1986), 228.

22. Barbara Christian, *Black Feminist Criticism: Perspectives on Black Women Writers* (New York: Pergamon, 1985), 87.

23. Faith Pullin, "Landscapes of Reality: The Fiction of Contemporary Afro-American Women," in *Black Fiction: New Studies in the Afro-American Novel since 1945*, ed. A. Robert Lee (New York: Barnes and Noble, 1980), 185.

24. Walker, *In Search of Our Mothers' Gardens*, 257–60.

Chapter 3

1. For a discussion of this theme, as differentiated from "lighting out for the territory" in Euro-American culture, see William Bevis, "Native American Novels: Homing In," in *Recovering the Word: Essays on Native American Literature*, ed. Brian Swann and Arnold Krupat (Berkeley: University of California Press, 1987), 580–620.

2. Arnold Krupat, *The Voice in the Margin: Native American Literature and the Canon* (Berkeley: University of California Press, 1989), 214.

3. Nancy Feyl Chavkin and Allan Chavkin, "An Interview with Michael Dorris," in their *Conversations with Louise Erdrich and Michael Dorris* (Jackson: University Press of Mississippi, 1994), 202.

4. Hertha D. Wong, "An Interview with Louise Erdrich and Michael Dorris," in Chavkin and Chavkin, 41.

5. Eric Konigsberg, "Michael Dorris's Troubled Sleep," *New York*, 16 June 1997, 33, 37.

6. Michael Dorris, "Native American Literature in Ethnohistorical Context," *College English* 41 (October 1979): 156.

7. Wong, "An Interview with Louise Erdrich and Michael Dorris," 40.

8. According to Robert Silberman, in "Opening the Text: *Love Medicine* and the Return of the Native American Woman," in *Narrative Chance: Postmodern Discourse on Native American Literatures*, ed. Gerald Vizenor (Albuquerque: University of New Mexico

Press, 1989), "the duplication of episodes is not entirely compensated for by the insights gained from different perspectives" (119n15). It should be obvious that I disagree with this assessment. Dorris pursues empathic fullness, not epistemological iconoclasm.

9. Dorris told the Chavkins that Ray was originally Raymond, but because he did not want to write yet another boy's coming of age story, he gradually realized, at the prompting of Erdrich, that the character needed to be a girl (Chavkin and Chavkin, 201–2), a complement to the other female narrators. A story told in women's voices, *Yellow Raft* will remind some readers of Christa Wolf's *Cassandra*, another meditation on survival after a cultural disaster, as experienced and articulated by women.

10. This was Dorris's starting point, both experientially and compositionally. As an eleven-year-old boy in eastern Montana, Dorris swam out to a yellow raft and got into conversation with a survivor of the Holocaust, a Polish Jew with a number tattooed on his arm. The author has remarked in interviews that he swam back from the raft a different person from the one he had been when he swam out to it. See Chavkin and Chavkin, 198, and Michael Schumacher, "Louise Erdrich and Michael Dorris: A Marriage of Minds," in Chavkin and Chavkin, 179.

11. Michael Dorris, *A Yellow Raft in Blue Water* (New York: Henry Holt, 1987), 104. Hereafter cited parenthetically.

12. Another example of this dual perspective is provided by Louis Owen, who in *Other Destinies: Understanding the American Indian Novel* (Norman: University of Oklahoma Press, 1992) notes that Christine is illegitimate only from a Eurocentric point of view. "It is ironic that among many tribes . . . it was once common for a man to take his wife's sisters as additional wives, especially if his first wife was in need of assistance and one of her sisters, like Clara, needed a home. According to traditional tribal values, at one time there might have been nothing at all improper about Clara bearing the child of her sister's husband had the situation been handled correctly" (221–22).

13. Fredric Jameson, "Third-World Literature in the Era of Multinational Capital," *Social Text* 15 (1986): 69. I am indebted to Krupat, *Voice in the Margin* (213) for this citation. Gilles Deleuze and Felix Guattari assert something similar in their *Kafka: Toward a Minor Literature*: a "characteristic of minor literatures is that everything in them is political" (17).

14. It is striking to think, in the wake of allegations that he sexually abused his own children, that Dorris might consciously or unconsciously have identified with Father Novak. One must keep in mind, of course, that immoral artists often—like Chaucer's Pardoner—produce tales of exemplary humanity.

15. For the pope's letter and the expected end of the world, Dorris has drawn on his own recollections of parochial school. See Wong, "An Interview with Louise Erdrich and Michael Dorris," 40–41.

16. This is one of the reasons the Erdrich-signed novels are frequently set in the past, in a time of magical spirituality.

17. By the same token, Ray's Uncle Lee, martyred in Vietnam, may remind the reader of Tayo's brother Rocky, killed in the Second World War. Both of the dead men are remembered as exemplary representatives of Native American culture.

18. Arnold Krupat, *Ethnocriticism: Ethnography History Literature* (Berkeley: University of California Press, 1991), 179.

Chapter 4

1. Naylor knows the Bible and Christian belief system well, having been involved, according to Virginia Fowler, with the Jehovah's Witnesses from about 1963 until 1975. For the last seven years she was a minister/missionary. In *Gloria Naylor: In Search of Sanctuary* (New York: Twayne, 1996), Fowler suggests that this denomination, with its apocalyptic expectations, had a "profound" effect on "Naylor's identity" and perhaps also "the directions taken by her art" (6).

2. See Naylor's untitled remarks in *Writers Dreaming*, ed. Naomi Epel (New York: Carol Southern Books, 1993), 170.

3. Kiswana, who has discarded the name of her grandmother, knows how to play the dozens, as one sees in the exchange with C. C. Baker, and in her sympathetic portrait one suspects Naylor of similarly playing the dozens with—that is, Signifyin(g) on—Alice Walker, so unsympathetic toward the central character in "Everyday Use," Wangero Leewanika Kimanjo (née Dee Johnson), who has also rejected the name that descended to her through her grandmother in favor of a cognomen more African, more authentic. Fowler suggests (Gloria Naylor, 166n13) that the Seven Days, the black terrorists in Morrison's *Song of Solomon*, provide a similar target for Naylor's imagining of the seven Days born to Sapphira Wade. Missy Dehn Kubitschek argues that Naylor engages with and revises Morrison at a number of points. Indeed, her essay "Toward a New Order: Shakespeare, Morrison, and Gloria Naylor's *Mama Day*," *MELUS* 19 (Fall 1994): 75–90, strikes an admirable balance of attention between the frequently noticed Shakespearean appropriations (see below) and the less exhaustively discussed debts to other African American writers, including Zora Neale Hurston, Ralph Ellison, Ernest J. Gaines, and Walker, as well as Morrison.

4. Gloria Naylor, *Linden Hills* (New York: Ticknor & Fields, 1985), 28. Hereafter cited parenthetically.

5. The literary antecedents notwithstanding, it is worth noting that the unnamed hurricane that provides the novel's climax takes place in 1985, which was the year of a fierce category 4 storm named Hurricane Gloria (16 September–2 October).

6. See, for example, Elaine Showalter's brief but insightful remarks in *Sister's Choice: Tradition and Change in American Women's Writing* (New York: Oxford, 1991): "Naylor's Miranda is created in the wake of the Third World Caliban, and is both a critique of the phallocentric Prospero-Caliban relation, and an effort to rewrite *The Tempest* as a

revolutionary text for women" (38–39). Peter Erickson, in a more extended analysis, suggests that "by putting into play both positive and critical attitudes towards Shakespeare, Naylor's work dramatizes with particular fullness the conflict between established and emergent traditions." See *Rewriting Shakespeare, Rewriting Ourselves* (Berkeley: University of California Press, 1991), 126. Valerie Traub concurs, noting that "the structural ambivalence with which Naylor relates to the Shakespearean repertoire—the mixture of admiration and resentment her novel reveals—maps the outlines of one possible strategy for negotiating the field of white Western aesthetic production." She concludes that "the novel's overall project (represented by the structural and thematic revision of *The Tempest*) is to educate us in reading for a diversity of historical and racial pasts." See "Rainbows of Darkness: Deconstructing Shakespeare in the Work of Gloria Naylor and Zora Neale Hurston," in *Cross-Cultural Performances: Differences in Women's Re-Visions of Shakespeare*, ed. Marianne Novy (Urbana: University of Illinois Press, 1993), 161. Interestingly, Traub sees Sapphira as a sympathetic, more resourceful Sycorax and associates Bascombe Wade and his fellow slaveholders with Prospero (155). See also Gary Storhoff, "'The Only Voice Is Your Own': Gloria Naylor's Revision of *The Tempest*," *African American Review* 29 (Spring 1995): 35–45.

7. Gloria Naylor, *Mama Day* (New York: Ticknor & Fields, 1988), 5. Hereafter cited parenthetically.

8. W. E. B. Du Bois, *Writings* (New York: Library of America, 1986), 364. Naylor actually quotes this passage in the opening sentence of her essay "Love and Sex in the Afro-American Novel," *Yale Review* 78 (1988): 19.

9. For discussions of African ancestor-consciousness in Willow Springs, see Joycelyn Hazelwood Donlon, "Hearing Is Believing: Southern Racial Communities and Strategies of Story-Listening in Gloria Naylor and Lee Smith," *Twentieth Century Literature* 41 (Spring 1995), especially 23–25, and Lindsay Tucker, "Recovering the Conjure Woman: Texts and Contexts in Gloria Naylor's *Mama Day*," *African American Review* 28 (1994): 180–81.

10. Gloria Naylor, *Bailey's Café* (New York: Harcourt Brace Jovanovich, 1992), 159, 160.

11. Perhaps, to adduce yet another Shakespearean analogue, the influence of Sapphira on Bascombe Wade was something like that of Cleopatra on Antony. Like that earlier African temptress, Sapphira subsequently becomes the kind of pure legend of which E. M. Forster speaks in his lyrical gloss on Plutarch, Shakespeare, and Dryden:

> It is almost impossible to think of the later Cleopatra as an ordinary person. She has joined the company of Helen and Iseult. . . . Voluptuous but watchful, she treated her new lover as she had treated her old. She never bored him, and since grossness means monotony she sharpened his mind to those more delicate delights, where sense verges into spirit. Her infinite variety lay in that. She was the last of a secluded and subtle race, she was a flower that Alexandria had taken three hundred years to produce and that eternity cannot wither, and she unfolded herself to a simple but intelligent Roman soldier.
> —See *Alexandria: A History and a Guide* (New York: Oxford, 1986), 28.

12. E. O. James, *The Cult of the Mother Goddess* (London: Thames and Hudson, 1959), 228.

13. One of the most readable accounts of that displacement is Mary Renault's 1958 novel *The King Must Die*, in which the Greek hero Theseus, born into a civilization dominated by the goddess, proves instrumental in overthrowing her in region after region of his Mediterranean world—from the Troezen of his birth to the Crete of his greatest triumph. The climactic sequence of his early adventures concerns his successful rebellion against the gynocratic order that first distinguishes him as royal consort for a year, then ordains his present sacrifice.

For an account of *Gilgamesh* as a similar narrative of patriarchal aggression, see Monica Sjöö and Barbara Mor, *The Great Cosmic Mother* (New York: Harper and Row, 1987), 246.

14. Jane Ellen Harrison, *Prolegomena to the Study of Greek Religion*, 3rd ed. (New York: Arno, 1975), 261.

15. Sjöö and Mor, *Great Cosmic Mother*, 21.

16. As Tucker points out, the Gullah culture of the Sea Islands that include Willow Springs seems to represent the survival of beliefs and customs originating in "the Kongo-Angolan area" and "the Windward coast." See "Recovering the Conjure Woman," 180–81.

17. Pierre Verger, "Yoruba Myths and Religion, and Their Afro-American Extensions," trans. Gerald Honingsblum, in Yves Bonnefoy, comp., *Mythologies*, "A Restructured Translation of *Dictionnaire des mythologies et des religions des societies traditionelles et du monde antique*" (1981; Chicago: University of Chicago Press, 1991), vol. 1: 60.

18. By the same token, Karla F. Holloway, in *Moorings and Metaphors: Figures of Culture and Gender in Black Women's Literature* (New Brunswick, NJ: Rutgers University Press, 1992), surely errs in saying that "Miranda (Mama) Day . . . must sacrifice George if she is to save her niece Cocoa" (139). Holloway is more helpful in her general emphasis on the goddess—literal or "figurative" (154)—that she identifies as an element common to works by "twentieth-century West African writers" and "African-American women writers whose work focuses on the recovery of an ancestral figure" (2). In the work of the latter, "the idea and presence of the ancestor indicate two important concepts: first, the textual perseverance of a primary (African) culture where the ancestor and the deity can inhabit the same metaphysical space, and second, the belief that a spiritual metaphor can center the metaphysics of a creative literature. . . . The image of a goddess is a constant thread." (149).

19. Erich Neumann, *The Great Mother: An Analysis of the Archetype*, trans. Ralph Mannheim, 2nd ed. (London: Routledge, 1996), 313.

20. Julia Kristeva, "La femme, ce n'est jamais ça," *Tel Quel* 59 (Autumn 1974): 21. Quoted (and translated) in Toril Moi, *Sexual/Textual Politics: Feminist Literary Theory* (New York: Methuen, 1985), 163.

Chapter 5

1. "Pynchon is a little like Joyce. His influence is so pervasive these days that you can't help but be influenced by him." James Mx Lane, "Steve Erickson," *BOMB* 20 (Summer 1987), http://bombmagazine.org/article/948/ (accessed 3 July 2014).

2. Louis Althusser, "Ideology and Ideological State Apparatuses (Notes Towards an Investigation)," in *Lenin and Philosophy and Other Essays*, trans. Ben Brewster (London: New Left Books, 1971), 127–86.

3. "I guess my first five novels culminated in *Arc d'X*–that's what they were all evolving towards." See Larry McCaffery and Takayuki Tatsumi, "Finding a Way to Obliterate the Barriers: An Interview with Steve Erickson," *Contemporary Literature* 38.3 (Autumn 1997): 397.

4. I have sought only to situate this novel within one kind of genre tradition. Rightly noting other affinities, Lee Spinks characterizes it as "simultaneously a historical novel, a work of science fiction, a meditation upon the nature of historicity, an autobiography, and a confession." See "Jefferson at the Millennial Gates: History and Apocalypse in the Fiction of Steve Erickson," *Contemporary Literature* 40.2 (Summer 1999): 226.

5. Steve Erickson, *Arc d'X* (New York: Poseidon Press, 1993), 212. Hereafter cited parenthetically.

6. Spinks, "Jefferson at the Millennial Gates," 215.

7. Jim Murphy, "Pursuits and Revolutions: History's Figures in Steve Erickson's *Arc d'X*," *Modern Fiction Studies* 46.2 (2000): 453, 464.

8. Thomas Pynchon, *The Crying of Lot 49* (Philadelphia, Lippincott, 1966), 125–26.

9. Steve Erickson, "American Weimar," *Los Angeles Times Sunday Magazine*, January 8, 1995, http://www.studiolarz.com/erickson/articles/weimar.html (accessed 24 January 2005).

10. R. W. B. Lewis, *The American Adam: Innocence, Tragedy, and Tradition in the Nineteenth Century* (Chicago: University of Chicago Press, 1955), 5.

11. Erickson, "American Weimar."

12. McCaffery and Tatsumi, "An Interview with Steve Erickson," 406. Erickson also contrasts "our false innocence and our true idealism" in *American Nomad* (New York: Holt, 1997), 32.

13. Thomas Pynchon, *Vineland* (New York: Little, Brown, 1990), 221–22.

14. Jacques Derrida, *De la grammatologie* (Paris: Les Éditions de Minuit, 1967), 296. I am indebted here to Spivak's translation, though I have departed from it somewhat in rendering Derrida's phrase "*L'estampe, qui copie les modèles de l'art*" (Spivak renders this as "copies the models of art"). See Derrida, *Of Grammatology*, trans. Gayatri Chakravorty Spivak (Baltimore: Johns Hopkins University Press, 1976), 208.

15. Benjamin views all the techniques of making images in quantity—from woodcuts to etchings to engravings to lithography to photography as merely steps in the attenuation of "aura." See Walter Benjamin, "The Work of Art in the Age of Mechanical

Reproduction," in *Illuminations*, trans. Harry Zohn (New York: Schocken, 1969), 218–19.

16. See John Barth, "The Literature of Exhaustion," in *The Friday Book* (New York: Putnam's, 1984), 72, and Jorge Luis Borges, "Pierre Menard, Author of the *Quixote*," in *Labyrinths*, ed. Donald A. Yates and James E. Irby (New York: New Directions, 1964), 42.

Chapter 6

1. See Gerald Howard, "Pynchon from A to V," *Bookforum* (June–September 2005), 29.

2. Richard Powers, *Operation Wandering Soul* (New York: William Morrow, 1993), 43. Hereafter cited parenthetically.

3. Richard Powers, *Galatea 2.2* (New York: Farrar, Straus and Giroux, 1995), 54.

4. Aristotle, *Poetics*, trans. S. H. Butcher (New York: Hill and Wang, 1961), 68.

5. Richard Powers, *Three Farmers on Their Way to a Dance* (New York: Beech Tree Books, 1985), 333, 206.

6. Cleo McNelly Kearns, "The Harrowing Grace of Truthful Fiction: A Review of Richard Powers's *Operation Wandering Soul*," *Theology Today* 51 (January 1995): 589.

7. Richard Powers, *The Gold Bug Variations* (New York: William Morrow, 1991), 76.

8. Kevin Berger, "The Art of Fiction CLXXV: Richard Powers," *Paris Review* 164 (Winter 2003): 108.

9. Powers, *Galatea 2.2*, 206, 32.

10. Powers, *Galatea 2.2*, 7, 117.

11. Jim Neilson, "An Interview with Richard Powers," *Review of Contemporary Fiction* 183 (Fall 1998), http://www.dalkeyarchive.com/a-conversation-with-richard-powers-by-jim-neilson/ (accessed 29 January 2014).

12. Jeffrey Williams, "The Last Generalist: An Interview with Richard Powers," *Minnesota Review*, n.s., 52–54 (2001): 100.

13. Ann Pancake, "'The Wheel's Worst Illusion': The Spatial Politics of *Operation Wandering Soul*," *Review of Contemporary Fiction* 183: 80. Like Pancake, April Lindner, in "Narrative as Necessary Evil in Richard Powers's *Operation Wandering Soul*," *Critique* 38 (Fall 1996), suggests that "the ultimate effect" of the relentlessly harsh narratives embedded in *Operation Wandering Soul* may be "anesthetic" (75). Pancake looks chiefly at the spatial, topographic, and cartographic conceits in this text; Lindner reads Powers's novel against selected psychological and sociological views of narrative's role in the development of children, citing the work of Bruno Bettelheim, James Hillman, and Joyce Thomas.

14. See W. H. Auden, "West's Disease," in *The Dyer's Hand* (New York: Random House, 1962).

15. Powers may have learned from Pynchon (especially *V.*) to develop narratives that

unfold parallel to each other but at a temporal—indeed, historical—remove. "All of his novels," observes Patrick O'Donnell in his study *The American Novel Now: Reading Contemporary American Fiction Since 1980* (Chichester, UK: Wiley-Blackwell, 2010), "are concerned with the phenomenon of the historical parallel, or how a sequence of events and related contexts in the past affect a similar sequence in the present, and, thus, how the past is prologue" (126).

16. Powers, *The Gold Bug Variations*, 330.

17. See Jacques Derrida, "Plato's Pharmacy," in *Dissemination*, trans. Barbara Johnson (Chicago: University of Chicago Press, 1981).

18. Powers, *Galatea 2.2*, 5, 206.

19. These remarks appeared as an online supplement—"The *Esquire* Conversation: Richard Powers and Sven Birkerts"—to Birkerts's July 2000 *Esquire* review of *Plowing the Dark*. Though no longer available online, the interview is quoted in Joseph Dewey, *Understanding Richard Powers* (Columbia: University of South Carolina Press, 2002), 160n1, and, in the slightly longer excerpt that I cite, in Charles B. Harris, "Technoromanticism and the Limits of Representationalism: Richard Powers's *Plowing the Dark*," in *Science, Technology, and the Humanities in Recent American Fiction*, ed. Harris and Peter Freese (Essen: Blaue Eule, 2004), 274–275n41.

20. Joseph Dewey, "Dwelling in Possibility: The Fiction of Richard Powers," *Hollins Critic* 33.2 (April 1996): 14.

21. The story appears in *Acta Sanctorum*, *Aurea Legenda*, and other hagiographic writings. See the online *Catholic Encyclopedia*: http://www.newadvent.org/cathen/03728a.htm (accessed 29 January 2014).

22. Dewey, *Understanding Richard Powers*, 80.

23. See Herbert A. Friedman, "The Wandering Soul Psyop Tape of Vietnam," http://www.psywarrior.com/wanderingsoul.html (accessed 29 January 2014).

24. Powers, *Three Farmers on Their Way to a Dance*, 212.

25. Walter Benjamin, "Theses on the Philosophy of History," in *Illuminations*, trans. Harry Zohn, ed. Hannah Arendt (New York: Schocken, 1969), 257.

26. Sigmund Freud, *Beyond the Pleasure Principle*, trans. James Strachey, in *The Standard Edition of the Complete Psychological Works of Sigmund Freud*, ed. Strachey (London: Hogarth Press, 1953–74), 18: 16, 23.

Chapter 7

1. Pliny the Elder, *The Natural History*, ed. John Bostock and H. T. Riley, Perseus Digital Library, http://www.perseus.tufts.edu/hopper/text?doc=Perseus%3Atext%3A 1999.02.0137%3Abook%3D35%3Achapter%3D43 (accessed 29 January 2014).

2. Flannery O'Connor, "The Fiction Writer and His Country," in *Mystery and Manners* (New York: Farrar, Straus and Giroux, 1961), 34.

3. Chuck Palahniuk, *Choke* (New York: Anchor Doubleday, 2001), 150, 149. Hereafter cited parenthetically.

4. Laura Miller, Review of *Diary*, by Chuck Palahniuk, Salon.com, 20 August 2003, http://dir.salon.com/books/review/2003/08/20/palahniuk/index.html (accessed 26 September 2014).

5. Janet Maslin, "An Immature Con Man with a Mom Problem" (Review of *Choke*, by Chuck *Palahniuk*), *New York Times*, 24 May 2001, http://www.nytimes.com/2001/05/24/books/books-of-the-times-an-immature-con-man-with-a-mom-problem.html?ref=chuckpalahniuk (accessed 29 January 2014).

6. Chuck Palahniuk, *Fight Club* (New York: W. W. Norton, 1996), 149, 166. Hereafter cited parenthetically.

7. F. Scott Fitzgerald, *This Side of Paradise* (New York: Scribners, 1921), 304.

8. John Updike, *Rabbit, Run* (New York: Knopf, 1960), 106.

9. Walker Percy, "The Man on the Train," in *The Message in the Bottle: How Queer Man Is, How Queer Language Is, and What One Has to Do with the Other* (New York: Farrar, Straus and Giroux, 1975), 83.

10. Jean Baudrillard, "The Precession of Simulacra," in *Simulations*, trans. Paul Foss, Paul Patton, and Philip Bleitchman (New York: Semiotext[e], 1983), 25.

11. Louis Marin, *Utopics: Spatial Play*, trans. Robert A. Vollrath (Atlantic Highlands, NJ: Humanities Press, 1984), 239, 248, 253.

12. Baudrillard, "Simulacra," 23.

13. Thomas Pynchon, *Gravity's Rainbow* (New York: Viking, 1973), 348.

14. Vladimir Nabokov, *Pnin* (New York: Vintage, 1984), 90.

15. Pausanias, *The Description of Greece*, vol. 1, trans. Thomas Taylor (London: Priestley and Weale, 1824), 13.

16. Henry Wadsworth Longfellow, "Kéramos," in *Kéramos and Other Poems* (London: George Routledge, 1878), 18.

17. Edward FitzGerald, *Rubáiyát of Omar Khayyám: A Critical Edition*, ed. Christopher Decker (Charlottesville: University Press of Virginia, 1997), 19, 18.

18. Alex E. Blazer, "The Phony 'Martyrdom of Saint Me': *Choke*, *The Catcher in the Rye*, and the Problem of Postmodern Narcissistic Nihilism," in *Reading Chuck Palahniuk: American Monsters and Literary Mayhem*, ed. Cynthia Kuhn and Lance Rubin (New York: Routledge, 2009), 148.

19. Jorge Luis Borges, "Kafka and His Precursors," in *Labyrinths* (New York: New Directions, 2007), 201.

20. DeLillo, *Mao II*, 24.

21. Antonio Casado de Rocha, "Disease and Community in Chuck Palahniuk's Early Fiction," *Stirrings Still: The International Journal of Existential Literature* 2.2 (Fall/Winter 2005): 106.

22. G. Christopher Williams, "Nihilism and Buddhism in a Blender: The Religion of

Chuck Palahniuk," in *Reading Chuck Palahniuk: American Monsters and Literary Mayhem*, ed. Cynthia Kuhn and Lance Rubin (New York: Routledge, 2009), 170.

23. Jean-François Lyotard, *The Postmodern Condition: A Report on Knowledge*, trans. Geoff Bennington and Brian Massumi (Minneapolis: University of Minnesota Press, 1984), 81.

24. Carter's remarks were quoted in Seth Mnookin, "In Disaster's Aftermath, Once-Cocky Media Culture Disses the Age of Irony," *Inside.com*, 18 September 2001. While Graydon Carter's remarks were widely quoted, the complete URL and relevant webpage is no longer available.

25. Roger Rosenblatt, "The Age of Irony Comes to an End," *Time*, 24 September 2001, http://www.time.com/time/magazine/article/0,9171,1000893,00.html (accessed 30 January 2014).

Chapter 8

1. Rabindranath Tagore, "Broken Song," in *Selected Poems*, trans. William Radice (New York: Penguin, 1994), 53–55.

2. See the 2010 *Wall Street Journal* interview with Alexandra Alter, http://online.wsj.com/article/SB10001424052748704094304575029673526948334.html (accessed 29 January 2014).

3. Ann Patchett, "Constantly Plagiarizing Myself," in *Conversations with American Women Writers*, conducted and ed. Sarah Anne Johnson (Hanover, NH: University Press of New England, 2004), 172.

4. Thomas Pynchon, Introduction, *Slow Learner: Early Stories* (Boston: Little, Brown, 1984), 21.

5. Harvey Blume, "Two Geeks on Their Way to Byzantium: A Conversation with Richard Powers," *Atlantic Unbound*, 28 June 2000, http://www.theatlantic.com/past/docs/unbound/interviews/ba2000-06-28.htm (accessed 29 January 2014).

6. Powers, *Galatea 2.2*, 137.

7. Powers, *The Gold Bug Variations*, 156–57.

8. Ann Patchett, *Bel Canto* (New York: HarperCollins, 2001), 152–53. Hereafter cited parenthetically.

9. Willa Sibert Cather, *The Song of the Lark* (Boston: Houghton Mifflin, 1915), 477.

10. Aristotle, *Poetics*, 101.

11. Robert Frost, "The Aim Was Song," in *Collected Poems, Prose and Plays* (New York: Library of America, 1995), 207.

12. Robert Frost, "The Figure a Poem Makes," in *Collected Poems, Prose and Plays* (New York: Library of America, 1995), 777.

13. Deborah Weisgall, "The Magic Opera," *Radcliffe Quarterly* (Summer 2001): 27.

14. Alex Clark, "Danger Arias" [Review of *Bel Canto*, by Ann Patchett], *Guardian* 13

July 2001, http://www.guardian.co.uk/books/2001/jul/14/fiction.reviews1 (accessed 29 January 2014). This quibble notwithstanding, Clark's review is quite positive.

15. See Dana Jean Schemo, "As a Rebel's Path Ends, Hard Turf but Soft Hearts," *New York Times*, 29 April 1997, http://www.nytimes.com/1997/04/29/world/as-a-rebel-s-path-ends-hard-turf-but-soft-hearts.html (accessed 29 January 2014).

16. Patchett refers to "'The Host Country' instead of Peru," she explains, "because I thought by the time this book comes out no one is going to remember this. Tragedy, in my experience, is always replaced by tragedy. We hold one crisis close to our heart until the next crisis comes along and it obliterates the one before. So we tend not to remember things that happened six years ago in South America." See "Conversation: Ann Patchett," *Online Newshour*, 2 July 2002, http://www.pbs.org/newshour/conversation/july-dec02/patchett_7–02.html (accessed 29 January 2014).

17. Daniel Mendelsohn, "Ransom Notes" [Review of *Bel Canto*, by Ann Patchett], *New York*, 18 June 2001, http://nymag.com/nymetro/arts/books/reviews/4804/ (accessed 29 January 2014).

18. Patchett made this observation during a public talk given at the University of South Carolina, 28 March 2012.

19. See "A Conversation with Ann Patchett, Author of *Bel Canto*," http://www.bookbrowse.com/author_interviews/full/index.cfm/author_number/645/ann-patchett (accessed 29 January 2014).

20. Hastings's reflections appear in an essay appended to the book, which is, as its title implies, an ethical and religious argument. See "*Bel Canto* Forgiveness Narrative: Terror and the Philosophy of Conflict Resolution," in Hastings, *Nonviolent Response to Terrorism* (Jefferson, NC: McFarland, 2004), 225.

21. "Conversation: Ann Patchett," *Online Newshour*.

22. For these and additional details of Peru's history and culture, see the country profile on the U.S. Department of State's website: http://www.state.gov/r/pa/ei/bgn/35762.htm#history (accessed 29 January 2014).

23. Patchett, "Constantly Plagiarizing Myself," 173.

24. The interview on the BookBrowse website contains the most succinct account of the author's self-education. See "A Conversation with Ann Patchett, Author of *Bel Canto*."

25. Long before their actually meeting, Mr. Hosokawa sees Roxane in *Sonnambula* three nights running (6). Its 2009 staging by the Metropolitan Opera, which starred Juan Diego Flóres, featured an extra element of reflexivity. According to the Met's own synopsis: "*La Sonnambula* is set in a Swiss village. Mary Zimmerman's new production is set in a rehearsal room where singers are rehearsing a production of *La Sonnambula* set in a Swiss village. The story, actions and characters of the village are all coincident with those of the rehearsal room." http://www.metoperafamily.org/metopera/history/stories/synopsis.aspx?id=268 (accessed 29 January 2014). For more on self-referential

features in this genre, see Olivia Giovetti, "Operas about Operas: Compelling or Confounding?" http://www.wqxr.org/#!/blogs/operavore/2012/mar/15/operas-about-operas/ (accessed 29 January 2014).

26. "A Conversation with Ann Patchett, Author of *Bel Canto*."

27. Jane Marcus-Delgado, "Destructive Persistence of Myths and Stereotypes: Civilization and Barbarism Redux in Ann Patchett's *Bel Canto*," *Letras Hispanas* 2.1 (Spring 2005): 52. The argument here would be more persuasive if it were buttressed by citations from opera's most cogent feminist critic, Catherine Clément, whose 1979 study *L'Opéra ou la Défaite des femmes* (translated into English in 1988 as *Opera; or, the Undoing of Women*) is less scattershot in its critique. Clément observes and deplores and theorizes the high mortality rate among operatic heroines.

28. Marcus-Delgado, "Destructive Persistence," 48.

29. Marcus-Delgado, "Destructive Persistence," 53.

30. Willa Sibert Cather, "Three American Singers: Louise Homer, Geraldine Farrar, Olive Fremstad," *McClure's Magazine* 42.2 (December 1913): 35, 41.

31. Not that operatic tradition lacks odd linguistic features. In her 1920 novel *The Age of Innocence* (New York: D. Appleton and Company), Edith Wharton gently satirizes the nineteenth-century New York custom of presenting opera in Italian, without regard for the language of the original libretto. When her characters attend such a performance of *Faust*, the narrator wryly notes that "an unalterable and unquestioned law of the musical world required that the German text of French operas sung by Swedish artists should be translated into Italian for the clearer understanding of English-speaking audiences" (3).

32. Richard Powers, *Plowing the Dark* (New York: Farrar, Straus and Giroux, 2000), 30.

33. T. S. Eliot, "The Waste Land," in *Collected Poems 1909–1962* (London: Faber, 1963), 79.

34. Vladimir Nabokov, *Strong Opinions* (New York: McGraw-Hill, 1973), 66.

35. "[A] wise reader reads the book of genius not with his heart, not so much with his brain, but with his spine," Nabokov observes. "Although we read with our minds, the seat of artistic delight is between the shoulder blades. . . . The brain only continues the spine: the wick really goes through the whole length of the candle." See Vladimir Nabokov, *Lectures on Literature* (New York: Harcourt Brace Jovanovich, 1980), 6, 64.

36. Adam Levin, *The Instructions* (San Francisco: McSweeney's, 2010), 390.

Chapter 9

1. Lyotard, *The Postmodern Condition*, 79.

2. Jameson, *Postmodernism, or, The Cultural Logic of Late Capitalism*, 9.

3. See Elliot Braha, "Menippean Form in *Gravity's Rainbow* and in Other Contemporary American Texts" (PhD diss., Columbia University, 1979), and Theodore D. Kharp-

ertian, *A Hand to Turn the Time: The Menippean Satires of Thomas Pynchon* (Madison, NJ: Fairleigh Dickinson University Press, 1990). A number of critics note the Fellini connection. In *La Strada*, Zampanò is a thuggish strong man, more marginal street performer than circus star. As such, he is Fellini's negative self-projection, the jejune entertainer he wants, as an artist, not to be. It may be significant that Anthony Quinn, who played Zampanò in the Fellini film, was the contemporary of Danielewski's Zampanò: the actor was born in 1915, Zampanò ca 1913. Quinn would die a few months after publication of Danielewski's novel.

4. Mark Z. Danielewski, *House of Leaves* (New York: Pantheon, 2000), 350. Hereafter cited parenthetically.

5. Wallace Stevens, "Man Carrying Thing," in *Collected Poetry and Prose*, ed. Frank Kermode and Joan Richardson (New York: Library of America, 1984), 306.

6. Joyce's mysterious period appears below the last of the questions in "Ithaca": "Where?" (607). The round, black dot signifies an answer: here, on the earth. The similar black dot that appears earlier in the Danielewski text (312) may represent the dwindling circle on the screen of older televisions when switched off.

7. "I didn't write *House of Leaves* on a word processor. In fact, I wrote out the entire thing in pencil!" See Larry McCaffery and Sinda Gregory, "Haunted House—An Interview with Mark Z. Danielewski," *Critique* 44.2 (Winter 2003): 117.

8. Richard Grusin and Jay David Bolter, *Remediation: Understanding New Media* (Cambridge: MIT Press, 2000), 5. I am indebted to my colleague Susan Vanderborg for bringing the work of Grusin and Bolter to my attention.

9. N. Katherine Hayles, "Saving The Subject: Remediation in *House of Leaves*," *American Literature* 74.4 (2002): 781. For a discussion of the novel's "orthographic" framing of digital mediation, see Mark B. N. Hansen, "The Digital Topography of Mark Z. Danielewski's *House of Leaves*," *Contemporary Literature* 45.4 (2004): 597–636. For scrutiny of the novel's affinities with hypertext, with considerable attention to the *House of Leaves* website (houseofleaves.com) and to the website devoted to *Haunted*, the recording by Danielewski's sister Poe, see Jessica Pressman, "*House of Leaves*: Reading the Networked Novel," *Studies in American Fiction* 34.1 (Spring 2006): 107–28. Noting that "the massive print novel barely mentions digital technology" (111) yet features "hypertextual heteroglossia" (109) and "contains an extensive hypertextual navigation system connecting multiple narratives and reading paths" (107), Pressman argues a certain disingenuousness in Danielewski's assertions "that his novel showcases the power of print textuality" (121).

10. Pressman, "Reading the Networked Novel" (119–20), provides an account of the novel's having really appeared on the Internet before print publication by Random House.

11. Will Slocombe, "'This is Not for You': Nihilism and the House That Jacques Built," *Modern Fiction Studies* 51.1 (2005): 102.

12. Hansen, "Digital Topography," 621, 606n7.

13. Stanley Fish, *Self-Consuming Artifacts* (Berkeley: University of California Press, 1972), 3. Such a text, says Fish, "requires of its readers a searching and rigorous scrutiny of everything they believe in and live by" (1). Fish always emphasizes what happens in the mind of the reader, and what happens to Navidson is distilled in the act in which he and the reader in real life undertake to grasp ideas that may call into question much of their daylight world.

14. Hayles, "Saving the Subject," 799. "Just as the House walls endlessly rearrange themselves, so the ontological distinctions that separate Navidson from Zampanò, Zampanò from Johnny, Johnny from Danielewski, and Danielewski from the reader keep shifting and changing" (800). As Natalie Hamilton observes, "[t]he question of authenticity pervades the book, and the suggestion is not only that *The Navidson Record* may be the invention of Zampanò, but that Zampanò may be the invention of Truant to enable him to face the demons of his past. . . . Danielewski creates a labyrinth out of the levels of narration, one so intricate that it is impossible to divine any semblance of a hierarchy." See "The A-Mazing House: The Labyrinth as Theme and Form in Mark Z. Danielewski's *House of Leaves*," *Critique* 50.1 (Fall 2008): 9.

15. In a 1935 letter to W. H. D. Rowse, Pound wrote: "The Nekuia shouts aloud that it is *older* than the rest, all that island, Cretan, etc., hinter-time that is *not* Praxiteles, not Athens of Pericles, but Odysseus." *Letters of Ezra Pound 1907–1941*, ed. D. D. Paige (London: Faber, 1951), 363.

16. Jacques Derrida, *Archive Fever: A Freudian Impression*, trans. Eric Prenowitz (Chicago: University of Chicago Press, 1996), 37.

17. Derrida, *Archive Fever*, 90, 91.

18. Franz Kafka, Letter to Oskar Pollak, 27 January 1904. In Kafka, *Letters to Friends, Family, and Editors*, trans. Richard and Clara Winston (New York: Schocken Books, 1977).

19. Faulkner so characterized the county in Mississippi that he created. See also Zora Neale Hurston, "Characteristics of Negro Expression," in *Negro*, ed. Nancy Cunard (New York: Negro Universities Press, 1934), 43. Danielewski observes of his novel: "The notion of authenticity or originality is constantly refuted." He is perfectly aware, moreover, that his playful parerga—annotations, notes, appendices, indices, exergues, and paratexts galore—have become fairly routine in contemporary fiction from Barth to Nabokov and from Nicholson Baker to William Vollmann and David Foster Wallace. See McCaffery and Gregory, "Haunted House," 121, 114.

20. McCaffery and Gregory, "Haunted House," 115.

21. Nick Lord, "The Labyrinth and the Lacuna: Metafiction, the Symbolic, and the Real in Mark Z. Danielewski's *House of Leaves*," *Critique* 55, no. 4 (2014): 465, 471–72. Pressman in "Reading the Networked Novel" (115–16) has mounted the most ambitious attempt to determine whether one of the voices in *House of Leaves* is responsible for the others. Relying on hints in Poe's obviously *House of Leaves*–related song "Time & a Half Minute Hallway," she argues for Pelafina as the novel's true puppet master

or Woman Behind the Curtain. Yet one still objects: every piece of evidence advanced for Pelafina-as-Author works as well on behalf of the other candidates for that honor. *Pace* Pressman and other Thesean navigators of the textual labyrinth, a point comes at which one must quit the game: "Within the world of the fiction," as Kathryn Hume observes, "the reality of various authors" remains "problematic in the extreme." See *Aggressive Fictions: Reading the Contemporary American Novel* (Ithaca: Cornell University Press, 2012), 152.

22. McCaffery and Gregory, "Haunted House," 114.

23. Steven Belletto makes the point that *Pale Fire* predicates its scholarly apparatus on an artifact tangibly before the reader—who can read Shade's poem and decide about the legitimacy of Kinbote's commentary. A reader cannot, however, visit the Navidson house, which can be experienced *only* through layers of mediation and commentary. See "Rescuing Interpretation with Mark Danielewski: The Genre of Scholarship in *House of Leaves,*" *Genre* 42.3–4 (Fall/Winter 2009): 106.

24. F. O. Matthiessen, *American Renaissance: Art and Expression in the Age of Emerson and Whitman* (New York: Oxford University Press, 1941), 547.

25. Vladimir Nabokov, *The Real Life of Sebastian Knight* (London: Weidenfeld and Nicholson, 1941), 175. As Natalie Hamilton points out, this conceit also recalls that of Borges in "The Garden of Forking Paths": "the book and the labyrinth were one and the same" (Borges, *Collected Fictions,* trans. Andrew Hurley [New York: Viking, 1998], 124). See Hamilton, "The A-Mazing House," 15.

26. Walt Whitman, "Song of Myself" 51, in *Leaves of Grass: Comprehensive Reader's Edition,* ed. Harold W. Blodgett and Sculley Bradley (New York: New York University Press, 1963), 88. All quotations from Whitman here refer to this edition.

27. Hegel called the sphinx "the symbol of the symbolic itself." See Georg Wilhelm Friedrich Hegel, *Aesthetics: Lectures on Fine Art,* trans. T. M. Knox, vol. 2 (Oxford: Clarendon, 1975), 360.

28. Vladimir Nabokov, *Speak, Memory: An Autobiography Revisited* (New York: Putnam's, 1966), 19.

29. "Pater, ait," thinks Stephen, echoing Ovid's account of Icarus's doom. James Joyce, *Ulysses,* ed. Hans Walter Gabler with Wolfhard Steppe and Claus Melchior (New York: Vintage, 1986), 173.

30. Joyce, *Ulysses,* 7.

31. Harold Bloom, *The Anxiety of Influence: A Theory of Poetry* (New York: Oxford University Press, 1973), 14.

32. Bloom, *Anxiety of Influence,* 30.

33. The German word evidently derives from the Fellini film. According to Mund-Mische.de, the word implies that in reality there's nothing beneath the façade ("in Wahrheit steckt nichts dahinter")—an apt phrase for Danielewski's hall of mirrors. http:// mundmische.de/bedeutung/26478-Zampano (accessed 30 January 2014). I am indebted to Theda Wrede for help with this term.

34. Josh Toth, "Healing Postmodern America: Plasticity and Renewal in Danielewski's *House of Leaves*," *Critique* 54.2 (2013): 182, 185.

35. Thomas Pynchon, *Mason & Dixon* (New York: Henry Holt, 1997), 354

36. Thomas Pynchon, *Inherent Vice* (New York: Penguin, 2009), 21, 251. I was reminded of these examples in Bill Millard's "Pynchon's Coast: *Inherent Vice* and the Twilight of the Spatially Specific," *College Hill Review*, no. 4 (Fall 2009), http://www.collegehillreview.com/004/0040501.html (accessed 30 January 2014).

37. Attempting for whatever reason to restore Zampanoan mythography, Johnny Truant himself drifts from one mythological identification to another. He is Icarus, he is Theseus, he is the Minotaur. As an abandoned or abused son, at once source and victim of parental shame, the Minotaur presents itself as kindred spirit to the unhappy Johnny, who eventually declares: "I will become, I have become, a creature unstirred by history, no longer moved by the present, just hungry, blind and at long last full of mindless wrath" (497). Johnny's self-recognition seems to date from his stumbling upon "a particularly disturbing coincidence" that he does not explain. Hayles has pointed out that the "disturbing coincidence" seems to lie in the anagram buried in the phrase "The Minotaur," but her unpacking of it as "O Im he Truant" ("Saving the Subject," 798) is unwieldy. Rearranged, the letters more plausibly spell: "Truant homie." In short, "wanting to turn The Minotaur into a homie" (336–337n298), Johnny figuratively discovers the monster in his own mirror.

38. McCaffery and Gregory, "Haunted House," 112.

Chapter 10

1. Richard Powers, *Orfeo* (New York: W. W. Norton, 2014), 172

2. William Faulkner, *The Sound and the Fury* (New York: Vintage, 1990), 85.

3. Robert Frost, "West-Running Brook," in *Collected Poems, Prose and Plays* (New York: Library of America, 1995), 238.

4. T. S. Eliot, *Four Quartets* (New York: Harcourt, 1971), 3.

5. Ursula Heise, *Chronoschisms: Time, Narrative, and Postmodernism* (Cambridge: Cambridge University Press, 1997), 7. For another argument regarding the displacement of the spatial by the temporal, see Hikaru Fujii, *Outside, America: The Temporal Turn in Contemporary American Fiction* (London: Bloomsbury, 2013). Fujii observes a near obsession, among contemporary writers, with Los Angeles as the place where America's westward expansion has perforce ended: "with the exhaustion of the spatial notion of freedom, a preoccupation with time emerges—the 'outside' appears as a temporal dimension in contemporary literary imaginings" (x).

6. Pynchon, *Inherent Vice*, 341.

7. Don DeLillo, *The Body Artist* (New York: Scribner, 2001), 98, 99, 100.

8. "The Proust factor was huge," she remarks in an interview with Jane Ciabattari. See "The Book on Aging Rockers," *Daily Beast*, 29 June 2010, http://www.thedailybeast.

com/articles/2010/06/29/jennifer-egan-interview-a-visit-from-the-goon-squad.html (accessed 29 January 2014).

9. Jennifer Egan, *A Visit from the Goon Squad* (New York: Knopf, 2010), 172. Hereafter cited parenthetically.

10. The lines are from *La prisonnière* (in English *The Prisoner* or *The Captive*), volume five of *À la recherche du temps perdu*.

11. Edmund Wilson, *Axel's Castle: A Study in the Imaginative Literature of 1870–1930* (New York: Scribner's, 1931), 159.

12. Jameson, *Postmodernism, or, The Cultural Logic of Late Capitalism*, 4.

13. Germaine Brée and Margaret Guiton, *An Age of Fiction: The French Novel from Gide to Camus* (New Brunswick, NJ: Rutgers University Press, 1957), 43.

14. See, for example, Will Blythe, "To Their Own Beat," *New York Times Book Review*, 8 July 2010, http://www.nytimes.com/2010/07/11/books/review/Blythe-t.html?pagewanted=all&_r=0 (accessed 29 January 2014) or Joe Gross, "In Egan's 'Goon Squad,' Stories Spanning Decades Come Together in Unexpected Ways," *Austin American-Statesman*, 12 October 2010, http://www.statesman.com/news/entertainment/books-literature/in-egans-goon-squad-stories-spanning-decades-com-1/nRydz/ (accessed 29 January 2014). Arranged in chronological order, the earliest part of Egan's narrative would be chapter 4, "Safari" (set in 1973), followed by chapter 3, "Ask Me if I Care" (1979); chapter 11, "Goodbye, My Love" (1990); chapter 10, "Out of Body" (1993); chapter 6, "X's and O's" (1997); chapter 9, "Forty-Minute Lunch" (1999?); chapter 7, "A to B" (2004?); chapter 5, "You (Plural)" (2005); chapter 2, "Gold Cure" (2006); chapter 1, "Found Objects" (2006); chapter 8, "Selling the General" (2008?); chapter 12 "Great Rock and Roll Pauses" (early 2020s); and chapter 13, "Pure Language" (Winter 2021–22).

15. Lyotard, *The Postmodern Condition*, xxiv, 81.

16. T. S. Eliot, "The Metaphysical Poets," in *Selected Prose of T. S. Eliot*, ed. Frank Kermode (New York: Harcourt, Brace & World, 1975), 65.

17. W. H. Auden, "As I Walked Out One Evening," in *Collected Poems*, ed. Edward Mendelson (New York: Random House, 2007), 134–35.

18. Wallace Stevens, "Sunday Morning," in *The Collected Poems of Wallace Stevens* (New York: Random House, 2011), 68, 69.

19. Geoffrey Chaucer, "General Prologue," *The Canterbury Tales*, in *The Works of Geoffrey Chaucer*, ed. F. N. Robinson (Boston: Houghton Mifflin, 1961), 21.

20. Chaucer, "General, Prologue," 17.

21. Chaucer, "The Parson's Prologue," 228.

22. In this detail, Egan resists the too-positive symbolism of the fish given to Kitty's family by the angel Rogni in Kathryn Harris's first novel, *Labrador* (1988).

23. Faulkner, *The Sound and the Fury*, 124.

24. Ezra Pound, "Homage to Sextus Propertius," in *Personae: The Collected Poems of Ezra Pound* (New York: New Directions, 1926), 216.

25. Cristina García, *Dreaming in Cuban* (New York: Knopf, 1992), 141.

26. For example, Sarah Churchwell, "A *Visit from the Goon Squad* by Jennifer Egan—review," *Guardian*, 12 March 2011, http://www.theguardian.com/books/2011/mar/13/jennifer-egan-visit-goon-squad (accessed 30 January 2014). See also Will Blythe, "To Their Own Beat." Wallace having committed suicide in 2008, as she was working on *Goon Squad*, Egan may have intended homage more than parody.

27. See Christopher Cox, "At Work: Jennifer Egan," *Paris Review Daily*, 25 June 2010, http://www.theparisreview.org/blog/2010/06/25/qa-jennifer-egan/ (accessed 30 January 2014).

28. Dick Hebdige, *Subculture: The Meaning of Style* (New York: Methuen, 1977), 3, 2.

29. Hunter S. Thompson, *Fear and Loathing in Las Vegas: A Savage Journey to the Heart of the American Dream* (New York: Knopf, 1971), 68.

30. Carly Schwartz, "Jennifer Egan on Growing Up in San Francisco, Finding Inspiration, and Experiencing the 'Sixties Hangover,'" *Huffington Post*, 10 October 2011, http://www.huffingtonpost.com/2011/10/10/jennifer-egan-my-sf_n_1001091.html (accessed 30 January 2014).

31. Pynchon, *Crying of Lot 49*, 105.

32. John Gardner, *Grendel* (New York: Knopf, 1972), 133, 159.

33. Heise, *Chronoschisms*, 53–55.

34. T. S. Eliot, "Philip Massinger," in *Selected Essays 1917–1932* (New York: Harcourt, Brace & World, 1964), 182.

Conclusion

1. Benjamin, "Theses on the Philosophy of History," 255.

2. James Boswell, *The Life of Samuel Johnson, LL.D.* (1791; Oxford: Oxford University Press, 1953), 315.

3. Richard Ellmann, *Yeats: The Man and the Masks* (New York: Macmillan, 1948), 212.

4. In *Every Love Story Is a Ghost Story: A Life of David Foster Wallace* (New York: Penguin, 2013), D. T. Max reports: "On the wall over the desk of his single [room]," the young writer hung "the famous photograph of Pynchon as a buck-toothed undergraduate at Cornell" (43). There is, however, no known picture of Pynchon as a Cornell undergraduate—Wallace's personal icon was presumably the photograph I myself published in 1980: the author as boot camp trainee, taken when he interrupted his undergraduate education for a hitch in the Navy (see the dust jacket of my *Thomas Pynchon: The Art of Allusion*). Pynchon also appears orthodontically challenged in the photographs from his high school yearbook, but these were not published until 1989, four years after Wallace graduated from Amherst.

5. Karl Kraus, *The Kraus Project. Essays by Karl Kraus*, ed. and trans. Jonathan Franzen (New York: Farrar, Straus and Giroux, 2013), 173n26, 174n26.

6. Stephen J. Burn, "The Art of Fiction CCVII: Jonathan Franzen," *Paris Review* 195 (Winter 2010). Franzen's Fulbright sojourn in Germany took place in 1981–82, some years before the 1988 appearance of his first novel, *The Twenty-Seventh City*, which he would later characterize as "a conversation with the literary figures of my parents' generation. The great '60s and '70s postmoderns. I wanted to feel like I belonged with them, much as I'd spent my childhood trying to be friends with my parents and their friends. A darker way of looking at it is that I was trying to impress them." See Donald Antrim, "Jonathan Franzen," *BOMB* 77 (2001), http://bombmagazine.org/article/2437/jonathan-franzen (accessed 1 August 2014).

7. Jonathan Franzen, *Freedom* (New York: Farrar, Straus and Giroux, 2010), 67.

8. Michael Robbins, "'Bleeding Edge' by Thomas Pynchon," *Chicago Tribune*, 15 September 2013, http://www.chicagotribune.com/lifestyles/books/ct-prj-0915-bleeding-edge-thomas-pynchon-2-20130915-story.html (accessed 23 July 2014). The poem takes its title—"Günter Glieben Glauchen Glöben"—from nonsense German lyrics affected by the rock group Def Leppard and *its* epigones. (The Def Leppard website gives the lyrics as "Gunter, Glieben, Glausen, Globen.") The poem appears in Michael Robbins, *The Second Sex* (New York: Penguin, 2014), 13.

9. David Foster Wallace, "I Unibus Pluram: Television and U. S. Fiction," in *A Supposedly Fun Thing I'll Never Do Again* (New York: Little, Brown, 1997), 81–82.

10. I am indebted for this list to Larry Daw's website, The Modern Word. http://www.themodernword.com/

11. Robert Brenner, "Pale Kings: Thomas Pynchon on David Foster Wallace," OpenSalon.com, 5 April 2011, http://open.salon.com/blog/robert_brenner/2011/04/01/pale_kings_thomas_pynchon_on_david_foster_wallace (accessed 25 July 2014).

12. Max, *Every Love Story Is a Ghost Story*, 157. Max effectively charts the course of Wallace's views of Pynchon, which became negative after *Vineland*. He also suggests that the remarks about irony might be aimed more at its invasion of the marketplace than at its literary legitimacy.

13. Thomas Pynchon, *Bleeding Edge* (London: Jonathan Cape, 2013), 335.

14. Mary K. Holland, *Succeeding Postmodernism: Language and Humanism in Contemporary American Literature* (London: Bloomsbury, 2013), 17.

Bibliography

Adams, Rachel. "The Ends of America, the Ends of Postmodernism." *Twentieth-Century Literature* 53.3 (Fall 2007): 233–47.

Alter, Alexandra. "What Don DeLillo's Books Tell Him." *Wall Street Journal*, 30 January 2010. http://online.wsj.com/news/articles/ SB10001424052748704094304575029673526948334?mg=re no64-wsj&url=http%3A%2F%2Fonline.wsj.com%2Farticle%2F SB10001424052748704094304575029673526948334.html (accessed 29 January 2014).

Althusser, Louis. "Ideology and Ideological States Apparatuses (Notes Towards an Investigation)." In *Lenin and Philosophy and Other Essays*, translated by Ben Brewster, 127–86. London: New Left Books, 1971.

Amis, Martin. "Survivors of the Cold War." Review of *Underworld*, by Don DeLillo. *New York Times Book Review*, 5 October 1997, 12–13.

Antrim, Donald. "Jonathan Franzen." *BOMB* 77 (2001). http://bombmaga-zine.org/article/2437/jonathan-franzen (accessed 1 August 2014).

Aristotle. *Poetics*. Translated by S. H. Butcher. New York: Hill and Wang, 1961.

Auden, W. H. "As I Walked Out One Evening." In *Collected Poems*, edited by Edward Mendelson, 134–35. New York: Random House, 2007.

Auden, W. H. "West's Disease." In *The Dyer's Hand*, 238–45. New York: Random House, 1962.

Azorín [José Martínez Ruiz]. "Dos Generaciones." In *Obras Completas*, vol. 5, 1136–40. Madrid: M. Aguilar, 1954.

Bach, Rebecca Ann. "*Mrs. Caliban*: A Feminist Postmodernist Tempest?" *Critique* 41.4 (Summer 2000): 391–402.

Baker, Houston, and Charlotte Pierce-Baker. "Patches: Quilts and Community in Alice Walker's 'Everyday Use.'" In *Alice Walker: Critical Perspectives Past and Present*, edited by Henry Louis Gates and K. A. Appiah, 309–16. New York: Amistad, 1993.

Barth, John. "The Literature of Exhaustion." In *The Friday Book*, 62–76. New York: Putnam's, 1984.

Baudrillard, Jean. "The Precession of Simulacra." In *Simulations*, translated by Paul Foss, Paul Patton, and Philip Bleitchman. New York: Semiotext[e], 1983.

Bauer, Margaret D. "Alice Walker: Another Southern Writer Criticizing Codes Not Put to 'Everyday Use.'" *Studies in Short Fiction* 29.2 (1992): 143–51.

Beatty, Jack. "Discovery." *Atlantic*, April 1986, 16–18.

Begley, Adam. "Don DeLillo: *Americana, Mao II,* and *Underworld.*" *Southwest Review* 82.4 (1997): 478–505.

Belletto, Steven. "Rescuing Interpretation with Mark Danielewski: The Genre of Scholarship in *House of Leaves.*" *Genre* 42.3–4 (Fall/Winter 2009): 99–117.

Benjamin, Walter. "Theses on the Philosophy of History." In *Illuminations*, translated by Harry Zohn, edited by Hannah Arendt, 253–64. New York: Schocken, 1969.

Benjamin, Walter. "The Work of Art in the Age of Mechanical Reproduction." In *Illuminations*, translated by Harry Zohn, edited by Hannah Arendt, 217–52. New York: Schocken, 1969.

Berger, Kevin. "The Art of Fiction CLXXV: Richard Powers." *Paris Review* 164 (Winter 2002–03): 106–138.

Bettelheim, Bruno. *The Uses of Enchantment: The Meaning and Importance of Fairy Tales.* New York: Knopf, 1976.

Bevis, William. "Native American Novels: Homing In." In *Recovering the Word: Essays on Native American Literature*, edited by Brian Swann and Arnold Krupat, 580–620. Berkeley: University of California Press, 1987.

Binyon, Laurence. *Selected Poems of Laurence Binyon.* New York: Macmillan, 1922.

Birkerts, Sven. "The *Esquire* Conversation: Richard Powers and Sven Birkerts." See Harris.

Blazer, Alex E. "The Phony 'Martyrdom of Saint Me': *Choke, The Catcher in the Rye,* and the Problem of Postmodern Narcissistic Nihilism." In *Reading Chuck Palahniuk: American Monsters and Literary Mayhem*, edited by Cynthia Kuhn and Lance Rubin, 143–56. New York: Routledge, 2009.

Bloom, Harold. *The Anxiety of Influence: A Theory of Poetry*. New York: Oxford, 1973.

Blume, Harvey. "Two Geeks on Their Way to Byzantium: A Conversation with Richard Powers." *Atlantic Unbound*, 28 June 2000. http://www.theatlantic.com/past/docs/unbound/interviews/ba2000–06–28.htm (accessed 29 January 2014).

Blythe, Will. "To Their Own Beat." Review of *A Visit from the Goon Squad*, by Jennifer Egan. *New York Times Book Review*, 8 July 2010. http://www.nytimes.com/2010/07/11/books/review/Blythe-t.html?pagewanted=all&_r=0 (accessed 29 January 2014).

Borges, Jorge Luis. "Kafka and His Precursors." In *Labyrinths*, edited by Donald A. Yates and James E. Irby, 199–201. New York: New Directions, 2007.

Borges, Jorge Luis. "Pierre Menard, Author of the *Quixote*." In *Labyrinths*, edited by Donald A. Yates and James E. Irby, 36–44. New York: New Directions, 1964.

Boswell, James. *The Life of Samuel Johnson, LL.D.* 1791. Oxford: Oxford University Press, 1953.

Braha, Elliot. "Menippean Form in *Gravity's Rainbow* and in Other Contemporary American Texts." PhD diss., Columbia University, 1979.

Brée, Germaine, and Margaret Guiton. *An Age of Fiction: The French Novel from Gide to Camus*. New Brunswick, NJ: Rutgers University Press, 1957.

Brenner, Robert. "Pale Kings: Thomas Pynchon on David Foster Wallace." OpenSalon.com, 5 April 2011, http://open.salon.com/blog/robert_brenner/2011/04/01/pale_kings_thomas_pynchon_on_david_foster_wallace (accessed 25 July 2014).

Burn, Stephen J. "The Art of Fiction CCVII: Jonathan Franzen." *Paris Review* 195 (Winter 2010): 38–79.

Burn, Stephen J. *Jonathan Franzen at the End of Postmodernism*. London: Continuum, 2008.

Carruthers, Mary. "Imagining Women: Notes Towards a Feminist Poetic." *Massachusetts Review* 20.2 (1979): 281–307.

Casado de Rocha, Antonio. "Disease and Community in Chuck Palahniuk's Early Fiction." *Stirrings Still: The International Journal of Existential Literature* 2.2 (Fall/Winter 2005): 105–15.

Cather, Willa Sibert. *The Song of the Lark*. Boston: Houghton Mifflin, 1915.

Cather, Willa Sibert. "Three American Singers: Louise Homer, Geraldine Farrar, Olive Fremstad." *McClure's Magazine* 42 (December 1913): 33–48.

Chaucer, Geoffrey. *The Canterbury Tales*. In *The Works of Geoffrey Chaucer*, edited by F. N. Robinson. Boston: Houghton Mifflin, 1961.

Chaucer, Geoffrey. "General Prologue." *The Canterbury Tales.* In *The Works of Geoffrey Chaucer,* edited by F. N. Robinson. Boston: Houghton Mifflin, 1961.

Chaucer, Geoffrey. "The Parson's Prologue." *The Canterbury Tales.* In *The Works of Geoffrey Chaucer,* edited by F. N. Robinson. Boston: Houghton Mifflin, 1961.

Chavkin, Nancy Feyl, and Allan Chavkin, eds. *Conversations with Louise Erdrich and Michael Dorris.* Jackson: University Press of Mississippi, 1994.

Chavkin, Nancy Feyl, and Allan Chavkin. "An Interview with Michael Dorris." In Chavkin and Chavkin, *Conversations with Louise Erdrich and Michael Dorris,* 184–219.

Christian, Barbara. *Black Feminist Criticism: Perspectives on Black Women Writers.* New York: Pergamon, 1985.

Churchwell, Sarah ."*A Visit from the Goon Squad* by Jennifer Egan—Review." *Guardian,* 12 March 2011. http://www.theguardian.com/books/2011/mar/13/jennifer-egan-visit-goon-squad (accessed 30 January 2014).

Ciabattari, Jane. "The Book on Aging Rockers." Interview with Jennifer Egan. *Daily Beast,* 29 June 2010. http://www.thedailybeast.com/articles/2010/06/29/jennifer-egan-interview-a-visit-from-the-goon-squad.html (accessed 29 January 2014).

Cixous, Hélène. "The Laugh of the Medusa." Translated by Keith Cohen and Paula Cohen. *Signs* 1 (Summer 1976): 875–93.

Clark, Alex. "Danger Arias." Review of *Bel Canto,* by Ann Patchett. *Guardian,* 13 July 2001. http://www.guardian.co.uk/books/2001/jul/14/fiction.reviews1 (accessed 29 January 2014).

Clément, Catherine. *Opera; or, the Undoing of Women.* Translated by Betsy Wing. Minneapolis: University of Minnesota, 1988.

Cowart, David. *History and the Contemporary Novel.* Carbondale: Southern Illinois University Press, 1989.

Cowart, David. *Thomas Pynchon: The Art of Allusion.* Carbondale: Southern Illinois University Press, 1980.

Cowart, David. *Trailing Clouds: Immigrant Fiction in Contemporary America.* Ithaca, NY: Cornell University Press, 2006.

Cox, Christopher. "At Work: Jennifer Egan." *Paris Review Daily,* 25 June 2010. http://www.theparisreview.org/blog/2010/06/25/qa-jennifer-egan/ (accessed 30 January 2014).

Craig, Hardin, ed. *The Complete Works of Shakespeare.* Chicago: Scott Foresman, 1961.

Danielewski, Mark Z. *House of Leaves.* New York: Pantheon, 2000.

Deleuze, Gilles, and Félix Guattari. *Kafka: Toward a Minor Literature.* Minneapolis: University of Minnesota Press, 1986.

DeLillo, Don. *The Body Artist.* New York: Scribner, 2001.

DeLillo, Don. *Libra.* New York: Viking, 1988.

DeLillo, Don. *Mao II.* New York: Viking, 1991.

DeLillo, Don. *The Names.* New York: Knopf, 1982.

Derrida, Jacques. *Archive Fever: A Freudian Impression.* Translated by Eric Prenowitz. Chicago: University of Chicago Press, 1996.

Derrida, Jacques. *De la grammatologie.* Paris: Les Éditions de Minuit, 1967.

Derrida, Jacques. *Dissemination.* Translated by Barbara Johnson. Chicago: University of Chicago Press, 1981.

Derrida, Jacques. *Of Grammatology.* Translated by Gayatri Chakravorty Spivak. Baltimore: Johns Hopkins University Press, 1976.

De Tocqueville, Alexis. *Democracy in America.* Edited by Isaac Kramnick. New York: W. W. Norton, 2007.

Dewey, Joseph. "Dwelling in Possibility: The Fiction of Richard Powers." *Hollins Critic* 33.2 (April 1996): 3–16.

Dewey, Joseph. *Understanding Richard Powers.* Columbia: University of South Carolina Press, 2002.

Docherty, Thomas. "Postmodernism: An Introduction." In *Postmodernism: A Reader,* edited by Docherty, 1–31. New York: Columbia University Press, 1993.

Donlon, Joycelyn Hazelwood. "Hearing Is Believing: Southern Racial Communities and Strategies of Story-Listening in Gloria Naylor and Lee Smith." *Twentieth Century Literature* 41 (Spring 1995): 16–35.

Dorris, Michael. "Native American Literature in Ethnohistorical Context." *College English* 41 (October 1979): 147–62.

Dorris, Michael. *A Yellow Raft in Blue Water.* New York: Henry Holt, 1987.

Du Bois, W. E. B. *Writings.* New York: Library of America, 1986.

Egan, Jennifer. *A Visit from the Goon Squad.* New York: Knopf, 2010.

Eliot, T. S. *Four Quartets.* New York: Harcourt, 1971.

Eliot, T. S. "The Metaphysical Poets." *Selected Prose of T. S. Eliot,* edited by Frank Kermode, 59–67. New York: Harcourt, Brace & World, 1975.

Eliot, T. S. "Philip Massinger." *Selected Essays 1917–1932,* 181–98. New York: Harcourt, Brace & World, 1964.

Eliot, T. S. Preface. *For Lancelot Andrewes: Essays on Style and Order,* xi–xii. Garden City, N.Y.: Doubleday, Doran and Company, 1929.

Eliot, T. S. "*Ulysses*, Order, and Myth." Review of *Ulysses*, by James Joyce. *Selected Prose of T. S. Eliot*, edited by Frank Kermode, 175–78. New York: Harcourt, Brace & World, 1975.

Eliot, T. S. *The Waste Land. Collected Poems 1909–1962*. London: Faber, 1963.

Ellison, Ralph. *Shadow and Act*. New York: Random House, 1964.

Ellmann, Richard. *Yeats: The Man and the Masks*. New York: Macmillan, 1948.

Enck, John. "John Hawkes: An Interview." *Wisconsin Studies in Contemporary Literature* 6 (1965): 141–55.

Erickson, Peter. *Rewriting Shakespeare, Rewriting Ourselves*. Berkeley: University of California Press, 1991.

Erickson, Steve. *American Nomad*. New York: Holt, 1997.

Erickson, Steve. "American Weimar." *Los Angeles Times Sunday Magazine*, 8 January 1995. http://www.steveerickson.org/articles/weimar.html (accessed 29 January 2014).

Erickson, Steve. *Arc d'X*. New York: Poseidon Press, 1993.

Faulkner, William. *The Sound and the Fury*. New York: Vintage, 1990.

Fish, Stanley. *Self-Consuming Artifacts*. Berkeley: University of California Press, 1972.

FitzGerald, Edward. *Rubáiyát of Omar Khayyám: A Critical Edition*. Edited by Christopher Decker. Charlottesville: University Press of Virginia, 1997.

Fitzgerald, F. Scott. *The Last Tycoon: An Unfinished Novel*. 1941. New York: Scribner's, 1969.

Fitzgerald, F. Scott. *This Side of Paradise*. New York: Scribner's, 1921.

Forster, E. M. *Alexandria: A History and a Guide*. 1922. 2nd American edition, "with revised Afterword and Notes by Michael Haag." New York: Oxford, 1986.

Fowler, Virginia. *Gloria Naylor: In Search of Sanctuary*. New York: Twayne, 1996.

Franzen, Jonathan. *Freedom*. New York: Farrar, Straus and Giroux, 2010.

Franzen, Jonathan. "Perchance to Dream." *Harper's Magazine*, April 1996, 35–54.

Freud, Sigmund. *Beyond the Pleasure Principle*. Edited and translated by James Strachey. Vol 18 of *The Standard Edition of the Complete Psychological Works of Sigmund Freud*. 24 vols. London: Hogarth Press, 1953–74.

Friedman, Herbert A. "The Wandering Soul Psyop Tape of Vietnam." http:www.psywarrior.com/wanderingsoul.html (accessed 29 January 2014).

Frost, Robert. "The Aim Was Song." *Collected Poems, Prose, and Plays*, 207. New York: Library of America, 1995.

Frost, Robert. "The Figure a Poem Makes." *Collected Poems, Prose, and Plays*, 776–78. New York: Library of America, 1995.

Frost, Robert. "West-Running Brook." *Collected Poems, Prose, and Plays*, 236–38. New York: Library of America, 1995.

Fujii, Hikaru. *Outside, America: The Temporal Turn in Contemporary American Fiction*. London: Bloomsbury, 2013.

García, Cristina. *Dreaming in Cuban*. New York: Knopf, 1992.

Gardner, John. *Grendel*. New York: Knopf, 1972.

Gates, Henry Louis. *The Signifying Monkey: A Theory of African-American Literary Criticism*. New York: Oxford, 1988.

Gates, Henry Louis, and K. A. Appiah. *Gloria Naylor: Critical Perspectives*. New York: Amistad, 1993.

Gilbert, Sandra M., and Susan Gubar. *The Madwoman in the Attic*. New Haven: Yale, 1979.

Giovetti, Olivia. "Operas about Operas: Compelling or Confounding?" http://www.wqxr.org/#!/story/192472-operas-about-operas/ (accessed 29 January 2014).

Greiner, Donald J. "'The God Itch': An Interview with Janette Turner Hospital." *Critique* 48.4 (Summer 2007): 331–43.

Gross, Joe. "In Egan's 'Goon Squad,' Stories Spanning Decades Come Together in Unexpected Ways." *Austin American-Statesman*, 12 October 2010. http://www.statesman.com/news/entertainment/books-literature/in-egans-goon-squad-stories-spanning-decades-com-1/nRydz/ (accessed 29 January 2014).

Grossman, Lev. "Who's the Voice of This Generation?" *Time*, 10 July 2006, 60–63.

Grusin, Richard, and Jay David Bolter. *Remediation: Understanding New Media*. Cambridge: MIT Press, 2000.

Hamilton, Natalie. "The A-Mazing House: The Labyrinth as Theme and Form in Mark Z. Danielewski's *House of Leaves*." *Critique* 50.1 (Fall 2008): 3–15.

Hansen, Mark B. N. "The Digital Topography of Mark Z. Danielewski's *House of Leaves*." *Contemporary Literature* 45.4 (2004): 597–636.

Harris, Charles B. "Technoromanticism and the Limits of Representationalism: Richard Powers's *Plowing the Dark*." In *Science, Technology, and the Humanities in Recent American Fiction*, edited by Harris and Peter Freese, 249–78. Essen: Blaue Eule, 2004.

Harrison, Jane Ellen. *Prolegomena to the Study of Greek Religion*. 3rd ed. 1922. New York: Arno, 1975.

Hastings, Tom H. *Nonviolent Response to Terrorism.* Jefferson, NC: McFarland, 2004.

Hayles, N. Katherine. "Saving the Subject: Remediation in *House of Leaves.*" *American Literature* 74.4 (2002): 779–806.

Hebdige, Dick. *Subculture: The Meaning of Style.* New York: Methuen, 1977.

Hegel, Georg Wilhelm Friedrich. *Aesthetics: Lectures on Fine Art.* Translated by T. M. Knox. Vol. 2. Oxford: Clarendon, 1975.

Heise, Ursula. *Chronoschisms: Time, Narrative, and Postmodernism.* Cambridge: Cambridge University Press, 1997.

Hirsch, Marianne. "Clytemnestra's Anger: Writing (Out) the Mother's Anger." In *Alice Walker,* edited by Harold Bloom, 195–213. New York: Chelsea House, 1989.

Hoberek, Andrew. "Introduction: After Postmodernism." *Twentieth-Century Literature* 53.3 (Fall 2007): 233–47.

Holland, Mary K. *Succeeding Postmodernism: Language and Humanism in Contemporary American Literature.* London: Bloomsbury, 2013.

Holloway, Karla F. C. *Moorings and Metaphors: Figures of Culture and Gender in Black Women's Literature.* New Brunswick, NJ: Rutgers University Press, 1992.

Howard, Gerald, et al. "Pynchon from A to V." *Bookforum* (June–September 2005): 29–40.

Hulley, Kathleen. "Interview with Grace Paley." *Delta: Revue du Centre d'Etude et de Recherche sur les Ecrivains du Sud aux Etats-Unis* 14 (1982): 19–40.

Hume, Kathryn. *Aggressive Fictions: Reading the Contemporary American Novel.* Ithaca, NY: Cornell, 2012.

Hume, Kathryn. *American Dream, American Nightmare: Fiction since 1960.* Urbana: Illinois University Press, 2000.

Hurston, Zora Neale. "Characteristics of Negro Expression." In *Negro,* edited by Nancy Cunard, 39–46. New York: Negro Universities Press, 1934.

Huyssen, Andreas. *After the Great Divide: Modernism, Mass Culture, Postmodernism (Theories of Representation and Difference).* Bloomington: Indiana University Press, 1986.

Ifill, Gwen. "Conversation: Ann Patchett." *Online Newshour,* 2 July 2002. http://www.pbs.org/newshour/conversation/july-dec02/patchett_7-02.html (accessed 29 January 2014).

Ingalls, Rachel. *Mrs. Caliban.* Boston: Harvard Common Press, 1983.

Jaeger, Hans. "Generations in History: Reflections on a Controversial Concept." *History and Theory* 24.3 (October 1985): 273–92.

James, E. O. *The Cult of the Mother Goddess*. London: Thames and Hudson, 1959.

Jameson, Fredric. *Postmodernism, or, The Cultural Logic of Late Capitalism*. Durham: Duke University Press, 1991.

Jameson, Fredric. "Third-World Literature in the Era of Multinational Capital." *Social Text* 15 (1986): 65–88.

Joyce, James. *Ulysses*. Edited by Hans Walter Gabler with Wolfhard Steppe and Claus Melchior. New York: Vintage, 1986.

Kafka, Oscar. *Letters to Friends, Family, and Editors*. Translated by Richard and Clara Winston. New York: Schocken Books, 1977.

Kearns, Cleo McNelly. "The Harrowing Grace of Truthful Fiction: A Review of Richard Powers's *Operation Wandering Soul*." *Theology Today* 51 (January 1995): 588–93.

Kelly, Adam. *American Fiction in Transition: Observer-Hero Narrative, the 1990s, and Postmodernism*. London: Bloomsbury, 2013

Kelly, Kevin. "Who Is Rachel Ingalls? And Why Is She Writing about Love with a Sea Monster?" *Chicago Tribune*, 11 October 1987. http://articles.chicagotribune.com/1987–10–11/features/8703180184_1_dorothy-larry-wittgenstein (accessed 29 June 2014).

Kharpertian, Theodore D. *A Hand to Turn the Time: The Menippean Satires of Thomas Pynchon*. Madison, NJ: Fairleigh Dickinson University Press, 1990.

Konigsberg, Eric. "Michael Dorris's Troubled Sleep." *New York*, 16 June 1997, 30–37.

Kraus, Karl. *The Kraus Project: Essays by Karl Kraus*. Edited and translated by Jonathan Franzen. New York: Farrar, Straus and Giroux, 2013.

Kristeva, Julia. "La femme, ce n'est jamais ça." *Tel Quel* 59 (Autumn 1974): 19–24.

Krupat, Arnold. *Ethnocriticism: Ethnography History Literature*. Berkeley: University of California Press, 1991.

Krupat, Arnold. *The Voice in the Margin: Native American Literature and the Canon*. Berkeley: University of California Press, 1989.

Kubitschek, Missy Dehn. "Toward a New Order: Shakespeare, Morrison, and Gloria Naylor's *Mama Day*." *MELUS* 19 (Fall 1994): 75–90.

Lane, James Mx. "Steve Erickson." *BOMB* 20 (Summer 1987), http://bomb-magazine.org/article/948/ (accessed 3 July 2014).

LeClair, Tom. "An Interview with Don DeLillo." In *Anything Can Happen: Interviews with Contemporary American Novelists*, conducted and edited by LeClair and Larry McCaffery, 79–90. Urbana: University of Illinois Press, 1983.

LeClair, Tom. "The Prodigious Fiction of Richard Powers, William Vollmann, and David Foster Wallace." *Critique* 38.1 (Fall 1996): 12–37.

Lee, Chang-rae. *On Such a Full Sea*. New York: Riverhead, 2014.

Levin, Adam. *The Instructions*. San Francisco: McSweeney's, 2010.

Lewis, R. W. B. *The American Adam: Innocence, Tragedy, and Tradition in the Nineteenth Century*. Chicago: University of Chicago Press, 1955.

Lindner, April. "Narrative as Necessary Evil in Richard Powers's *Operation Wandering Soul*." *Critique* 38 (Fall 1996): 68–79.

Longfellow, Henry Wadsworth. "Kéramos." In *Kéramos and Other Poems*, 11–33. London: George Routledge, 1878.

Lord, Nick. "The Labyrinth and the Lacuna: Metafiction, the Symbolic, and the Real in Mark Z. Danielewski's *House of Leaves*." *Critique* 55, no. 4 (2014): 465–76.

Lyotard, Jean-François. *The Postmodern Condition: A Report on Knowledge*. Translated by Geoff Bennington and Brian Massumi. Minneapolis: University of Minnesota Press, 1984.

Mailer, Norman. *Advertisements for Myself*. New York: Berkley Medallion, 1959.

Mannheim, Karl. *Essays on the Sociology of Knowledge*. Translated by Paul Kecskemeti. New York: Oxford University Press, 1952.

Marcus-Delgado, Jane. "Destructive Persistence of Myths and Stereotypes: Civilization and Barbarism Redux in Ann Patchett's *Bel Canto*." *Letras Hispanas* 2.1 (Spring 2005): 48–58.

Marin, Louis. *Utopics: Spatial Play*. Translated by Robert A. Vollrath. Atlantic Highlands, NJ: Humanities Press, 1984.

Maslin, Janet. "An Immature Con Man with a Mom Problem." Review of *Choke*, by Chuck Palahniuk. *New York Times*, May 24, 2001. http://www.nytimes.com/2001/05/24/books/books-of-the-times-an-immature-con-man-with-a-mom-problem.html?ref=chuckpalahniuk (accessed 29 January 2014).

Matthiessen, F. O. *American Renaissance: Art and Expression in the Age of Emerson and Whitman*. New York: Oxford, 1941.

Max, D. T. *Every Love Story Is a Ghost Story: A Life of David Foster Wallace*. New York: Penguin, 2013.

McCaffery, Larry, and Sinda Gregory. "Haunted House—an Interview with Mark Z. Danielewski." *Critique* 44.2 (Winter 2003): 99–135.

McCaffery, Larry, and Takayuki Tatsumi. "Finding a Way to Obliterate the Barriers: An Interview with Steve Erickson." *Contemporary Literature* 38.3 (1997): 395–421.

McHale, Brian. *The Cambridge Introduction to Postmodernism*. New York: Cambridge University Press, 2015.

McHale, Brian. *Constructing Postmodernism*. New York: Routledge. 1992.

McHale, Brian. *Postmodernist Fiction*. New York: Methuen, 1987.

McHale, Brian. "What Was Postmodernism." *electronic book review*, 20 January 2007, http://www.electronicbookreview.com/thread/fictionspresent/tense (accessed 29 January 2014).

Mendelsohn, Daniel. "Ransom Notes." Review of *Bel Canto*, by Ann Patchett. *New York*, 18 June 2001. http://nymag.com/nymetro/arts/books/reviews/4804/ (accessed 29 January 2014).

Millard, Bill. "Pynchon's Coast: *Inherent Vice* and the Twilight of the Spatially Specific." *College Hill Review*, no. 4 (Fall 2009). http://www.colleghillreview.com/004/0040501.html (accessed 30 January 2014).

Miller, Laura. Review of *Diary*, by Chuck Palahniuk. Salon.com, 20 August 2003. http://dir.salon.com/books/review/2003/08/20/palahniuk/index.html (accessed 26 September 2014).

Mnookin, Seth. "In Disaster's Aftermath, Once-Cocky Media Culture Disses the Age of Irony." *Inside.com*, 18 September 2001.

Moi, Toril. *Sexual/Textual Politics: Feminist Literary Theory*. New York: Methuen, 1985.

Moraru, Christian. *Cosmodernism: American Narrative, Late Globalization, and the New Cultural Imaginary*. Ann Arbor: University of Michigan Press, 2011.

Murphy, Jim. "Pursuits and Revolutions: History's Figures in Steve Erickson's *Arc d'X*." *Modern Fiction Studies* 46.2 (2000): 451–79.

Nabokov, Vladimir. *Lectures on Literature*. New York: Harcourt Brace Jovanovich, 1980.

Nabokov, Vladimir. *Pnin*. New York: Vintage, 1984.

Nabokov, Vladimir. *The Real Life of Sebastian Knight*. New York: New Directions, 1941.

Nabokov, Vladimir. *Speak, Memory: An Autobiography Revisited*. New York: Putnam's, 1966.

Nabokov, Vladimir. *Strong Opinions*. New York: McGraw-Hill, 1973.

Naylor, Gloria. *Bailey's Cafe*. New York: Harcourt Brace Jovanovich, 1992.

Naylor, Gloria. *Linden Hills*. New York: Ticknor & Fields, 1985.

Naylor, Gloria. "Love and Sex in the Afro-American Novel." *Yale Review* 78 (1988): 19–31.

Naylor, Gloria. *Mama Day*. New York: Ticknor & Fields, 1988.

Naylor, Gloria. [Untitled.] In *Writers Dreaming*, edited by Naomi Epel, 167–77. New York: Carol Southern Books, 1993.

Naylor, Gloria. *The Women of Brewster Place*. New York: Viking, 1983.

Neilson, Jim. "An Interview with Richard Powers." *Review of Contemporary Fiction* 18.3 (Fall 1998): 18–23. http://www.dalkeyarchive.com/a-conversation-with-richard-powers-by-jim-neilson/ (accessed 29 January 2014).

Neumann, Erich. *The Great Mother: An Analysis of the Archetype*. 2nd ed. Translated by Ralph Mannheim. London: Routledge, 1996.

O'Connor, Flannery. "The Fiction Writer and His Country." In *Mystery and Manners*, 25–50. New York: Farrar, Straus and Giroux, 1961.

O'Donnell, Patrick. *The American Novel Now: Reading Contemporary American Fiction since 1980*. Chichester, UK: Wiley-Blackwell, 2010.

Ortega y Gasset, José. *Man and Crisis*. 1933. Translated by Mildred Adams. New York: W. W. Norton, 1958.

Ortega y Gasset, José. *The Modern Theme*. 1923. Translated by James Cleugh. New York: Harper & Brothers, 1961.

Owen, Louis. *Other Destinies: Understanding the American Indian Novel*. Norman: University of Oklahoma Press, 1992.

Palahniuk, Chuck. *Choke*. New York: Anchor Doubleday, 2001.

Palahniuk, Chuck. *Fight Club*. New York: W. W. Norton, 1996.

Pancake, Ann. "'The Wheel's Worst Illusion': The Spatial Politics of *Operation Wandering Soul*." *Review of Contemporary Fiction* 18.3 (Fall 1998): 72–83.

Patchett, Ann. *Bel Canto*. New York: HarperCollins, 2001.

Patchett, Ann. "Constantly Plagiarizing Myself." In *Conversations with American Women Writers*, conducted and edited by Sarah Anne Johnson, 167–85. Hanover, NH: University Press of New England, 2004.

Patchett, Ann. "An Interview with Ann Patchett." *BookBrowse*. http://www.bookbrowse.com/author_interviews/full/index.cfm/author_number/645/ann-patchett (accessed 29 January 2014).

Pausanias. *The Description of Greece*. Vol. 1. Translated by Thomas Taylor. London: Priestley and Weale, 1824.

Percy, Walker. "The Man on the Train." In *The Message in the Bottle: How Queer Man Is, How Queer Language Is, and What One Has to Do with the Other*, 83–100. New York: Farrar, Straus and Giroux, 1975.

"Peru." U.S. Department of State website. http://www.state.gov/r/pa/ei/bgn/35762.htm#history (accessed 29 January 2014).

Petersen, Julius. "Die literarischen Generationen." In *Philosophie der liter-*

aturwissenschaft, edited by Emil Ermatinger, 130–87. Berlin: Junker und Dunnhaupt Verlag, 1930.

Petry, Alice Hall. "Alice Walker: The Achievement of the Short Fiction." *Modern Language Studies* 19.1 (Winter 1989): 12–27.

Pickle, Linda S. "Christa Wolf's *Cassandra*: Parallels to Feminism in the West." *Critique* 28.3 (Spring 1987): 149–57.

Pifer, Ellen. "Toni Morrison's *Beloved*: Twain's Mississippi Recollected and Rewritten." In *Le fleuve et ses métamorphoses: Actes du colloque international tenu à l'Université Lyon 3-Jean-Moulin, les 13, 14 et 15 mai 1992*, edited by François Piquet, 511–14. Paris: Didier, 1993.

Pliny the Elder. *The Natural History*. Edited by John Bostock and H. T. Riley. Perseus Digital Library. http://www.perseus.tufts.edu/hopper/text ?doc=Perseus%3Atext%3A1999.02.0137%3Abook%3D35%3Achapte r%3D43 (accessed 29 January 2014).

Pound, Ezra. *Letters of Ezra Pound 1907–1941*. Edited by D. D. Paige. London: Faber, 1951.

Powers, Richard. *Galatea 2.2*. New York: Farrar, Straus and Giroux, 1995.

Powers, Richard. *The Gold Bug Variations*. New York: William Morrow, 1991.

Powers, Richard. *Operation Wandering Soul*. New York: William Morrow, 1993.

Powers, Richard. *Orfeo*. New York: W. W. Norton, 2014.

Powers, Richard. *Plowing the Dark*. New York: Farrar, Straus and Giroux, 2000.

Powers, Richard. *Three Farmers on Their Way to a Dance*. New York: Beech Tree Books, 1987.

Pressman, Jessica. "*House of Leaves*: Reading the Networked Novel." *Studies in American Fiction* 34.1 (Spring 2006): 107–28.

Pullin, Faith. "Landscapes of Reality: The Fiction of Contemporary Afro-American Women." In *Black Fiction: New Studies in the Afro-American Novel since 1945*, edited by A. Robert Lee, 173–203. New York: Barnes and Noble, 1980.

Pynchon, Thomas. *Against the Day*. New York: Penguin, 2006.

Pynchon, Thomas. *Bleeding Edge*. London: Jonathan Cape, 2013.

Pynchon, Thomas. *The Crying of Lot 49*. Philadelphia: Lippincott, 1966.

Pynchon, Thomas. *Gravity's Rainbow*. New York: Viking, 1973.

Pynchon, Thomas. *Inherent Vice*. New York: Penguin, 2009.

Pynchon, Thomas. "Introduction." In *Slow Learner: Early Stories*, 3–23. Boston: Little, Brown, 1984.

Pynchon, Thomas. *Mason & Dixon*. New York: Henry Holt, 1997.

Pynchon, Thomas. *Vineland*. New York: Little, Brown, 1990.

Robbins, Michael. "'Bleeding Edge' by Thomas Pynchon." *Chicago Tribune*, 15 September 2013. http://www.chicagotribune.com/lifestyles/books/ct-prj-0915-bleeding-edge-thomas-pynchon-2–20130915-story.html (accessed 23 July 2014).

Robbins, Michael. *The Second Sex*. New York: Penguin, 2014.

Rosenblatt, Roger. "The Age of Irony Comes to an End." *Time*, 24 September 2001. http://www.time.com/time/magazine/article/0,9171,1000893,00.html (accessed 30 January 2014).

Roth, Philip. "Writing American Fiction." *Commentary* 21 (March 1961): 223–33.

"Saint Christopher." *Catholic Encyclopedia*. http://www.newadvent.org/cathen/03728a.htm (accessed 29 January 2014).

Schemo, Dana Jean. "As a Rebel's Path Ends, Hard Turf but Soft Hearts." *New York Times*, 29 April 1997. http://www.nytimes.com/1997/04/29/world/as-a-rebel-s-path-ends-hard-turf-but-soft-hearts.html (accessed 29 January 2014).

Schumacher, Michael. "Louise Erdrich and Michael Dorris: A Marriage of Minds." In Chavkin and Chavkin, *Conversations with Louise Erdrich and Michael Dorris*, 173–83.

Schwartz, Carly. "Jennifer Egan on Growing Up in San Francisco, Finding Inspiration, and Experiencing the 'Sixties Hangover.'" *Huffington Post*, 10 October 2011. http://www.huffingtonpost.com/2011/10/10/jennifer-egan-my-sf_n_1001091.html (accessed 30 January 2014).

Sexton, Anne. *The Complete Poems*. Boston: Houghton Mifflin, 1981.

Shklovsky, Viktor. *Literature and Cinematography*. 1923. Translated by Irina Masinovsky. Champaign: Dalkey Archive Press, 2008.

Showalter, Elaine. "Piecing and Writing." In *The Poetics of Gender*, edited by Nancy K. Miller, 222–47. New York: Columbia University Press, 1986.

Showalter, Elaine. *Sister's Choice: Tradition and Change in American Women's Writing*. New York: Oxford, 1991.

Silberman, Robert. "Opening the Text: *Love Medicine* and the Return of the Native American Woman." In *Narrative Chance: Postmodern Discourse on Native American Literatures*, edited by Gerald Vizenor, 101–20. Albuquerque: University of New Mexico Press, 1989.

Silko, Leslie Marmon. *Ceremony*. New York: Penguin, 1977.

Sjöö, Monica, and Barbara Mor. *The Great Cosmic Mother*. New York: Harper and Row, 1987.

Slocombe, Will. "'This Is Not for You': Nihilism and the House That Jacques Built." *Modern Fiction Studies* 51.1 (2005): 88–109.

La Sonnambula. Metropolitan Opera website, http://www.metoperafamily. org/metopera/history/stories/synopsis.aspx?id=268 (accessed 29 January 2014).

Spinks, Lee. "Jefferson at the Millennial Gates: History and Apocalypse in the Fiction of Steve Erickson." *Contemporary Literature* 40.2 (Summer 1999): 214–39.

Spitzer, Alan B. "The Historical Problem of Generations." *American Historical Review* 78 (1973): 1353–85.

Stevens, Wallace. "Man Carrying Thing." In *Collected Poetry and Prose*, edited by Frank Kermode and Joan Richardson, 306. New York: Library of America, 1984.

Stevens, Wallace. "Sunday Morning." In *The Collected Poems of Wallace Stevens*, 68–69. New York: Random House, 2011.

Storhoff, Gary. "'The Only Voice Is Your Own': Gloria Naylor's Revision of *The Tempest*." *African American Review* 29 (Spring 1995): 35–45.

Tagore, Rabindranath. "Broken Song." In *Selected Poems*, translated by William Radice, 53–55. New York: Penguin, 1994.

Thompson, Hunter S. *Fear and Loathing in Las Vegas: A Savage Journey to the Heart of the American Dream*. New York: Knopf, 1971.

Toth, Josh. "Healing Postmodern America: Plasticity and Renewal in Danielewski's *House of Leaves*." *Critique* 54.2 (2013): 181–97.

Traub, Valerie. "Rainbows of Darkness: Deconstructing Shakespeare in the Work of Gloria Naylor and Zora Neale Hurston." In *Cross-Cultural Performances: Differences in Women's Re-Visions of Shakespeare*, edited by Marianne Novy, 150–64. Urbana: University of Illinois Press, 1993.

Tucker, Lindsay. "Recovering the Conjure Woman: Texts and Contexts in Gloria Naylor's *Mama Day*." *African American Review* 28 (1994): 173–88.

Updike, John. *Rabbit, Run*. New York: Knopf, 1960.

Verger, Pierre. "Yoruba Myths and Religion, and Their Afro-American Extensions." Translated by Gerald Honingsblum. In *Mythologies*, compiled by Yves Bonnefoy, "A Restructured Translation of *Dictionnaire des mythologies et des religions des sociétés traditionelles et du monde antique*," 1981. Prepared under the direction of Wendy Doniger. Translated by Gerald

Honigsblum et al. 2 vols. Volume 1, 52–62. Chicago: University of Chicago Press, 1991.

Walker, Alice. *In Love and Trouble: Stories of Black Women.* New York: Harcourt Brace Jovanovich, 1973.

Walker, Alice. *In Search of Our Mothers' Gardens.* San Diego: Harcourt Brace Jovanovich, 1983.

Walker, Alice. *Living By the Word: Selected Writings 1973–1987.* San Diego: Harcourt Brace Jovanovich, 1988.

Walker, Alice. *Revolutionary Petunias and Other Poems.* New York: Harcourt Brace Jovanovich, 1973.

Wallace, David Foster. "I Unibus Pluram: Television and U. S. Fiction." In *A Supposedly Fun Thing I'll Never Do Again: Essays and Arguments*, 21–82. New York: Little, Brown, 1997.

Weisgall, Deborah. "The Magic Opera." *Radcliffe Quarterly* (Summer 2001): 27.

Wharton, Edith. *The Age of Innocence.* New York: D. Appleton and Company, 1920.

Whitman, Walt. *Song of Myself.* In *Leaves of Grass: Comprehensive Reader's Edition*, edited by Harold W. Blodgett and Sculley Bradley. New York: New York University Press, 1963.

Williams, G. Christopher. "Nihilism and Buddhism in a Blender: The Religion of Chuck Palahniuk." In *Reading Chuck Palahniuk: American Monsters and Literary Mayhem*, edited by Cynthia Kuhn and Lance Rubin, 170–82. New York: Routledge, 2009.

Williams, Jeffrey. "The Last Generalist: An Interview with Richard Powers." *Minnesota Review*, n.s., 52–54 (2001): 95–114.

Williams, William Carlos. "Asphodel, That Greeny Flower." In *Selected Poems*, 142–55. New York: New Directions, 1968.

Wilson, Edmund. *Axel's Castle: A Study in the Imaginative Literature of 1870–1930.* New York: Scribner's, 1931.

Winchell, Donna Haisty. *Alice Walker.* Boston: Twayne, 1990.

Wong, Hertha D. "An Interview with Louise Erdrich and Michael Dorris." In Chavkin and Chavkin, *Conversations with Louise Erdrich and Michael Dorris*, 30–53.

"Zampano." MundMische. http://mundmische.de/bedeutung/26478-Zampano (accessed 30 January 2014).

Index

Printed and bound by CPI Group (UK) Ltd, Croydon, CR0 4YY

09/06/2025

14685669-0003